EYEWITNESS *TRAVEL GUIDES*

LISBON

Main Contributor: SUSIE BOULTON

DORLING KINDERSLEY

LONDON • NEW YORK • SYDNEY • MOSCOW

A DORLING KINDERSLEY BOOK

PROJECT EDITORS Claire Folkard, Ferdie McDonald
ART EDITORS Jim Evoy, Vanessa Hamilton
EDITORS Francesca Machiavelli, Rebecca Miles,
Alice Peebles, Alison Stace
DESIGNERS Anthea Forlee, Carolyn Hewitson,
Nicola Rodway, Dooty Williams
MAP CO-ORDINATORS Emily Green, David Pugh
PICTURE RESEARCH Brigitte Arora
DTP DESIGNER Sarah Martin
LANGUAGE CONSULTANT Paula Tomé
PRODUCTION David Proffit

MANAGING EDITOR Georgina Matthews
MANAGING ART EDITOR Annette Jacobs
DEPUTY EDITORIAL DIRECTOR Douglas Amrine
DEPUTY ART DIRECTOR Gillian Allan

CONTRIBUTORS AND CONSULTANTS
Clive Gilbert, Peter Gilbert, Sarah McAlister,
Norman Renouf, Joe Staines, Martin Symington

MAPS
Neil Cook, Maria Donnelly (Colourmap Scanning Ltd)
David Murphy, Phil Rose Jennifer Skelley,
Leanne Wright (Lovell Johns Ltd)

PHOTOGRAPHERS
Linda Whitwam, Peter Wilson

ILLUSTRATORS
Javier Gomez Morata/Acanto Arquitectura y Urbanismo S.L.,
Paul Guest, Claire Littlejohn, John Woodcock, Martin Woodward

Text film output by Graphical Innovations (London)
Reproduced by Colourscan (Singapore)
Printed and bound by G. Canale (Italy)

First published in Great Britain in 1997
by Dorling Kindersley Limited
9 Henrietta Street, London WC2E 8PS

Copyright 1997 © Dorling Kindersley Limited, London

Visit us on the World Wide Web at http://www.dk.com

Every effort has been made to ensure that the information in this
book is as up-to-date as possible at the time of going to press.
However, details such as telephone numbers, opening hours,
prices, gallery hanging arrangements and travel information are
liable to change. The publishers cannot accept responsibility for
any consequences arising from the use of this book.

We would be delighted to receive any corrections and
suggestions for incorporation in the next edition. Please write to:
Deputy Editorial Director, Eyewitness Travel Guides,
Dorling Kindersley, 9 Henrietta Street, London WC2E 8PS.

◁ **View of the Castelo de São Jorge at night**

CONTENTS

**Manueline vaulting in the cloister
in the Mosteiro dos Jerónimos**

INTRODUCING
LISBON

**A statue of St Antony, dressed up
for his feast day celebrations**

View to the Sé across the Baixa from the Elevador de Santa Justa

Atmospheric houses in the old Moorish district of Alfama

Porco à alentejana, a popular dish in Lisbon

The Monument to the Discoveries

Palácio da Pena, Sintra

HOW TO USE THIS GUIDE

THIS GUIDE helps you get the most from a visit to Lisbon, providing expert recommendations as well as detailed practical information. The opening chapter *Introducing Lisbon* maps the city and sets it in its historical and cultural context. Each of the five area chapters, plus *The Lisbon Coast*, describe important sights, using maps, pictures and illustrations. Hotel and restaurant recommendations plus features on subjects such as entertainment and food and drink can be found in *Travellers' Needs*. The *Survival Guide* contains practical information on everything from transport to personal safety.

LISBON

Lisbon has been divided into five main sightseeing areas. Each of these areas has its own chapter, which opens with a list of the major sights described. All sights are numbered and plotted on an *Area Map*. Information on the sights is easy to locate as the order in which they appear in the chapter follows the numerical order used on the map.

Sights at a Glance
lists the chapter's sights by category: Churches, Museums and Galleries, Historic Buildings, Parks and Gardens.

1 Area Map
For easy reference, the sights covered in the chapter are numbered and located on a map. The sights are also marked on the Street Finder *maps on pages 164–77.*

A locator map shows clearly where the area is in relation to other parts of the city.

Each area is indicated by a colour-coded thumb tab (see inside front cover).

2 Street-by-Street Map
This gives a bird's-eye view of the heart of each of the sightseeing areas.

A suggested route for a walk is shown in red.

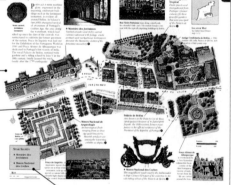

Stars indicate the sights that no visitor should miss.

3 Detailed Information
All the sights in Lisbon are described individually. Addresses and practical information are provided. The key to the symbols used in the information block is shown on the back flap.

THE LISBON COAST

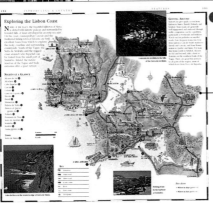

1 Introduction to The Lisbon Coast
The Lisbon Coast has its own introduction, which provides an overview of the history and character of the coast and countryside around Lisbon and outline what it has to offer the visitor today. The area covered by this section is highlighted on the map of Portugal shown on page 89. It covers coastal resorts and local wildlife, as well as beautiful palaces and historic towns.

2 Pictorial Map
This shows the main road network and gives an illustrated overview of the region. All entries are numbered and there are also useful tips on getting around the region.

The Lisbon Coast chapter is indicated by a green thumb tab.

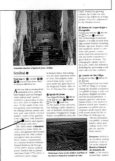

3 Detailed Information
All the important towns and other places to visit are described individually. They are listed in order, following the numbering given on the Pictorial Map. Within each entry, there is further detailed information on important buildings and other sights.

Story boxes explore specific subjects further.

For all the top sights, a Visitors' Checklist provides the practical information you need to plan your visit.

4 The Top Sights
These are given two or more full pages. Historic buildings are dissected to reveal their interiors; museums and galleries have colour-coded floorplans to help you locate the most interesting exhibits.

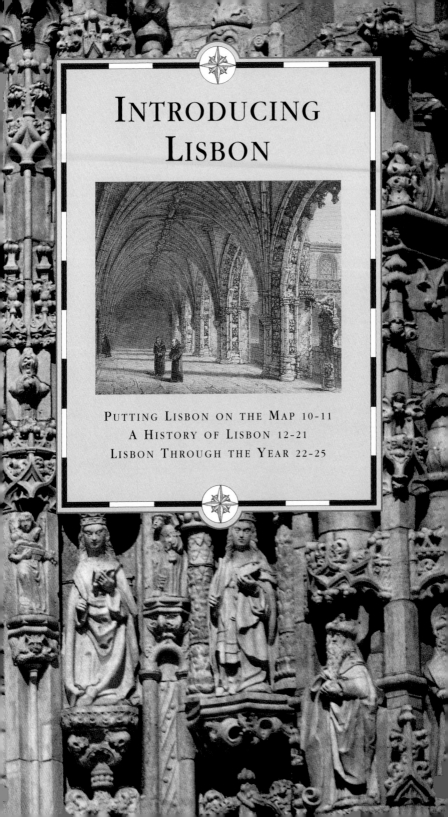

Introducing
Lisbon

Putting Lisbon on the Map

L ISBON, the capital of Portugal, is situated on the
Atlantic coast, in the southwest of the country.
It is approximately 300 km (180 miles) from the
Algarve in the south and around 400 km (250 miles)
from the Minho in the north. The political, economic
and cultural centre of Portugal, the city lies on the
steep hills on the north bank of the Tagus. The
greater Lisbon area occupies around 1,000 sq km
(300 sq miles) and has a population of 2.1 million.
Well-served by international flights, the city is now
becoming popular as a holiday destination and its
proximity to the coast makes it an ideal choice for
both sightseeing and sunbathing.

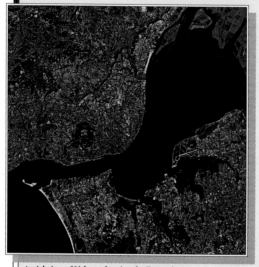

Aerial view of Lisbon, showing the Tagus river

| 0 kilometres | 100 |
| 0 miles | 50 |

KEY

✈	Airport
⚓	Port
▬	Motorway
▬	Major road
=	Minor road
—	Main railway line
▬ ∙	National boundary

ATLANTIC

OCEAN

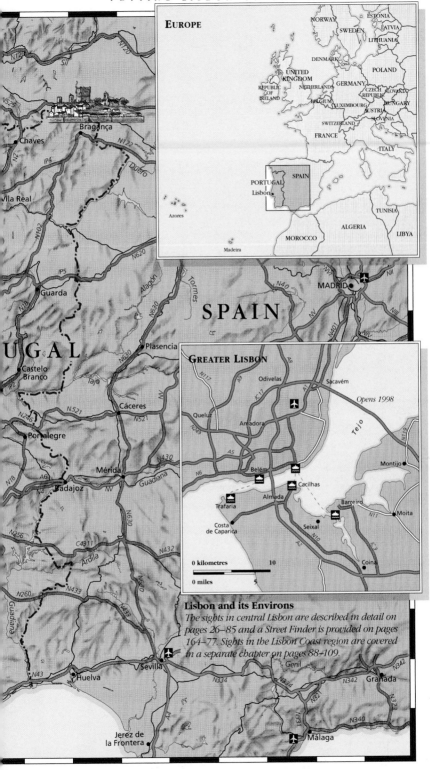

EUROPE

NORWAY
SWEDEN
ESTONIA
LATVIA
LITHUANIA
DENMARK
UNITED KINGDOM
POLAND
REPUBLIC OF IRELAND
NETHERLANDS
GERMANY
CZECH REPUBLIC
SLOVAKIA
BELGIUM
LUXEMBOURG
AUSTRIA
HUNGARY
SWITZERLAND
SLOVENIA
FRANCE
ITALY
PORTUGAL
SPAIN
Lisbon
Azores
TUNISIA
MOROCCO
ALGERIA
LIBYA
Madeira

Chaves
Bragança
Vila Real
Duero
Guarda
IP5
N620
N630
IP2
UGAL
Castelo Branco
Tajo
Plasencia
SPAIN
Cáceres
N521
N521
MADRID
Mérida
Guadiana
Badajoz
N630
Portalegre
N256
N433
N432
Huelva
Sevilla
Jerez de la Frontera
Genil
N334
Málaga
N340
Granada
N342
N331

GREATER LISBON

N117
A9
Odivelas
Sacavém
Opens 1998
Queluz
Amadora
A5
Belém
Cacilhas
Almada
Trafaria
Barreiro
Moita
Costa de Caparica
Seixal
Coina
Tejo
Montijo

0 kilometres   10
0 miles   5

Lisbon and its Environs
The sights in central Lisbon are described in detail on pages 26–85 and a Street Finder is provided on pages 164–77. Sights in the Lisbon Coast region are covered in a separate chapter on pages 88–109.

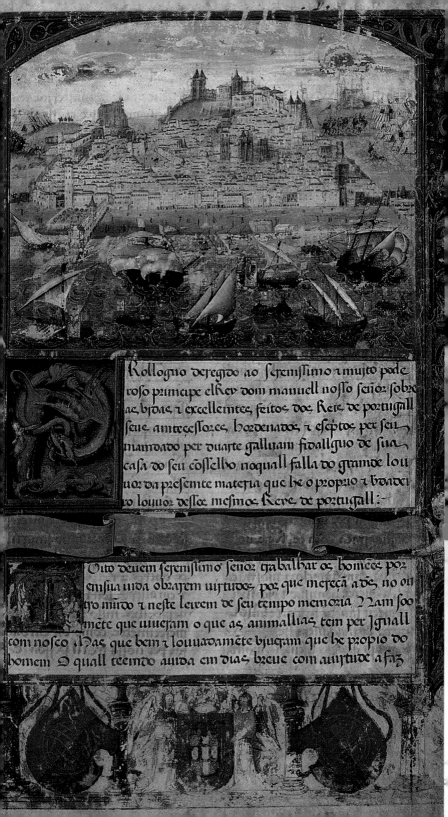

Rolloguo deregido ao serenissimo i muito pode
roso primcipe elRev dom manuell nosso senor sobre
as bvdas i excellentes feitos dos Reis de portugall
seus antecessores hordenados i escriptos per seu
mandado per duarte galluam fidallguo de sua
casa do seu cossellho noquall falla do grande lou
uor da presente materia que he o propuo i vvdadei
ro louuor desste mesmos Reys de portugall:~

Oito deuem serenissimo senor trabalhar os homees por
emsua vida obrarem vistudes por que mereça a des no ou
tro mudo i neste leixem de seu tempo memoria Nam soo
mete que viueram o que as animallias tem per iguall
com nosco Mas que bem i louuadamete biueram que he propuo do
homem O quall teeendo auida em dias breue com austide a faz

THE HISTORY OF LISBON

O VER THE CENTURIES, *Lisbon has both flourished and suffered. The city is most famous for its history of maritime successes, in particular the voyages of Vasco da Gama who first navigated a sea route to India. In recent years the city has flourished again, and is now a major European centre of commerce.*

According to myth, the Greek hero Odysseus (also known as Ulysses) founded Lisbon on his journey home from Troy. The Phoenicians are known to have established a trading post on the site in around 1200 BC. From 205 BC the town was in Roman hands, reaching the height of its importance when Julius Caesar became the governor in 60 BC. **St Vincent**

With the collapse of the Roman Empire, barbarian tribes invaded from northern Europe. The Alans, who conquered the city in around AD 409, were superseded by the Suevi who in turn were driven out by the Visigoths. None of these tribes were primarily town-dwellers and Lisbon began to decline. In 711 North African Muslim invaders, the Moors, overran the peninsula and occupied the city for some 450 years. Lisbon was an important trading centre under the Moors and their legacy is evident today in the Castelo de São Jorge and the streets of the Alfama district.

The first king of Portugal, Afonso Henriques, finally ousted the Moors from Lisbon in 1147. Among those who helped was the English Crusader Gilbert of Hastings, who became Lisbon's first bishop. A new cathedral was built below the castle and, shortly afterwards, the remains of St Vincent, the patron saint of Portugal, were brought there. Lisbon received its charter early in the 13th century, but it was not until 1256, under Afonso III, that it became the capital.

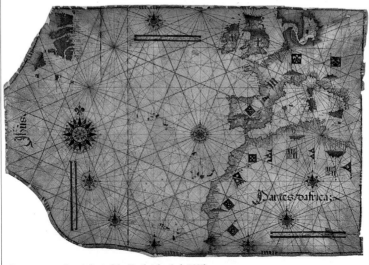

Portuguese mariners' chart of the North Atlantic (c.1550)

◁ Illuminated page from the *Chronica de Dom Afonso Henriques*, showing Lisbon in the 16th century

THE REIGN OF KING DINIS

Under King Dinis, the son of Afonso III, the court at Lisbon became a centre of culture and in 1290 the University of Lisbon was founded. Dinis extended the city away from the castle, developing the Baixa, and Lisbon flourished as trade with Europe grew.

In the 14th century, the city continued to expand westwards along the river, despite the ruin caused by the Black Death, which spread throughout Portugal from Lisbon. In 1373, after Lisbon was sacked by Enrique II of Castile, Fernando I built a new line of fortifications to protect his 40,000 citizens and to redefine the boundaries of the growing city. When Fernando died without an heir, the throne was claimed by his illegitimate half brother, João of Avis, who defeated Juan of Castile, in 1385.

Statue of Manuel I and St Jerome on the Mosteiro dos Jerónimos

Musicians at the court of King Dinis

THE DISCOVERIES

Periodic outbreaks of plague continued to destabilize the economy and led to riots in Lisbon over grain shortages. Prosperity returned during the Age of Discovery *(see pp18–19)* when Vasco da Gama, setting out from Belém in 1497, successfully navigated a sea route to India. The resulting wealth from the spice trade made Lisbon the mercantile centre of Europe. In gratitude for this newfound prosperity, Manuel I ordered the building of the Torre de Belém *(see p70)* and the magnificent Mosteiro dos Jerónimos in Belém *(see pp66–7)*; their ornate late-Gothic style, known as Manueline after the king, reflects the Discoveries in the exotic and nautical nature of the detailed sculpture on the two monuments.

The 16th century saw major developments: a new square, the Terreiro do Paço (now the Praça do Comércio), was built on the waterfront, and a new district, the Bairro Alto, sprang up to house the many merchants drawn to Lisbon. The Inquisition, a Catholic movement which persecuted heretics and non-believers, began a reign of terror. Mass trials and executions of those that were condemned took place regularly in the Terreiro do Paço.

SPANISH CONTROL

The young King Sebastião I was killed at the battle of Alcácer-Quibir in a doomed attempt to invade Morocco in 1578. The lack of an heir led to conquest by Spain in 1580. Ignoring his advisers, Philip II of Spain refused to make Lisbon the capital of his extended kingdom and left the government of Portugal to a viceroy. The Spanish were ousted in 1640 and the Duke of Bragança crowned João IV.

With the discovery of Brazilian gold in 1697, Lisbon enjoyed a new wave of prosperity. From 1706, João V began an ambitious building programme in the city. The most valuable addition to Lisbon at this time was the Águas Livres aqueduct *(see p84)*,

The battle of Alcácer-Quibir in Morocco, where 8,000 men were killed and 15,000 captured

which was carrying water across the Alcântara valley just a few years before the devastating earthquake struck the city in 1755 *(see pp20–21).*

POMBAL'S VISION

Responsibility for rebuilding the ruined city fell to José I's chief minister, the Marquês de Pombal. Engineers drew up a plan that re-aligned Lisbon on a north–south axis and created a grid of streets with the Baixa at its heart. Pombal's vision was not continued by his successors; when the royal family fled to Brazil in 1807, ahead of Napoleon's invading army, Rio de Janeiro temporarily became the capital of the Portuguese empire, and Lisbon began to decline.

The Águas Livres aqueduct, completed in the 19th century

The Marquês de Pombal pointing to the new Lisbon

REGENERATION

In the second half of the 19th century a period of economic revival and industrialization commenced. Railways and new roads were built, trams were introduced, modern drains and sewers were constructed and work began on the embankment of the Tagus. In 1908 the king was assassinated and two years later the monarchy was overturned. Under António Salazar's lengthy dictatorship (1926–68), Lisbon's modernization continued at the expense of the rest of the country.

Soldiers in the Carnation Revolution of 1974 which ended the dictatorship

A suspension bridge across the Tagus was completed in 1966. Initially called the Ponte Salazar, it was later renamed Ponte 25 de Abril in commemoration of the peaceful Carnation Revolution in 1974 which finally ended the totalitarian regime instituted by Salazar.

MODERN LISBON

The years following the Revolution were a period of both euphoria and political chaos. Then, in 1986, Portugal joined the European Community and foreign companies began to set up in Lisbon. Under the leadership of the Social Democratic prime minister, Aníbal Cavaco Silva, Lisbon's economy recovered. Even the disastrous fire which swept through the Chiado district in 1988 failed to dampen the general optimism. To mastermind the rebuilding of this historic district, the city appointed Portugal's most prestigious architect, Álvaro Siza Vieira. Since then, Lisbon has enjoyed much prestige, and was voted European City of Culture in 1994. In 1998 the city will host a World Exposition on the theme of the Oceans, in celebration of its maritime history. Today, Lisbon is a cosmopolitan city where the influence of its previous African and South American colonies is still widely evident.

The Rulers of Portugal

Afonso Henriques declared himself Portugal's first
king in 1139, but his descendants' ties of marriage
to various Spanish kingdoms led to dynastic disputes.
João I's defeat of the Castilians in 1385 established the
House of Avis which presided over the golden age of
Portuguese imperialism. Then in 1580, in the absence
of a direct heir, Portugal was ruled by Spanish kings for
60 years before the Duke of Bragança became João IV.
A Republican uprising ended the monarchy in 1910.
However, in the first 16 years of the
Republic there were 40 different
governments, and in 1926 Portugal
became a dictatorship under the
eventual leadership of Salazar.
Democracy was restored by the
Carnation Revolution of 1974.

1481–95
João II

1211–23 Afonso II

1185–1211
Sancho I

1248–79
Afonso III

1279–1325 Dinis

1438–81
Afonso V

1100	1200	1300	1400	1500
HOUSE OF BURGUNDY			**AVIS**	
1100	1200	1300	1400	1500

1325–57 Afonso IV

1357–67 Pedro I

1367–83 Fernando I

1223–48
Sancho II

1139–85
Afonso
Henriques
(Afonso I)

1433–8
Duarte

1521–57
João III

1385–1433 João I

1495–1521 Manuel I

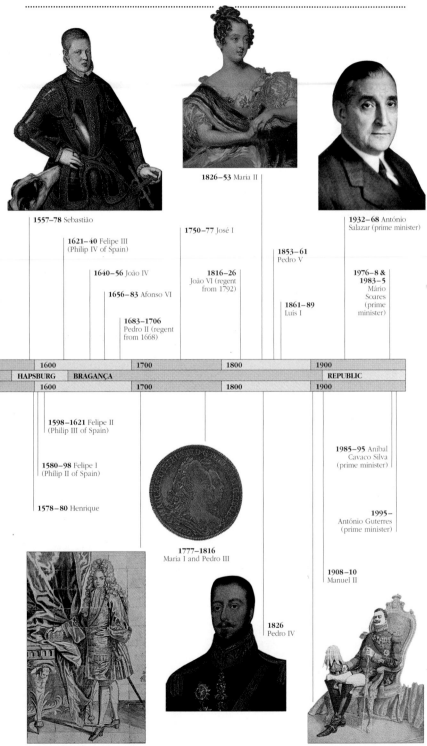

1826–53 Maria II

1557–78 Sebastião

1932–68 António
Salazar (prime minister)

1621–40 Felipe III
(Philip IV of Spain)

1750–77 José I

1853–61
Pedro V

1640–56 João IV

1816–26
João VI (regent
from 1792)

**1976–8 &
1983–5**
Mário
Soares
(prime
minister)

1656–83 Afonso VI

1861–89
Luís I

1683–1706
Pedro II (regent
from 1668)

1600	1700	1800	1900
HAPSBURG	BRAGANÇA		REPUBLIC
1600	1700	1800	1900

1598–1621 Felipe II
(Philip III of Spain)

1985–95 Aníbal
Cavaco Silva
(prime minister)

1580–98 Felipe I
(Philip II of Spain)

1995–
António Guterres
(prime minister)

1578–80 Henrique

1777–1816
Maria I and Pedro III

1908–10
Manuel II

1826
Pedro IV

1706–50 João V

1889–1908 Carlos I

The Age of Discovery

PORTUGAL'S ASTONISHING PERIOD of conquest and exploration began in 1415 with the capture of the North African city of Ceuta. Maritime expeditions into the Atlantic and along the West African coast followed, motivated by traditional Christian hostility towards Islam and the desire for commercial gain. Great riches were earned from the gold and slaves taken from the Guinea coast, but the real breakthrough for Portuguese imperialism occurred in 1498 when Vasco da Gama *(see p68)* reached India. Portugal soon controlled the Indian Ocean and the spice trade, and established an eastern capital at Goa. With Pedro Álvares Cabral's "discovery" of Brazil, Portugal became a mercantile super-power rivalled only by her neighbour Spain.

Portuguese padrão

Armillary Sphere
This celestial globe with the earth in its centre was used by navigators for measuring the positions of the stars. It became the personal emblem of Manuel I.

Magellan (c.1480–1521)
With Spanish funding, Portuguese sailor Fernão de Magalhães, known as Magellan, led the first circumnavigation of the globe (1519–22). He was killed in the Philippines before the voyage's end.

1500–1501 Gaspar Corte Real reaches Newfoundland.

1427 Diogo de Silves discovers the Azores.

1434 Gil Eanes rounds Cape Bojador (Western Sahara).

1460 Diogo Gomes discovers the Cape Verde archipelago.

1470s Discovery of island of São Tomé.

1482 Diogo Cão reaches the mouth of the Congo.

1485 On his third voyage Diogo Cão reaches Cape Cross (Namibia).

1488 Bartolomeu Dias rounds Cape of Good Hope.

1500 Pedro Álvares Cabral reaches Brazil.

The Adoration of the Magi
Painted for Viseu Cathedral shortly after Cabral returned from Brazil in 1500, this panel is attributed to the artist Grão Vasco (c.1475–1540). King Baltazar is depicted as a Tupi Indian.

African Ivory Salt Cellar
This 16th-century ivory carving shows Portuguese warriors supporting a globe and a ship. A sailor peers out from the crow's nest at the top.

Japanese Screen (c.1600)
This screen shows traders unloading a nau, *or great ship. Between 1575 and their expulsion in 1638, the Portuguese monopolized the carrying trade between China and Japan.*

HENRY THE NAVIGATOR

Although he did not sail himself, Henry (1394–1460), the third son of João I, laid the foundations for Portugal's maritime expansion that were later built upon by João II and consolidated by Manuel I. As Master of the wealthy Order of Christ and Governor of the Algarve, Henry was able to finance expeditions along the African coast. By the time he died he had a monopoly on all trade south of Cape Bojador. Legend tells that he founded a school of navigation in the Algarve, at either Sagres or Lagos.

KEY

- - - Discoverers' routes

1543 Portuguese arrive in Japan.

1513 Trading posts set up in China at Macau and Canton.

1510 Capture of Goa.

1498 Vasco da Gama reaches Calicut in India.

1518 Fortress built in Colombo (Sri Lanka).

1512 Portuguese reach Ternate in the Moluccas (Spice Islands).

Cloves
Pepper
Nutmeg
Cinnamon

The Spice Trade
Exotic spices were a great source of wealth for Portugal. The much-disputed Moluccas, or Spice Islands, were purchased from Spain in 1528.

PORTUGUESE DISCOVERIES

The systematic attempt to find a sea route to India, which led to a monopoly of the spice trade, began in 1482 with the first voyage of Diogo Cão, who planted a *padrão* (stone cross) on the shores where he landed.

Lateen-rigged Caravel
These ships with three triangular sails were favoured by the first Portuguese explorers who sailed close to the African coast. For later journeys across the open ocean, square sails were found more effective.

Crow's nest
Square sail on foremast
Cross of the Order of Christ

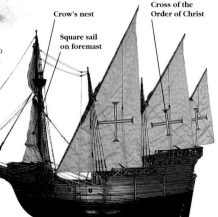

The 1755 Lisbon Earthquake

Ex-voto tile panel offered by survivors

THE FIRST TREMOR of the devastating earthquake was felt at 9:30am on 1 November. A few minutes later there was a second, far more violent shock, reducing over half the city to rubble. Although the epicentre was close to the Algarve, Lisbon, as the most populated area, bore the worst. Over 20 churches collapsed, crushing the crowds who had assembled for All Saints' Day. A third shock was followed by fires which quickly spread. An hour later, huge waves came rolling in from the Tagus and flooded the lower part of the city. Most of Portugal suffered damage and the shock was felt as far away as Italy. Perhaps 15,000 people lost their lives in Lisbon alone.

This anonymous painting of the arrival of a papal ambassador at court in 1693 shows how Terreiro do Paço looked before the earthquake.

Some buildings that might have survived an earthquake alone were destroyed by the fire that followed.

The old royal palace, the 16th-century Paço da Ribeira, was utterly ruined by the earthquake and ensuing flood.

The royal family was staying at the palace in Belém, a place far less affected than Lisbon, and survived the disaster unscathed. Here the king surveys the city's devastation.

Ships crammed full of people fleeing the fire were wrecked and anchors thrown up to water level.

This detail is from an ex-voto painting dedicated to Nossa Senhora da Estrela, given by a grateful father in thanks for the sparing of his daughter's life in the earthquake. The girl was found miraculously alive after being buried under rubble for seven hours.

THE RECONSTRUCTION OF LISBON

Marquês de Pombal (1699–1782)

No sooner had the tremors abated than Sebastião José de Carvalho e Melo, chief minister to José I and later to become Marquês de Pombal, was outlining ideas for rebuilding the city. While philosophers moralized, Pombal reacted with practicality. "Bury the dead and feed the living" was his initial response. He restored order, then began a progressive town-planning scheme. His efficient handling of the crisis gained him almost total political control.

REACTIONS TO THE DISASTER

The earthquake had a profound effect on European thought. Eyewitness accounts appeared in the papers, many written by foreigners living in Lisbon. A heated debate developed over whether the earthquake was a natural phenomenon or divine wrath. Pre-earthquake Lisbon had been a flourishing city, famed for its wealth – also for its Inquisition and idolatry. Interpreting the quake as punishment, preachers prophesied further catastrophes. Famous literary figures debated the significance of the event, among them the French writer Voltaire, who wrote a poem about the disaster, propounding his views that evil exists and man is weak and powerless, doomed to an unhappy fate on earth.

French author, Voltaire

The ancient castle walls succumbed to the reverberating shock waves.

Flames erupted as the candles lit for All Saints' Day ignited the city's churches. The fire raged for seven days.

Some of Lisbon's finest buildings were destroyed, along with gold, jewellery, priceless furniture, archives, books and paintings.

At 11am, tidal waves rolled into Terreiro do Paço. The Alcântara docks, to the west, bore the brunt of the impact.

Churches, homes and public buildings all suffered in the disaster. The Royal Opera House, here shown in ruins, was only completed in March the same year.

A CONTEMPORARY VIEW OF THE EARTHQUAKE

This anonymous German engraving of 1775 gives a vivid picture of the scale of the disaster. Many who fled the flames made for the Tagus, but were washed away in the huge waves which struck the Terreiro do Paço. The human and material losses were incalculable.

The reconstruction of the centre of Lisbon took place rapidly. By the end of November the Marquês de Pombal had devised a strikingly modern scheme for a grid of parallel streets running from the waterfront to Rossio. The new buildings are shown in yellow.

Modern-day Lisbon holds many reminders of the earthquake. Pombal's innovative grid system is clearly visible in this aerial view of the Baixa (see pp40–47). The scheme took many years to complete, and the triumphal arch that spans Rua Augusta was not finished until over a century later, in 1873.

LISBON THROUGH THE YEAR

WHILE THE SUMMER MONTHS are the most popular for visiting Lisbon and have many events on the calendar – the Festas dos Santos Populares, in June, are one of the highlights of the year – spring and autumn can also be rewarding if you want to tour the Lisbon Coast. In late winter, the colourful Carnaval celebrations attract many visitors to Lisbon. Other events during the year include music festivals, sporting fixtures and the many religious *festas*, which are great times of celebration for the Portuguese people.

SPRING

WITH THE ARRIVAL of springtime in Lisbon, the café and restaurant terraces begin to fill with people. Many events, such as concerts and markets, start to take place in the open air again as the weather improves. At the weekends the coastal resorts of Cascais and Estoril become livelier when on warm, bright days local people take day trips there to enjoy the seaside.

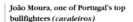

João Moura, one of Portugal's top bullfighters (*cavaleiros*)

MARCH

Concerto da Primavera
(*21 Mar*). This huge open-air music celebration takes place at the Cultural Centre of Belém. It includes rock and pop as well as classical music performances by both national and international artists.
Procissão dos Terceiros Franciscanos (*4th Sun before Easter*). The colourful

procession through the streets of Mafra (*see p92*) starts at the convent. The ceremonial robes worn in the procession were given to the church by João V, in the 18th century.

APRIL

Festa dos Merendeiros
(*4 Apr*). A traditional festival and procession held in Santo Isidoro, near Mafra (*see p92*). There is a ceremony to bless the bread and the fields in the hope of a successful harvest later on in the year.
Portuguese Open Tennis Championship (*first two weeks in Apr*). The best international players compete in Portugal's top tennis competition, held at the National Stadium in Lisbon.
Liberty Day (*25 Apr*). The annual celebration of the Carnation Revolution that ended 48 years of dictatorship in 1974 (*see p15*) is a major event in the

Lisbon calendar. Commemorations include a military parade and political speeches at the Praça do Império. The unions organize festivities that take place all over the city and a marathon is also held through the streets of Lisbon.
Beginning of the bull-fighting season (*Apr–Sep*). The vast Campo Pequeno bullring in Lisbon is the venue for this traditional entertainment. It takes place every Thursday, starting at the beginning of April and continuing throughout the summer months.
Festival Internacional de Teatro (FIT) (*Apr–May*). This theatre festival is held annually in Lisbon. Theatre companies from all over the world are invited to participate. The venue of the festival varies each year but details of the location and a programme of the productions being done can be obtained from tourist offices.

MAY

Dia do Trabalhador (*1 May*). Protest marches and political speeches throughout Lisbon are organized by the unions on Labour Day.
Festas do Senhor das Chagas (*3–5 May*). These religious celebrations held in Sesimbra (*see p106*) date back to the 18th century. The statue of the Senhor das Chagas (Our Lord of the Wounds) is carried in a procession from the seaside to the town.
Feira do Livro (*May–Jun*). One of the main literary events in Lisbon, this book fair offers numerous bargains, such as second-hand books and signed copies of recently published works. The event takes place either at the Praça do Comércio or the Parque Eduardo VII.

Formal military parades are held in Lisbon in celebration of Liberty Day

AVERAGE DAILY HOURS OF SUNSHINE

Hours

12
9
6
3
0

Jan Feb Mar Apr May Jun Jul Aug Sep Oct Nov Dec

Sunshine Chart
Although Lisbon enjoys a moderate amount of sunshine all year, the days are particularly hot and sunny in the summer months. Care should be taken to protect the skin against the sun, both when walking around Lisbon itself and when sunbathing along the coast on the beaches of Estoril or Cascais.

SUMMER

THE SUMMER MONTHS are a major holiday time in Lisbon, especially August when many Lisboetas retire to the coastal resorts, in particular Costa da Caparica and Cascais.

JUNE

Camões Day *(10 Jun).* This is the Portuguese National Day, known as *Dia de Portugal e das Comunidades*, referring to the Portuguese emigrants around the world. Flowers are laid by Camões's statue in Praça Luís de Camões, in Lisbon. Revered as the national poet, Camões (1524–80) wrote *Os Lusíadas*, an epic poem about the Discoveries.
Festas da Cidade *(throughout Jun).* A celebration of the city of Lisbon itself, that includes all sorts of events from rock concerts to drive-in films. The streets are all lit up and decorated for the event.

Celebrating Santo António, one of Lisbon's most important festivals

The beach at Estoril, just one of the many popular bays along the Lisbon Coast

Santo António *(12–13 Jun).* A major festival in Lisbon, honouring the city's patron saint, and the beginning of the Festas dos Santos Populares (Feasts of the People's Saints). Locals put up lanterns and streamers in the Alfama and bring out chairs for the hundreds who come for the wine and sardines.
São João *(23–24 Jun).* A similar festival to that of Santo António, forming part of the Festas dos Santos Populares.
Festival de Música de Sintra *(15 Jun–16 Jul).* A celebration of classical music in a series of concerts in the parks and palaces of Sintra *(see pp96–9).*
São Pedro *(25 Jun–1 Jul).* The end of the Festas dos Santos Populares. The fishing boats are blessed in Montijo, on the south bank of the Tagus.

JULY

FIA-Lisbon International Handicraft Exhibition *(early Jul).* This takes place at FIL, Lisbon's International Fair, a huge exhibition hall located by the river.
Festival Estoril Jazz *(early Jul).* A programme of jazz concerts, lasting about a week, takes place in locations in and around Lisbon.

Feira de Artesanato *(Jul–Aug).* This craft fair is held in Estoril *(see p102).* Craftwork is sold in the market and there is an exhibition of wine, food and traditional costumes.
Feira dos Alhos *(3rd Sun in Jul).* Located by the Convent of Mafra *(see p92),* this annual market includes the sale of local crafts, delicacies and the tasting of wine and cheese.
Festa de Santiago *(25 Jul).* Art exhibitions as well as musical and religious events are held at this annual festival in Sesimbra *(see p106).*
Feira Grande de São Pedro *(31 Jul).* A market of crafts, antiques and local delicacies, in Sintra *(see pp96–9).*
Música à Beira-Mar *(weekends in Jul–Sep).* Local musicians perform in the streets at night in the coastal town of Sesimbra *(see p106).*

AUGUST

Jazz em Agosto *(early Aug).* Jazz music is performed in the gardens of the Calouste Gulbenkian Cultural Centre.
Noites de Bailado em Seteais *(weekends throughout Aug).* Ballet performances are held at the palace of Seteais, near Sintra *(see pp96–7).*
Romaria de São Mamede *(14–22 Aug).* Farmers lead their animals around the chapel of Janas, north of Colares *(see p93),* to be blessed. The tradition originates in the fact that the site of the church was once that of a Roman temple dedicated to Diana, goddess of hunting and animals.

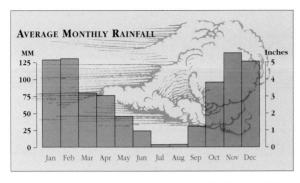

Rainfall Chart
Rainfall is fairly heavy in the winter months in Lisbon, and then drops steadily until the height of summer, when there is almost no rain at all. The autumn, although still warm, can produce some wet days, the wettest month on average being November.

AUTUMN

IN MANY WAYS, this is the best season for touring and sightseeing. The strong heat of the summer has passed but the weather is still pleasantly warm. The countryside around Sintra is particularly beautiful with the changing colours of the trees.

SEPTEMBER

Festa do Avante *(1st weekend in Sep)*. This lively *festa* in Seixal, south of the Tagus, attracts large crowds. It includes national and international music shows, exhibitions and cultural events.

Nossa Senhora da Luz *(2nd weekend of Sep)*. A religious *festa* held in honour of Our Lady of the Light in Sampaio, near Sesimbra *(see p106)*.

Festa das Vindimas *(2nd Sun of Sep)*. At the foot of Palmela's medieval castle *(see p106)*, the first grape harvest is blessed, amid traditional entertainment, wine-tasting and fireworks.

Nossa Senhora do Cabo Espichel *(last Sun of Sep)*. Local fishermen honour the Virgin Mary with a procession up to the church at Cabo Espichel *(see p103)*.

Portuguese Grand Prix *(date varies)*. The Formula One racing competition attracts huge crowds. It is held in the Autodromo just north of Estoril *(see p102)*.

Festival do Mar *(last 2 weeks of Sep–first 2 weeks of Oct)*. This festival in Sesimbra *(see p103)* promotes the town's local artists, traditions and gastronomic specialities.

Encontros Acarte *(throughout Sep)*. Organized by the Gulbenkian Foundation, this is a programme of activities designed to promote new talent in the arts. It runs all year round but a show is held in September. *Acarte* is an acronym standing for Animation, Creativity, Art and Education.

OCTOBER

Republic Day *(5 Oct)*. The revolution that brought the monarchy to an end in 1910 *(see p15)*, is commemorated annually in Lisbon with military parades.

Golf-Semana Internacional *(late Oct)*. A major golf tournament, in Estoril *(see p102)*.

An old lady laying flowers at a cemetery in Lisbon in honour of All Saints' Day

NOVEMBER

All Saints' Day *(1 Nov)*. An important festival in the Portuguese religious calendar, many families light candles and lay flowers in local cemeteries throughout the area, in honour of their dead relatives.

Feira de Todos os Santos *(1 Nov)*. Also known as the Chestnuts' Market, this is a lively fair held in Azureira, near Mafra *(see p92)*, on All Saints' Day. Nuts and dried fruits are the main trade of the market.

Circus *(late Nov–early Jan)*. As the Christmas season approaches, various circuses arrive in Lisbon. The main ones are set up in the bullring at Campo Pequeno *(see p80)* and others at the Coliseu dos Recreios. Check with tourist offices for exact dates.

Blessing the grape harvest at the Festa das Vindimas in Palmela

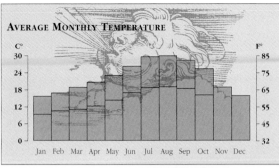

Temperature Chart
Lisbon is rarely very cold, and maintains a pleasantly mild climate, even during the winter months, making it a good city to visit in any season. However, the summer months bring days of consistent heat, and although the city is quiet in high summer, it can become humid and stifling.

WINTER

THOSE SEEKING MILD, sunny climes and an escape from the winter cold, will find this a good time of year to visit Lisbon. The nightlife is very lively and continues until the early hours, especially at weekends. Christmas is a time of great celebration and an important occasion for families to reunite and enjoy long meals together.

DECEMBER

Moda Lisboa *(early Dec).* Although the Lisbon fashion show only started fairly recently, it has rapidly become a major event and attracts huge crowds. The venue changes annually, so it is advisable to check the location with tourist offices.
Christmas *(24–25 Dec).* Throughout the Lisbon area, churches and shops display nativity scenes and cribs. The main celebrations take place on Christmas Eve, when families get together and go to midnight mass. They then return home for a large traditional meal of *bacalhau* (salted dried cod) and *sonhos* (small fried cakes similar to doughnuts, usually flavoured with pumpkin or orange).
Nossa Senhora da Conceição *(26 Dec).* A traditional religious procession held in honour of Our Lady of the Immaculate Conception, the saint protector of Alfarim, near Sesimbra *(see p106).*

Colourful parades during the annual Carnaval celebrations in Lisbon

JANUARY

New Year *(1 Jan).* In Lisbon, a spectacular firework display is held in Praça do Comércio to welcome in the New Year.
Epiphany *(6 Jan).* The traditional cake baked for the Epiphany is *bolo rei* (king's cake), a small fruit cake made with a lucky charm and a bean inside. Crown-shaped, it is topped with crystallized fruit, resembling gems. The person who gets the bean must then buy the next cake. *Bolo rei* is also made at Christmas time.

The celebratory cake, *bolo rei*

Opera season *(Jan–Nov).* The opera season commences at the Teatro Nacional de São Carlos *(see p53).*

FEBRUARY

Carnaval *(date varies).* This is celebrated throughout Portugal with spectacular costumes and floats; there is an especially colourful parade in Sesimbra *(see p106).*

Procissão do Senhor dos Passos da Graça *(second Sun in Lent).* The figure of Christ *(Senhor dos Passos)* is taken out of the Igreja da Graça *(see p37)* and carried through the streets of Graça, in Lisbon. The procession dates back to the 16th century.

PUBLIC HOLIDAYS

New Year's Day (1 Jan)
Carnaval (Feb)
Good Friday (Mar or Apr)
Dia 25 de Abril, *commemorating 1974 revolution* (25 Apr)
Dia do Trabalhador, *Labour Day* (1 May)
Corpus Christi (6 Jun)
Camões Day (10 Jun)
Assumption Day (15 Aug)
Republic Day (5 Oct)
All Saints' Day (1 Nov)
Dia da Restauração, *commemorating Independence from Spain, 1640* (1 Dec)
Immaculate Conception (8 Dec)
Christmas Day (25 Dec)

LISBON AREA
BY AREA

Lisbon at a Glance

Portugal's capital, a city of about 700,000 people, sits on the north bank of the Tagus estuary, 17 km (10 miles) from the Atlantic. Razed to the ground by the devastating earthquake of 1755 *(see pp20–21)*, the city centre, the Baixa, is essentially 18th century, with a carefully planned grid of elegant streets. On the hills on either side of the centre, the narrow streets of the Alfama and Bairro Alto make it a personal, approachable city. Since the construction of the bridge, Ponte 25 de Abril, in the 1960s, it has been possible for the city to expand to the Outra Banda (the other bank). Since its days of glory during the Age of Discovery, when Lisbon was at the forefront of world trade, the city has been an important port. Today the docks have moved, but in Belém, 6 km (4 miles) west along the river from the city centre, the Mosteiro dos Jerónimos and the Torre de Belém still bear witness to the city's maritime past.

The Museu Nacional de Arte Antiga houses paintings and sculpture. There are notable Flemish-influenced Portuguese works such as Jorge Afonso's Apparition of Christ to the Virgin *(see pp56–7).*

The Mosteiro dos Jerónimos is a magnificent 16th-century monastery. Commissioned by Manuel I, much of it is built in the peculiarly Portuguese style of architecture, known as Manueline. The extravagantly sculpted south portal of the church with its minute detailing was designed by João de Castilho in 1516. It is one of the finest examples of the style (see pp66–7).

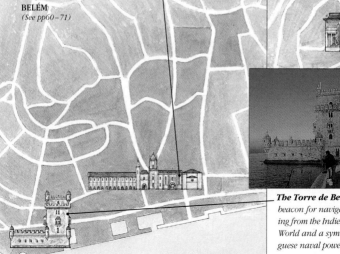

BELÉM
(See pp60–71)

The Torre de Belém was a beacon for navigators returning from the Indies and the New World and a symbol of Portuguese naval power (see p70).

◁ **View from the Tagus of Praça do Comércio with the statue of José I at the centre**

The Elevador de Santa Justa, *built at the turn of the century, is a wrought-iron lift decorated with delicate filigree that links the Baixa quarter with the Bairro Alto* (see p46).

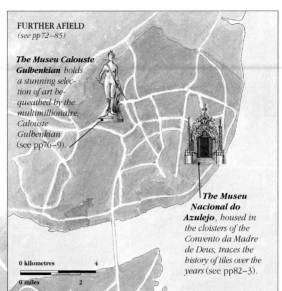

FURTHER AFIELD
(see pp72–85)

The Museu Calouste Gulbenkian *holds a stunning selection of art bequeathed by the multimillionaire, Calouste Gulbenkian* (see pp76–9).

The Museu Nacional do Azulejo, *housed in the cloisters of the Convento da Madre de Deus, traces the history of tiles over the years* (see pp82–3).

0 kilometres   4

0 miles   2

BAIXA
(See pp40–47)

ALFAMA
(See pp30–39)

BAIRRO ALTO AND ESTRELA
(See pp48–59)

The Castelo de São Jorge, *once a Moorish castle and then the abode of the Portuguese kings, was transformed in the 1930s into tranquil public gardens. The battlements afford spectacular views of the city* (see pp38–9).

0 metres   500

0 yards   500

The Sé, *the city's greatly restored cathedral, is a sturdy Romanesque building lit by a beautiful rose window. The relics of St Vincent, the city's patron saint, are among the religious objects on display in the treasury* (see p36).

ALFAMA

IT IS DIFFICULT TO BELIEVE that this humble neighbourhood was once the most desirable quarter of Lisbon. For the Moors, the tightly packed alleyways around the fortified castle comprised the whole city. The seeds of decline were sown in the Middle Ages when wealthy residents moved west for fear of earthquakes, leaving the quarter to fishermen and paupers. The buildings survived the 1755 earthquake *(see pp20–21)* and, although there are no Moorish houses still standing, the quarter retains its kasbah-like layout. Compact houses line steep streets and stairways, their façades strung with washing.

Portugal's coat of arms in the treasury of the Sé

Long-overdue restoration is under way in the most dilapidated areas, but daily life still revolves around local grocery stores and small, cellar-like tavernas.

Above the Alfama, the imposing Castelo de São Jorge crowns Lisbon's eastern hill. This natural vantage point, a defensive stronghold and royal palace until the 16th century, is today a popular promenade, with spectacular views from its greatly restored ramparts.

West of the Alfama stand the proud twin towers of the Sé. To the northeast, the domed church of Santa Engrácia and the white façade of São Vicente de Fora dominate the skyline.

SIGHTS AT A GLANCE

Museums and Galleries
Museu de Artes
  Decorativas **2**
Museu da Marioneta **11**
Museu Militar **6**

Historic Buildings
Casa dos Bicos **7**
Castelo de São Jorge pp38–9 **10**

Churches
Santo António à Sé **9**
Santa Engrácia **5**
São Vicente de Fora **3**
Sé **8**

Belvederes
Miradouro da Graça **12**
Miradouro de Santa Luzia **1**

Markets
Feira da Ladra **4**

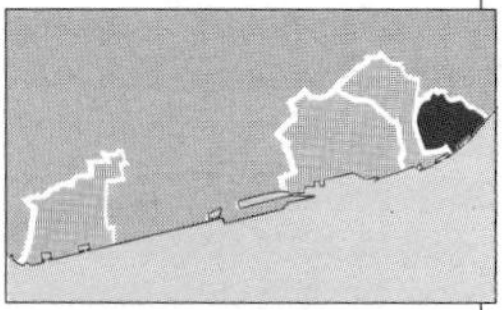

GETTING THERE
The 12 and 28 trams rattle up the narrow streets of the Alfama from the Baixa. Bus 37 does a circuit from the Castle to Rossio. Many buses run east along Avenida Dom Infante Henrique to Santa Apolónia station, and west to Belém.

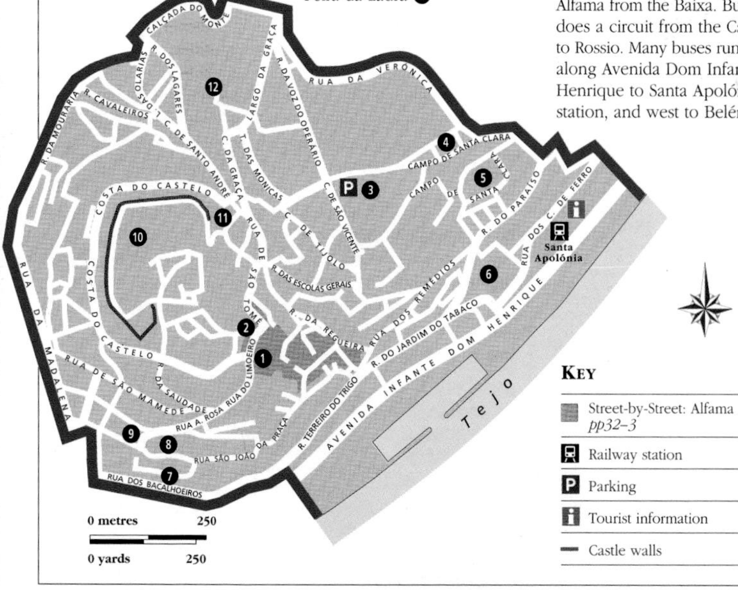

KEY

	Street-by-Street: Alfama *pp32–3*
🚉	Railway station
🅿	Parking
🛈	Tourist information
—	Castle walls

0 metres 250
0 yards 250

◁ **Ironwork balconies on a house in Rua dos Bacalhoeiros, beside the Casa dos Bicos**

Street-by-Street: Alfama

A FASCINATING QUARTER at any time of day, the Alfama comes to life in the late afternoon and early evening when the locals emerge at their doorways and the small tavernas start to fill. Many African immigrants live here and several venues play music from Mozambique and the Cape Verde Islands. Given the steep streets and steps of the quarter, the least strenuous approach is to start at the top and work your way down. A walk around the maze of winding alleyways will reveal picturesque corners and crumbling churches as well as panoramic views from the shady terraces, such as the Miradouro de Santa Luzia.

On Largo das Portas do Sol, café tables look out over the Alfama towards the Tagus estuary. Portas do Sol was one of the entrance gates to the old city.

The church of Santa Luzia has 18th-century blue and white *azulejo* panels on its south wall.

A modern statue of St Vincent holding the emblem of Lisbon, a boat with two ravens *(see p36)*, stands in Largo das Portas do Sol.

Castelo de São Jorge

★ **Museu de Artes Decorativas**
Set up as a museum by the banker Ricardo do Espírito Santo Silva, the 17th-century Palácio Azurara houses fine 17th- and 18th-century Portuguese furniture and decorative arts ❷

KEY

— — — Suggested route

0 metres   25

0 yards   25

STAR SIGHTS

★ **Miradouro de Santa Luzia**

★ **Museu de Artes Decorativas**

★ **Miradouro de Santa Luzia**
The view from this bougainvillea-clad terrace spans the tiled roofs of the Alfama toward the Tagus. This is a pleasant place to rest after a walk around the area's steep streets ❶

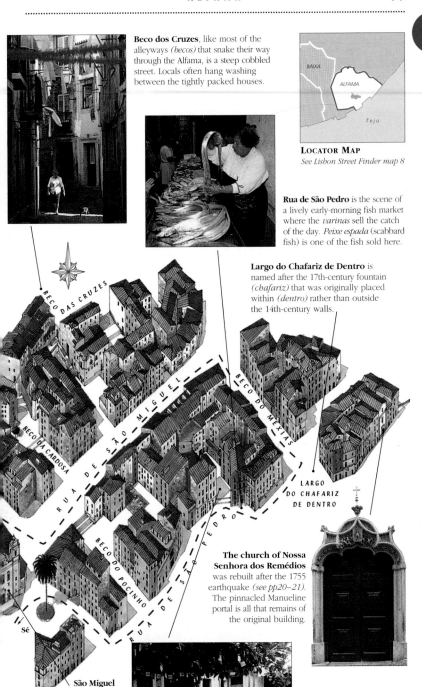

Beco dos Cruzes, like most of the alleyways *(becos)* that snake their way through the Alfama, is a steep cobbled street. Locals often hang washing between the tightly packed houses.

LOCATOR MAP
See Lisbon Street Finder map 8

Rua de São Pedro is the scene of a lively early-morning fish market where the *varinas* sell the catch of the day. *Peixe espada* (scabbard fish) is one of the fish sold here.

Largo do Chafariz de Dentro is named after the 17th-century fountain *(chafariz)* that was originally placed within *(dentro)* rather than outside the 14th-century walls.

BAIXA

ALFAMA

Tejo

BECO DAS CRUZES

BECO DA CARDOSA

RUA DE SÃO MIGUEL

BECO DO MEXIAS

BECO DO POCINHO

RUA DE SÃO PEDRO

LARGO DO CHAFARIZ DE DENTRO

Sé

The church of Nossa Senhora dos Remédios was rebuilt after the 1755 earthquake *(see pp20–21)*. The pinnacled Manueline portal is all that remains of the original building.

São Miguel was rebuilt after it was damaged in the 1755 earthquake. It retains a few earlier features, including a fine ceiling of Brazilian jacaranda wood.

Popular restaurants hidden in the labyrinth of alleyways spill out onto open-air patios. The *Lautasco (see p128)*, in Beco do Azinhal, serves excellent Portuguese food.

Tile panel showing pre-earthquake Praça do Comércio, Santa Luzia

Miradouro de Santa Luzia ➊

Rua do Limoeiro. **Map** 8 D4. 🚌 28.

THE TERRACE by the church of Santa Luzia provides a sweeping view over the Alfama and the River Tagus. Distinctive landmarks, from left to right, are the cupola of Santa Engrácia, the church of Santo Estêvão and the two startling white towers of São Miguel. While tourists admire the views, old men play cards under the bougainvillea-clad pergola. The south wall of Santa Luzia has two modern tiled panels, one of Praça do Comércio before it was flattened by the earthquake, the other showing the Christians attacking the Castelo de São Jorge (see pp38–9) in 1147.

Museu de Artes Decorativas ➋

Largo das Portas do Sol 2. **Map** 8 D3. 📞 01-886 21 83. 🚌 12, 28. ⏰ 10am–5pm Wed–Mon. ● 1 Jan, Easter, 1 May, 25 Dec. 🎫 ♿

ALSO KNOWN AS the Ricardo do Espírito Santo Silva Foundation, the museum was set up in 1953 to preserve the traditions and increase public awareness of the Portuguese decorative arts. The foundation was named after a banker who bought the 17th-century Palácio Azurara in 1947 to house his fine collection of furniture, textiles, silver and

ceramics. Among the 17th- and 18th-century antiques displayed in this handsome four-storey mansion are many fine pieces in exotic woods, including an 18th-century rosewood back-gammon and chess table. Also of note are the collections of 18th-century silver and Chinese porcelain, and the Arraiolos carpets. The spacious rooms still retain some original ceilings and *azulejo* panels.

18th-century china cutlery case, Museu de Artes Decorativas

Workshops are housed in the adjoining building, where visitors can watch artisans preserving the techniques of cabinet-making, gilding, book-binding and other traditional crafts. Temporary exhibitions, lectures and concerts are also held in the palace.

Stone figure of a woman praying by the tomb of Carlos I in São Vicente de Fora

São Vicente de Fora ➌

Largo de São Vicente. **Map** 8 E3. 📞 01-886 25 44. 🚌 28. ⏰ 9am–12:30pm, 3–6:30pm Tue–Sun. 🎫 📷 ♿ to cloisters.

ST VINCENT was proclaimed Lisbon's patron saint in 1173, when his relics, now in the Sé (see p36), were transferred from the Algarve, in southern Portugal, to a church on this site outside (fora) the city walls. Designed by Italian architect Filippo Terzi, and completed in 1627, the off-white Italianate façade is sober and symmetrical, with towers either side and statues of saints Augustine, Sebastian and Vincent over the entrance. Inside, the eye is drawn immediately to Machado de Castro's Baroque canopy over the altar, flanked by life-size wooden statues.

The adjoining former Augustinian monastery, reached via the nave, retains its 16th-century cistern and vestiges of the former cloister but is chiefly visited for its 18th-century *azulejos*. Among the panels in the entrance hall off the first cloister there are lively, though historically inaccurate, tile scenes of Afonso Henriques attacking Lisbon and Santarém. Around the cloisters the tiled rural scenes, surrounded by floral designs and cherubs, illustrate the fables of La Fontaine.

A passageway leads behind the church to the old refectory, transformed into the Bragança Pantheon in 1885. The stone sarcophagi of almost every king and queen are here, from the first of that dynasty, João IV, who died in 1656, to Manuel II, last king of Portugal. Only Maria I and Pedro IV are not buried here. A stone mourner kneels at the tomb of Carlos I and his son Luís Felipe, assassinated in Praça do Comércio in 1908.

Feira da Ladra 4

Campo de Santa Clara. **Map** 8 F2.
🔓 7:30am–1pm Tue & Sat. 🚌 28.

THE STALLS of the so-called
"Thieves' Market" have
occupied this site on the edge
of the Alfama for over a century, laid out under the shade
of trees or canopies. As the
fame of this flea market has
grown, bargains are increasingly hard to find amongst the
mass of bric-a-brac, but a few
of the vendors have interesting
wrought-iron work, prints and
tiles, as well as second-hand
clothes. The influence of the
African colonies can be seen
in some of the stalls selling
statuary, masks and jewellery.
Fish, vegetables and herbs are
sold in the nearby wrought-
iron marketplace.

Bric-a-brac for sale in the Feira da Ladra

Santa Engrácia 5

Campo de Santa Clara. **Map** 8 F2.
📞 01-888 15 29. 🚌 28. 🔓 10am–
5pm Tue–Sun. 🔴 1 Jan, Easter,
1 May, 25 Dec. 📷 🅾 ♿

ONE OF LISBON'S most striking
landmarks, the soaring
dome of Santa Engrácia punc-
tuates the skyline in the east
of the city. The original church
collapsed in a storm in 1681.
The first stone of the new
Baroque monument, laid in
1682, marked the beginning
of a 284-year saga which led
to the invention of a saying
that a Santa Engrácia job was
never done. The church was
not completed until 1966.
  The interior, paved with
coloured marble and crowned
by a giant cupola, emanates
a feeling of space. As the
National Pantheon, it houses
cenotaphs of heroes of Portuguese history, such as Vasco da

Gama (see p68) and Afonso
de Albuquerque, Viceroy of
India (1502–15) on the left,
and on the right Henry the
Navigator (see p19) and Luís
de Camões (see p23). On
request you can take the lift up
to the dome and enjoy a 360-
degree panorama of the city.

Museu Militar 6

Largo do Museu da Artilharia.
Map 8 F3. 📞 01-888 21 31. 🚌 12,
46, 107. 🚌 28. 🔓 10am–5pm
Tue–Sat. 🔴 public hols. 📷

APTLY LOCATED on the site of
a 16th-century cannon
foundry and arms depot, the
military museum contains an
extensive display of arms,
uniforms and historical military
documents. Visits begin in the
Vasco da Gama Room
with a collection of old
cannons and modern
murals depicting the dis-
covery of the sea route
to India. The Salas da
Grande Guerra, on the
first floor, display World
War I related exhibits.
Other rooms are de-
voted to the evolution
of weapons in Portugal,
from primitive flints
through spears to rifles.
  The large courtyard,
flanked by cannons, tells the
story of Portugal in tiled
panels, from the Christian Re-
conquest to World War I. The
Portuguese artillery section in
the oldest part of the museum
displays the wagon used to
transport the triumphal arch to
Rua Augusta (see p47).

The multicoloured marble interior
beneath Santa Engrácia's dome

Casa dos Bicos 7

Rua dos Bacalhoeiros. **Map** 8 D4.
📞 01-888 48 27. 🚌 1, 13, 46, 91.
🔓 for temporary exhibitions only.

THIS CONSPICUOUS house,
faced with diamond-shaped
stones (bicos), was built in
1523 for Brás de Albuquerque,
illegitimate son of Afonso,
Viceroy of India and conqueror
of Goa and Malacca. The
strange façade is an adaptation
of a style popular in Mediterranean Europe during the 16th
century. The two top storeys,
ruined in the earthquake of
1755, were only restored in
the 1980s, recreating the original from old views of Lisbon
in tile panels and engravings.
In the interim the building
was used for salting fish (Rua
dos Bacalhoeiros means street
of the cod fishermen). The
modern interior of the lower
floors is used as a venue for
temporary exhibitions.

The curiously faceted Casa dos Bicos, and surrounding buildings

The façade of the Sé, the city's cathedral

Sé 8

Largo da Sé. **Map** 8 D4. 01-886
67 52. 37. 28. 9am–5pm
daily. to cloister & treasury.

IN 1150, THREE YEARS after
Afonso Henriques recap-
tured Lisbon from the Moors,
he built a cathedral for the first
bishop of Lisbon, the English
crusader Gilbert of Hastings,
on the site of the old mosque.
Sé is short for Sedes Episco-
palis, the seat (or see) of a
bishop. Devasted by three
earth tremors in the 14th century, as well as the earthquake
of 1755, and renovated over
the centuries, the cathedral you
see today blends a variety of

architectural styles.
The façade, with
twin castellated
belltowers and a
splendid rose win-
dow, retains its
solid Romanesque
aspect. The gloomy
interior, for the most
part, is simple and
austere, and hardly
anything remains
of the embellish-
ment lavished
upon it by King
Joào V in the first
half of the 18th
century. Beyond
the renovated Ro-
manesque nave the
ambulatory has nine
Gothic chapels. The
Capela de Santo
Ildefonso contains
the 14th-century sarcophagi
of Lopo Fernandes Pacheco,
companion in arms to King
Afonso IV, and his wife, Maria
Vilalobos. The bearded figure
of the nobleman, sword in
hand, and his wife, clutching
a prayer book, are carved
onto the tombs with their
dogs sitting faithfully at their

**Detail of the Baroque nativity scene
by Joaquim Machado de Castro**

feet. In the adjacent chancel
are the tombs of Afonso IV
and his wife Dona Beatriz.

The Gothic **cloister**, reached
via the third chapel in the ambulatory, has elegant double
arches with some finely carved
capitals. One of the chapels is
still fitted with its 13th-century
wrought-iron gate. Archaeological excavations in the
cloister have unearthed various
Roman and other remains.

To the left of the cathedral
entrance the Franciscan chapel
contains the font where the
saint was baptized in 1195
and is decorated with a charming tiled scene of St
Antony preaching to
the fishes. The adja-
cent chapel contains
a Baroque nativity
scene made of cork,
wood and terracotta
by Machado de
Castro (1766).

The **treasury** is
at the top of the stair-
case on the right as you
enter. It houses a varied collection of silver, ecclesiastical
robes, statuary, illustrated
manuscripts and a selection
of relics associated with St
Vincent. The cathedral's most
prized possession is the casket
containing the remains of the
saint which were transferred to
Lisbon from Cape St Vincent
in southern Portugal in 1173.
Legend has it that two sacred
ravens kept a permanent vigil
over the boat that transported
the relics, and the raven became the symbol of Lisbon's
liberation from Muslim rule
used on the city's coat of
arms. The descendants of the
two ravens used to live in the
cloisters of the cathedral, but
the last one died in 1978.

**Tomb of the 14th-century nobleman Lopo
Fernandes Pacheco in the ambulatory**

SANTO ANTÓNIO (C.1195–1231)

To the chagrin of the Lisboetas, their best-loved
saint is known as St Antony of Padua. Although
born and brought up in Lisbon, he spent the
last months of his life in Padua, Italy.

St Antony joined the Franciscan Order in
1220, impressed by some crusading friars he
had met at Coimbra where he was studying.
The Franciscan friar was a learned and pas-
sionate preacher, renowned for his devotion
to the poor and his ability to convert heretics.
Many statues and paintings of St Antony depict
him carrying the Infant Jesus on a book, while
others show him preaching to the fishes, as
St Francis preached to the birds. He is also
often called upon to help find lost objects.

In 1934 Pope Pius XI declared St Antony
a patron saint of Portugal. The year 1995 saw
the 800th anniversary of his birth – a cause
for major celebrations throughout the city.

Santo António à Sé 9

Largo Santo António da Sé. **Map** 7 C4.
[] *01-886 91 45.* [] *37.* [] *28.*
[] *8am–7:30pm daily.* [] **Museu Antoniano** [] *01-886 04 47.*
[] *10am–1pm, 2–6pm Tue–Sun.* [[]]

THE POPULAR LITTLE church of Santo António allegedly stands on the site of the house in which St Antony was born. The crypt, reached via the tiled sacristy on the left of the church, is all that remains of the original church destroyed by the earthquake of 1755. Work began on the new church in 1757 headed by Mateus Vicente, architect of the Basilica da Estrela *(see p55)* and was partially funded by donations collected by local children with the cry "a small coin for St Antony". Even today the floor of the tiny chapel in the crypt is strewn with escudos and the walls are scrawled with devotional messages from worshippers.

The church's façade blends the undulating curves of the Baroque style with Neo-Classical Ionic columns on either side of the main portal. Inside, on the way down to the crypt, a modern *azulejo* panel commemorates the visit of Pope John Paul II in 1982. In 1995 the church was given a facelift for the saint's eighth centenary. It is traditional for young couples to visit the church on their wedding day and leave flowers for St Antony who is believed to bring good luck to new marriages.

Next door the small **Museu Antoniano** houses ex votos, images and manuscripts, all relating to St Antony, as well

20th-century tiled panel recording Pope John Paul II's visit to Santo António à Sé

as gold and silverware which used to decorate the church. The most charming exhibit is a 17th-century tiled panel of St Antony preaching to the fishes.

Castelo de São Jorge 10

See pp38–9.

Museu da Marioneta 11

Largo Rodrigues de Freitas 19.
Map 8 D3. [] *01-888 28 41.* [] *37.* [] *28.*
[] *10am–1pm, 3–6pm Tue–Sun.* [[]]

AN UNSALUBRIOUS entrance takes you up to this small, eccentric puppet museum. The collection includes characters from 17th- and 18th-century theatre and opera, among them knights, jesters, princesses, devils and satirical figures. The puppets are finely crafted but their gruesome, contorted features are unlikely to appeal to small children. The museum runs videos of puppet shows and there are occasionally live performances on the small stage set.

The Miradouro and Igreja da Graça seen from the Castelo de São Jorge

Grotesque puppet in Museu da Marioneta

Miradouro da Graça 12

Map 8 D2. [] *37.* [] *12, 28.*

THE WORKING-CLASS quarter of Graça developed at the end of the last century. Today, it is visited chiefly for the views from its *miradouro* (belvedere). The panorama of rooftops and skyscrapers is less spectacular than the view from the castle, but it is a popular spot, particularly in the early evenings when couples sit at café tables under the pines. Behind the *miradouro* stands an Augustinian monastery, founded in 1271 and rebuilt after the earthquake. Once a flourishing complex, the huge building is nowadays used as barracks but the church, the **Igreja da Graça**, can still be visited. Inside, in the right transept, is the *Senhor dos Passo*s, a representation of Christ carrying the cross on the way to Calvary. This figure, clad in brilliant purple clothes, is carried in a procession through Graça on the second Sunday in Lent. The *azulejos* on the altar front, dating from the 17th century, imitate the brocaded textiles usually draped over the altar.

Castelo de São Jorge ⓾

FOLLOWING THE RECAPTURE of Lisbon from the Moors in 1147, King Afonso Henriques transformed their hilltop citadel into the residence of the Portuguese kings. In 1511 Manuel I built a more lavish palace in what is now the Praça do Comércio and the castle was used variously as a theatre, prison and arms depot. After the 1755 earthquake the ramparts remained in ruins until 1938 when Salazar *(see p15)* began a complete renovation, rebuilding the "medieval" walls and adding gardens and wild-fowl. The castle may not be authentic but the gardens and the narrow streets of the Santa Cruz district within the walls make a pleasant stroll and the views are the finest in Lisbon.

Stone head of Martim Moniz

A steep stairway leads down to the outlying Torre de São Lourenço.

A statue of Afonso Henriques was placed here during Salazar's restoration.

★ Battlements
Visitors can climb the towers and walk along the reconstructed ramparts of the castle walls.

Casa do Leão Restaurant
Part of the former royal residence can be booked for evening meals and parties (see p128).

★ Observation Terrace
This large shaded square affords spectacular views over Lisbon and the Tagus. Local men play backgammon and cards under the trees.

KEY

– – –   Suggested route

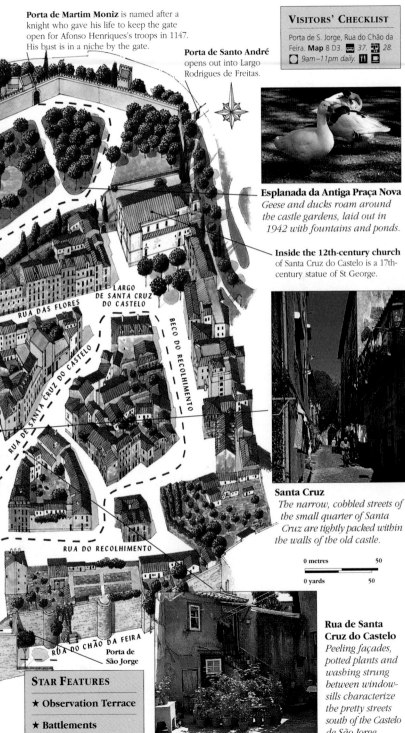

Porta de Martim Moniz is named after a knight who gave his life to keep the gate open for Afonso Henriques's troops in 1147. His bust is in a niche by the gate.

Porta de Santo André opens out into Largo Rodrigues de Freitas.

VISITORS' CHECKLIST

Porta de S. Jorge, Rua do Chão da Feira. **Map** 8 D3. 🚌 *37.* 🚋 *28.* ⏰ *9am–11pm daily.* 🍴 📷

Esplanada da Antiga Praça Nova
Geese and ducks roam around the castle gardens, laid out in 1942 with fountains and ponds.

Inside the 12th-century church of Santa Cruz do Castelo is a 17th-century statue of St George.

LARGO DE SANTA CRUZ DO CASTELO

RUA DAS FLORES

BECO DO RECOLHIMENTO

RUA DE SANTA CRUZ DO CASTELO

Santa Cruz
The narrow, cobbled streets of the small quarter of Santa Cruz are tightly packed within the walls of the old castle.

RUA DO RECOLHIMENTO

| 0 metres | 50 |
| 0 yards | 50 |

RUA DO CHÃO DA FEIRA
Porta de São Jorge

STAR FEATURES

★ **Observation Terrace**

★ **Battlements**

Rua de Santa Cruz do Castelo
Peeling façades, potted plants and washing strung between window-sills characterize the pretty streets south of the Castelo de São Jorge.

Baixa

From the ruins of Lisbon, devastated by the earthquake of 1755 *(see pp20–21)*, the Marquês de Pombal created an entirely new centre. Using a grid layout of streets, he linked the stately, arcaded Praça do Comércio beside the Tagus with the busy central square of Rossio. The streets were flanked by uniform, Neo-Classical buildings and named according to the shopkeepers and craftsmen who traded there.

Detail on statue of José I in Praça do Comércio

The Baixa (lower town) is still the commercial hub of the capital, housing banks, offices and shops. At its centre, Rossio is a popular meeting point with cafés, theatres and restaurants. The geometric layout of the area has been retained, but most of the buildings constructed since the mid-18th century have not adhered to Pombaline formality. The streets are crowded by day, particularly the lively Rua Augusta, but after dark the quarter is almost deserted.

Sights at a Glance

Museums and Galleries
Museu da Sociedade de Geografia 4

Churches
Nossa Senhora da Conceição Velha 9

Parks and Gardens
Jardim Botânico 1

Lifts
Elevador de Santa Justa 7

Historic Streets and Squares
Avenida da Liberdade 2
Praça do Comércio 10
Praça da Figueira 6
Praça dos Restauradores 3
Rossio 5
Rua Augusta 8

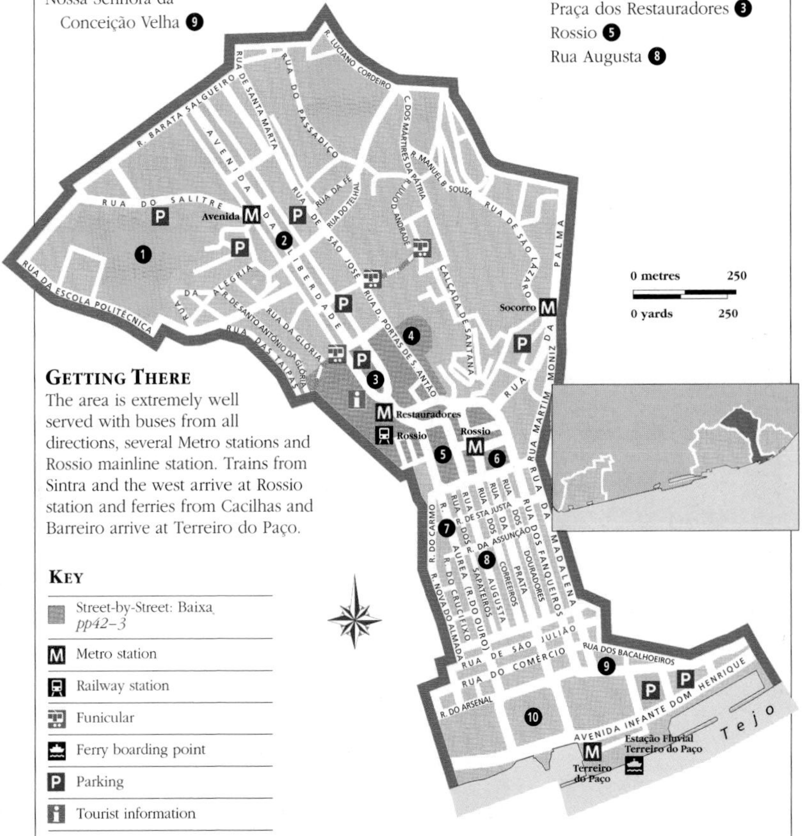

Getting There

The area is extremely well served with buses from all directions, several Metro stations and Rossio mainline station. Trains from Sintra and the west arrive at Rossio station and ferries from Cacilhas and Barreiro arrive at Terreiro do Paço.

Key

- Street-by-Street: Baixa *pp42–3*
- [M] Metro station
- Railway station
- Funicular
- Ferry boarding point
- [P] Parking
- [i] Tourist information

◁ **The triumphal arch in Praça do Comércio leading into Rua Augusta and the Baixa**

Street-by-Street: Baixa

THIS IS THE BUSIEST quarter of the city, in particular the central squares of Rossio and Praça da Figueira. Totally rebuilt after the earthquake of 1755 *(see pp20–21)*, the area was one of Europe's first examples of town planning. Today, the large Neo-Classical buildings along the wide avenues house business offices. The ambience and surroundings are best absorbed from one of the busy pavement cafés. The pedestrianized Rua das Portas de Santo Antão, where restaurants display tanks of live lobsters, is more relaxing for a stroll.

Tiled panel outside the Tabacaria Monaco

Palácio Foz, once a magnificent 18th-century palace built by the Italian architect Francesco Fabri, now houses the city's tourist office.

The Elevador da Glória is a bright yellow funicular that rattles up the hill to the Bairro Alto as far as the Miradouro de São Pedro de Alcântara *(see p54)*.

Restauradores

Praça dos Restauradores
This large tree-lined square, named after the men who died during the War of Restoration, is a busy through road with café terraces on the patterned pavements ❸

Restauradores

KEY

- - - Suggested route

STAR SIGHT

★ **Rossio**

Rossio station, designed by José Luís Monteiro, is an eye-catching Neo-Manueline building with horseshoe-arch doorways.

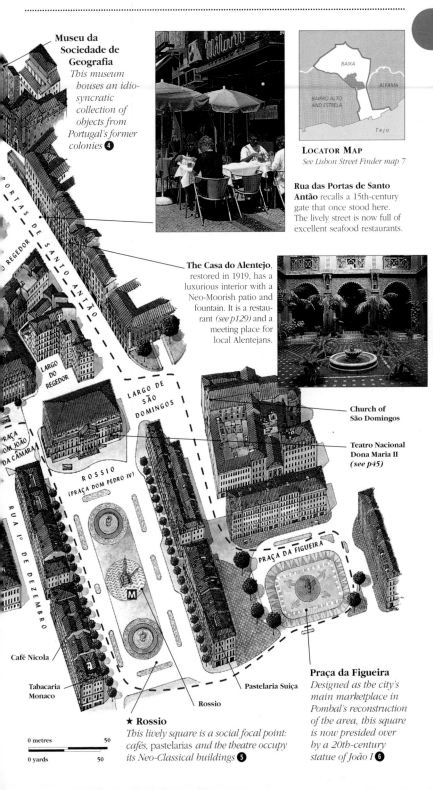

Museu da Sociedade de Geografia
This museum houses an idio-syncratic collection of objects from Portugal's former colonies ❹

See Lisbon Street Finder map 7

LOCATOR MAP

Rua das Portas de Santo Antão recalls a 15th-century gate that once stood here. The lively street is now full of excellent seafood restaurants.

The Casa do Alentejo, restored in 1919, has a luxurious interior with a Neo-Moorish patio and fountain. It is a restaurant *(see p129)* and a meeting place for local Alentejans.

Church of São Domingos

Teatro Nacional Dona Maria II *(see p45)*

Praça da Figueira
Designed as the city's main marketplace in Pombal's reconstruction of the area, this square is now presided over by a 20th-century statue of João I ❻

Café Nicola

Tabacaria Monaco

Pastelaria Suiça

Rossio

★ **Rossio**
This lively square is a social focal point: cafés, pastelarias and the theatre occupy its Neo-Classical buildings ❺

0 metres 50
0 yards 50

Bridge and pond shaded by trees in the Jardim Botânico

Jardim Botânico ❶

Rua da Escola Politécnica 56. **Map** 4 F1.
(01-396 15 21. ⬛ 15, 58, 100.
Ⓜ *Avenida.* **Gardens** ⭘ 9am–6pm
(Apr–Sep: 8pm) Mon–Fri, 10am–6pm
(Apr–Sep: 8pm) Sat & Sun. ⬤ 1 Jan,
25 Dec. ♿ ⭘ **Museu de História**
Natural ⭘ for exhibitions only. ♿
Museu da Ciência ⭘ 10am–1pm,
2–5pm Mon–Fri, 3–6pm Sat.
⬤ public hols. ♿

THE COMPLEX, owned by the university, comprises two museums and four hectares (10 acres) of gardens. The botanical gardens, which slope down from the upper level by the main entrance towards Rua da Alegria, have a distinct air of neglect. However, it is worth paying the entrance fee to wander among the exotic trees and dense shady paths of the gardens as they descend to the second entrance. A magnificent avenue of lofty palms connects the two different levels.

The **Museu de História Natural** (Natural History Museum) opens only for temporary exhibitions and these are well advertised throughout the city. The **Museu da Ciência** (Science Museum), whose exhibits demonstrate basic scientific principles, is popular with school children.

Avenida da Liberdade ❷

Map 7 A2. ⬛ 2, 9, 36 & many other routes. Ⓜ *Restauradores, Avenida.*

FOLLOWING THE earthquake of 1755 (see pp20–21), the Marquês de Pombal created the Passeio Público (public promenade) in the area now occupied by the lower part of Avenida da Liberdade and Praça dos Restauradores.

Despite its name, enjoyment of the park was restricted to Lisbon's high society and walls and gates ensured the exclusion of the lower classes. In 1821, when the Liberals came to power, the barriers were pulled down and the Avenida and square became open to all.

The boulevard you see today was built in 1879–82 in the style of the Champs-Elysées in Paris. The wide tree-lined avenue became a focus for pageants, festivities and demonstrations. A war memorial stands as a tribute to those who died in World War I. The avenue still retains a certain elegance with fountains and café tables shaded by trees, however, it no longer makes for a peaceful stroll. The once majestic thoroughfare, 90 m (295 ft) wide and decorated with abstract pavement patterns, is now divided by seven lanes of traffic linking Praça dos Restauradores and Praça Marquês de Pombal to the north. Some of the original mansions have been preserved, including the Neo-Classical Tivoli cinema at No. 188, with an original 1920s kiosk outside, and Casa Lambertini with its colourful mosaic decoration at No. 166. However, many of the Art Nouveau façades have unfortunately given way to newer ones occupied by offices, hotels or shopping complexes.

Detail from the memorial to the dead of World War I in Avenida da Liberdade

19th-century monument in honour of the Restoration in Praça dos Restauradores

Praça dos Restauradores ❸

Map 7 A2. ⬛ 2, 9, 36, 46 & many other routes. Ⓜ *Restauradores.*

THE SQUARE, distinguished by its soaring obelisk, erected in 1886, commemorates the country's liberation from the Spanish yoke in 1640. The bronze figures on the pedestal depict Victory, holding a palm and a crown, and Freedom. The names and dates that are inscribed on the sides of the obelisk are those of the battles of the War of Restoration.

On the west side the Palácio Foz, housing the main tourist office, was built by Francesco Savario Fabri in 1755–77 for the Marquês de Castelo-Melhor. It was renamed after the Marquês de Foz, who lived here in the last century. The smart Avenida Palace Hotel (see p115) stands on the southwest side of the square. This building was designed by José Lúis Monteiro (1849–1942), who also built Rossio railway station (see p42).

Museu da Sociedade de Geografia ❹

Rua das Portas de Santo Antão 100.
Map 7 A2. **C** 01-342 54 01. 9, 80, 90. **M** *Restauradores*. **O** 11am & 3pm Mon, Wed & Fri. **C** compulsory.

LOCATED in the Geographical Society building, the museum houses an idiosyncratic ethnographical collection brought back from Portugal's former colonies. On display are circumcision masks from Guinea Bissau, musical instruments and snake spears. From Angola there are neckrests to sustain coiffures and the original *padrão* – the stone pillar erected by the Portuguese in 1482 to mark their sovereignty over the colony. Most of the exhibits are arranged along the splendid Sala Portugal, a large hall used also for conferences.

Rossio ❺

Map 6 B3. 2, 36, 44, 45 & many other routes. **M** *Rossio*.

FORMALLY CALLED Praça de Dom Pedro IV, this large square has been the nerve centre of Lisbon for six centuries. During its history it has been the stage of bullfights, festivals, military parades and also the burning of heretics during the Inquisition *(see p14)*. Today there is little more than an occasional political rally

Teatro Nacional Dona Maria II in Rossio illuminated by night

and the sober Pombaline buildings, disfigured on the upper level by old neon advertisements, are occupied at street level by souvenir shops, jewellers and cafés. Centre stage stands a statue of Dom Pedro IV, the first emperor of independent Brazil. At the foot of the statue, the four female figures are allegories of Justice, Wisdom, Strength and Moderation – qualities dubiously attributed to Dom Pedro.

In the mid-19th century the square was paved with wave-patterned mosaics which gave it the nickname of "Rolling Motion Square". The hand-cut grey and white stone cubes were the first such designs to decorate the city's pavements. Today, only a small central section of the design survives.

On the north side of the square is the Teatro Nacional Dona Maria II, named after Dom Pedro's daughter. The Neo-Classical structure was built in the 1840s by the Italian architect Fortunato Lodi. On top of the pediment is Gil Vicente (1465–1536), the founder of Portuguese theatre.

Café Nicola on the west side of the square was a favourite meeting place among writers. A regular of the original café (the present one dates from 1929) was the poet Manuel du Bocage (1765–1805), who was notorious for his satires.

Praça da Figueira ❻

Map 6 B3. 14, 43, 59, 60 & many other routes. 15. **M** *Rossio*.

BEFORE THE 1755 earthquake *(see pp20–21)* the square next to Rossio was the site of the Hospital de Todos-os-Santos (All Saints). In Pombal's new design for the Baixa, the square took on the role of the city's central marketplace. In 1885 a covered market was introduced, but this was pulled down in the 1950s. Today, the four-storey buildings are given over to hotels, shops and cafés and the square is no longer a marketplace. Perhaps its most eye-catching feature is the multitude of pigeons that perch on the pedestal supporting Leopoldo de Almeida's bronze equestrian statue of João I, erected in 1971.

Bronze statue of King João I in Praça da Figueira

There are spectacular **views** of the Baixa from the platform.

Café

A walkway links the lift with Largo do Carmo.

The two cars that travel up and down can hold 25 people each.

Filigree motifs decorate the wrought-iron shaft.

Rua do Carmo

Steps down to Rua de Santa Justa

Ticket office

Entrance

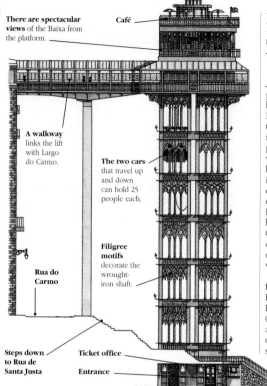

Elevador de Santa Justa ❼

Rua de Santa Justa & Largo do Carmo.
Map 7 B3. ☎ 01-363 20 21.
⏰ 7am–11pm Mon–Sat, 9am–11pm
Sun & public hols.

ALSO KNOWN as the Elevador do Carmo, this Neo-Gothic lift, built at the turn of the century by the French architect

Raoul Mesnier du Ponsard, an apprentice of Alexandre Gustave Eiffel, is one of the more eccentric features of the Baixa. Made of iron, and embellished with filigree, the lift within a tower provides a regular service between the Baixa and the Bairro Alto, 32 m (105 ft) above, and is the most convenient way to reach the upper part of town. Two smart wood-panelled cabins with brass fittings travel up and down within the tower depositing passengers on a walkway leading to the nearby Largo do Carmo and the ruined Igreja do Carmo (see p52).

The very top of the tower, reached via a tight spiral stairway, is given over to café tables. This high vantage point commands splendid views of Rossio, the grid pattern of the Baixa, the castle on the opposite hill, the river and the nearby ruins of the Carmo church. The fire that gutted the Chiado district in 1988 (see p52) was extinguished very close to the lift.

Café on the top platform of the Elevador de Santa Justa

Rua Augusta ❽

Map 7 B4. Ⓜ Rossio. 🚌 2, 14, 36, 40 & many other routes.

A LIVELY PEDESTRIANIZED street decorated with mosaic pavements and lined with boutiques and open-air cafés, Rua Augusta is the main tourist thoroughfare and the smartest in the Baixa. Street performers provide entertainment, while vendors sell lottery tickets, books and souvenirs. The eye is drawn to the triumphal Arco da Rua Augusta framing the equestrian statue of José I in Praça do Comércio. Designed by the architect Santos de Carvalho to commemorate the city's recovery from the earthquake (see pp20–21), the arch was completed only in 1873.

The other main thoroughfares of the Baixa are Rua da Prata (silversmiths' street) and Rua do Ouro or Rua Aurea (goldsmiths' street). Cutting across these main streets full of shops and banks are smaller streets that give glimpses up to the Bairro Alto to the west and the Castelo de São Jorge (see pp38–9) to the east. Many of the streets retain shops that gave them their name: there are jewellers in Rua da Prata and shoemakers in Rua dos Sapateiros and banks in Rua do Comércio.

The most incongruous sight in the heart of the Baixa is a small section of the Roman baths, located within the Banco Comercial Português in Rua dos Correeiros. The ruins and mosaics can be seen from the street window at the rear side of the bank; alternatively you can go on a Thursday when the "museum" is open.

Shoppers and strollers in the pedestrianized Rua Augusta

Nossa Senhora da Conceição Velha ❾

Rua da Alfândega. **Map** 7 C4.
🚌 9, 46, 90. 🚊 18. ⏰ 8am–1pm, 3–7pm daily. ⚫ Aug. ♿ 🔲 📷 ♿

T HE ELABORATE Manueline doorway of the church is the only feature that survived from the original 16th-century Nossa Senhora da Misericórdia, which stood here until the 1755 earthquake. The portal is decorated with a profusion of Manueline detail including angels, beasts, flowers, armillary spheres and the cross of the Order of Christ. In the tympanum, the Virgin Mary spreads her protective mantle over various contemporary figures. These include Pope Leo X, Manuel I and his sister, Queen Leonor, widow of João II. It was Leonor who founded the original Misericórdia (almshouse) on the site of a former synagogue.

Unfortunately, enjoyment of the portal is hampered by the

Detail from portal of Conceição Velha

constant stream of traffic hurtling along Rua da Alfândega and the cars that park right in front of the church. The gloomy interior has an unusual stucco ceiling; in the second chapel on the right is a statue of Our Lady of Restelo. This came from the Belém chapel where navigators prayed before embarking on their historic voyages east.

Praça do Comércio ❿

Map 7 C5. 🚌 2, 14, 40, 46 & many other routes. 🚊 15, 18.

M ORE COMMONLY known by the locals as *Terreiro do Paço* (Palace Square), this huge open space was the site of the royal palace for 400 years. Manuel I transferred the royal residence from Castelo de São Jorge to this more convenient location by the river in 1511. The first palace, along with its library and 70,000 books, was destroyed in the earthquake of 1755. In the rebuilding of the city, the square became the *pièce de résistance* of Pombal's Baixa design. The new palace occupied spacious arcaded buildings that extended around three sides of the square. After the revolution of 1910 *(see p15)* these were converted into government administrative offices and painted Republican pink. However, they have since been repainted royal yellow.

The south side, graced by two square towers, looks across the wide expanse of the Tagus. This has always been the finest gateway to Lisbon, where royalty and ambassadors would alight and take the marble steps up from the river. You can still experience the dramatic approach by taking a ferry across from Cacilhas on the southern bank. However, today the spectacle is spoilt by the busy Avenida Infante Dom Henrique, which runs along the waterfront. In the centre of Praça do Comércio is the equestrian statue of King José I erected in 1775 by Machado de Castro, the leading Portuguese sculptor of the 18th century. The bronze horse, depicted trampling on serpents, earned the square its third name of "Black Horse Square", used by English travellers and merchants. Over the years, however, the horse has acquired a green patina.

Shaded arcades along the north side of Praça do Comércio

The impressive triumphal arch on the north side of the square leads into Rua Augusta and is the gateway to the Baixa. The arch is decorated with statues of historical figures, including Vasco da Gama *(see p68)* and the Marquês de Pombal *(see p15)*. Nearby, in the northeast corner of the square, stands Lisbon's oldest café, the Martinho da Arcada, formerly a haunt of the city's literati.

On 1 February 1908, King Carlos and his son, Luís Felipe, were assassinated as they were passing through the square. In 1974 the square saw the first uprising of the Armed Forces Movement which overthrew the Caetano regime in a bloodless revolution *(see p15)*. For many years the area was requisitioned as a car park, but today it has been reclaimed for the use of open-air cafés and stalls.

Marble steps leading up to Praça do Comércio from the Tagus

BAIRRO ALTO AND ESTRELA

AID OUT IN A GRID pattern in the late 16th century, the hilltop Bairro Alto is one of the most picturesque districts of the city. First settled by rich citizens who moved out of the disreputable Alfama, by the 19th century it had become a run-down area frequented by prostitutes. Today, it retains a traditional way of life, with small workshops and family-run *tascas* (cheap restaurants).

Tile panel in Largo Rafael Bordalo Pinheiro, Bairro Alto

Very different in character to the heart of the Bairro Alto is the elegant commercial district known as the Chiado, where affluent Lisboetas do their shopping. To the north-west, the Estrela quarter is centred on the huge domed basilica and popular gardens. The mid-18th century district of Lapa, to the southwest, is home to foreign embassies and large, smart residences.

SIGHTS AT A GLANCE

Museums and Galleries
Museu do Chiado **5**
Museu Nacional de Arte Antiga pp56–9 **11**

Churches
Basílica da Estrela **13**
Igreja do Carmo **2**
São Roque **1**

Historic Buildings and Districts
Chiado **3**
Palácio de São Bento **10**
Solar do Vinho do Porto **7**
Teatro Nacional de São Carlos **4**

Markets
Mercado 24 de Julho **6**

Gardens and Belvederes
Jardim da Estrela **12**
Miradouro de São Pedro de Alcântara **8**
Praça do Príncipe Real **9**

GETTING THERE
This area is reached effortlessly with the Elevador da Glória from Praça dos Restauradores or the Elevador de Santa Justa from the Baixa. Otherwise it is a steep, but pleasant walk. There is also a metro station on Largo do Chiado. From Bairro Alto, trams 24 and 28 go to Estrela and Lapa.

KEY

▦	Street-by-Street: Bairro Alto *pp50–51*
Ⓜ	Metro station
Ⓡ	Railway station
🚡	Funicular
⛴	Ferry boarding point
Ⓟ	Parking
=	Railway line

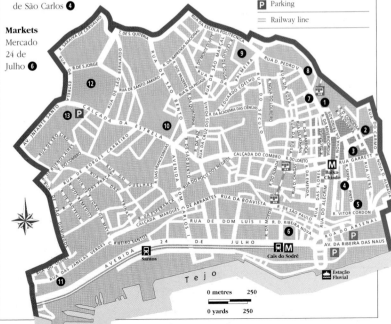

Street-by-Street: Bairro Alto

Baroque cherub,
Igreja do Carmo

THE BAIRRO ALTO (high quarter) is a fascinating area of cobbled streets, peeling houses and tiny grocery shops selling fruit and flasks of local wine. Traditionally a bohemian quarter, notorious for prostitution and gambling, today the Bairro Alto is a residential area, with the spirit of a close-knit community. In recent years it has become fashionable at night for its bars and *casas de fado (see pp142–3)*. In contrast, the Chiado is an area of elegant shops and old-style cafés that extends down from Praça Luís de Camões towards Rua do Carmo and the Baixa. Major renovation work has taken place since a fire in 1988 *(see p52)* destroyed many of the buildings.

Rua do Norte and Rua das Gáveas are at the heart of the traditional Bairro Alto where night-time revellers crowd the bars after dark.

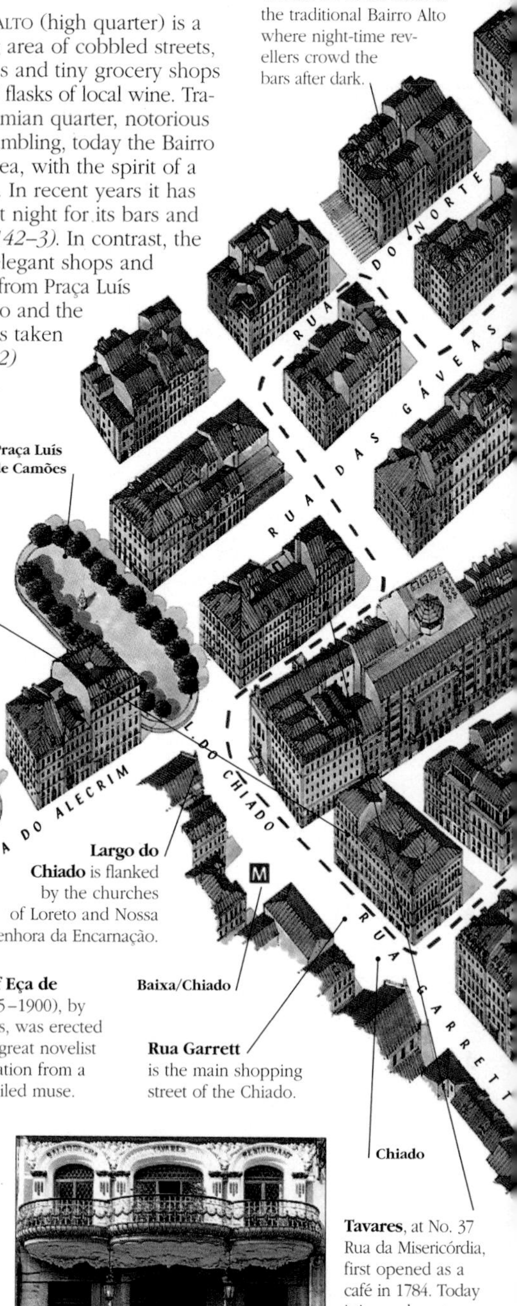

Praça Luís de Camões

Chiado
Once a haunt of writers and intellectuals, this area is now an elegant shopping district. The 1920s Brasileira café, on Largo do Chiado, is adorned with gilded mirrors ❸

Largo do Chiado is flanked by the churches of Loreto and Nossa Senhora da Encarnação.

The statue of Eça de Queirós (1845–1900), by Teixeira Lopes, was erected in 1903. The great novelist takes inspiration from a scantily veiled muse.

Baixa/Chiado

Rua Garrett is the main shopping street of the Chiado.

Chiado

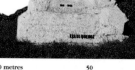

Tavares, at No. 37 Rua da Misericórdia, first opened as a café in 1784. Today it is an elegant restaurant *(see p129)* decorated at the turn of the century with mirrors and elaborate stucco designs.

0 metres	50
0 yards	50

KEY

‑ ‑ ‑ Suggested route

Elevador da Glória

The Museu de Arte Sacra has an interesting exhibition of religious artefacts and explains the history of the treasures in the church of São Roque next door.

LOCATOR MAP
See Lisbon Street Finder map 7

Cervejaria Trindade is a popular beer hall and restaurant decorated with *azulejo* panels.

★ **São Roque**
Opulent mosaics and semiprecious stones adorn the Baroque Capela de São João inside the 16th-century church of São Roque ❶

Teatro da Trindade

The tile decoration on the façade of this house, erected in 1864 on Largo Rafael Bordalo Pinheiro, features allegorical figures of Science, Agriculture Industry and Commerce.

★ **Igreja do Carmo**
The graceful skeletal arches of this Carmelite church, once the largest in Lisbon, stand as a reminder of the earthquake of 1755. The chancel, the only part that remains intact, holds an archaeological museum ❷

Elevador de Santa Justa *(see p46)*

The shops in Rua do Carmo are gradually being restored after the devastating fire in 1988 *(see p52).*

STAR SIGHTS
★ São Roque
★ Igreja do Carmo

Ruins of the 14th-century Igreja do Carmo seen from the Baixa

São Roque ❶

Largo Trindade Coelho. **Map** 7 A3.
🕻 01-346 03 61. 🚌 58, 100. 🚃 28.
⭕ 8:30am–5pm (public hols: 1pm)
daily. 🏛 **Museu de Arte Sacra**
⭕ 10am–5pm Tue–Sun. ⬤ public
hols. 🈳 ⭕

SÃO ROQUE's plain façade
belies a remarkably rich
interior. The church was
founded at the end of
the 16th century by
the Jesuit Order, then
at the peak of its
power. In 1742 the
Chapel of St John
the Baptist (last on
the left) was com-
missioned by the
prodigal João V from
the Italian architects
Luigi Vanvitelli and
Nicola Salvi. Con-
structed in Rome
and embellished with
lapis lazuli, agate, alabaster,
amethyst, precious marbles,
gold, silver and mosaics, the
chapel was given the Pope's
blessing in the church of
Sant'Antonio dei Portoghesi in
Rome, dismantled and sent to
Lisbon in three ships.

**Tile detail in the
Chapel of St Roch**

Among the many tiles in the
church, the oldest and most
interesting are those in the
third chapel on the right, dating
from the mid-16th century
and dedicated to São Roque
(St Roch), protector against
the plague. Other noteworthy
features of the church are the
painted *trompe l'oeil* ceiling,
showing a dome and scenes
of the Apocalypse, and the
sacristy, with its coffered
ceiling and painted panels of
the life of St Francis Xavier, the
16th-century Jesuit missionary.

Treasures from the Chapel of
St John, including the silver
and lapis lazuli altar front, can
be seen in the adjoining
Museu de Arte Sacra.

Igreja do Carmo ❷

Largo do Carmo. **Map** 7 B3. 🕻 01-
346 04 73. 🚃 28 & Santa Justa lift.
⭕ Apr–Sep: 10am–6pm Tue–Sun;
Oct–Mar: 10am–1pm, 2–5pm
Tue–Sun. ⬤ public hols. 🈳

THE GOTHIC RUINS
of this Carmelite
church, built on a
slope overlooking the
Baixa, are evocative
reminders of the dev-
astation left by the
earthquake of 1755.
Founded in the late
14th century by Nuno
Álvares Pereira, the
commander who
became a member of the
Carmelite Order, the church
was at one time the biggest in

Lisbon. Nowadays the roofless
nave, open to the sky, is all
that remains of the arches and
rubble that caved in on the
congregation as they were
attending mass. Roses grow
up its ancient pillars, pigeons
perch on the ruined arches
and cats wander among the
scattered statuary and capitals.
  The chancel, whose roof
withstood the shock, is now
an **archaeological museum**
with a small, heterogeneous
collection of sarcophagi,
statuary, ceramics and mosaics.
Among the more ancient finds
from Europe are a remnant
from a Visigothic pillar and a
Roman tomb carved with
reliefs depicting the Muses.
There are also finds from
Mexico and South America,
including ancient mummies.
  Outside the ruins, in the
Largo do Carmo, stands the
Chafariz do Carmo, an 18th-
century fountain designed by
Ângelo Belasco, elaborately
decorated with four dolphins.

Chiado ❸

Map 7 A4. 🚌 58. 🚃 28. Ⓜ Chiado.

HYPOTHESES abound for the
origin of the word Chiado,
in use since 1567. One of the
most interesting recalls the
creak *(chiar)* of the wheels of
the carts as they negotiated the
area's steep slopes. A second
theory refers to the nickname
given to the 16th-century poet
António Ribeiro, "O Chiado".
An area traditionally known

THE CHIADO FIRE

On 25 August 1988 a disastrous fire began in a store in
Rua do Carmo, the street that
links the Baixa with the Bairro
Alto. Fire engines were unable
to enter this pedestrianized
street and the fire spread into
Rua Garrett. Along with shops
and offices, many important
18th-century buildings were
destroyed, the worst damage
being in Rua do Carmo. The
renovation project, which will
preserve where possible the
original façades, is headed
by the leading Portuguese
architect, Álvaro Siza Vieira.

**Firemen attending the raging
fire in Rua do Carmo**

Stalls and circle of the 18th-century Teatro Nacional de São Carlos

for its intellectual associations, various statues of literary figures can be found here. Fernando Pessoa, Portugal's most famous 20th-century poet, is seated at a table outside the Café Brasileira. Established in the 1920s, this was a favourite rendezvous of intellectuals.

The name Chiado is often used to mean just Rua Garrett, the main shopping street of the area, named after the author and poet João Almeida Garrett (1799–1854). This elegant street, which descends from Largo do Chiado towards the Baixa, is known for its clothes shops, cafés and bookshops. Devastated by fire in 1988, the former elegance of this quarter is gradually being restored.

On Largo do Chiado stand two Baroque churches: the Italian church, Igreja do Loreto, on the north side and, opposite, Nossa Senhora da Encarnação, whose exterior walls are partly decorated with *azulejos*.

Teatro Nacional de São Carlos ❹

Rua Serpa Pinto 9. **Map** 7 A4. ☎ 01-346 84 08. 🚌 58. 🚋 28. Ⓜ Chiado. 🔲 for performances only.

REPLACING a former opera house which was ruined by the earthquake of 1755, the Teatro de São Carlos was built in 1792–5 by José da Costa e Silva. Designed on the lines of La Scala in Milan and the San Carlo in Naples, the building has a beautifully proportioned façade and an enchanting Rococo interior. Views of the exterior, however, are spoiled by the car park, invariably crammed, which occupies the square in front. The opera season lasts from September to June, but concerts and ballets are also staged here at other times of the year.

Museu do Chiado ❺

Rua Serpa Pinto 4–6. **Map** 7 A5. ☎ 01-343 21 48. 🚌 58. 🚋 24, 28. Ⓜ Chiado. 🔲 10am–6pm Wed–Sun, 2–6pm Tue. ⬤ 1 Jan, Easter, 1 May, 25 Dec. 🎫

THE NATIONAL MUSEUM of Contemporary Art, whose collection of 1850–1950 paintings could no longer be termed contemporary, changed its name in 1994 and moved to a stylishly restored warehouse. The paintings and sculpture, arranged in 12 rooms, each with a different theme, illustrate the development from Romanticism to Modernism. The majority are works by

Portuguese, often showing the marked influence from other European countries. This is particularly noticeable in the 19th-century landscape painters who had contact with artists from the French Barbizon School. The few international works of art include drawings by Rodin (1840–1917) and French sculpture from the late 19th century. Temporary exhibitions are held for "very new artists, preferably inspired by the permanent collection".

A vegetable stall holder in the daily Mercado 24 de Julho

Mercado 24 de Julho ❻

Avenida 24 de Julho. **Map** 4 F3. Ⓜ Cais do Sodré. 🚌 14, 32, 40. 🚋 15, 28. 🔲 3am–noon Mon–Sat.

FROM EARLY MORNING to noon this conspicuous, domed building is the scene of the food and flower market. The hall is packed with boxes of seasonal vegetables, fruit and bags of beans and nuts. Surrounding stalls sell cheese, meat, fresh fish and dried cod. Nowadays most of the produce arrives in the early morning by cart, truck or van, but you can still spot a few vendors disembarking from ferries, with crates of vegetables on their heads. A modern tiled scene in a fishmonger's is another reminder of bygone days when fresh fish was sold from the quay by the barefooted *varinas* or fishwives.

The café inside the market is popular with both traders and late-night revellers who come here to sober up in the early hours of the morning.

Art Nouveau façade of the popular Café Brasileira in the Chiado

The wide selection of port at the Solar do Vinho do Porto

Solar do Vinho do Porto ❼

Rua de São Pedro de Alcântara 45.
Map 4 F2. ☎ 01-347 57 07.
🚌 58. 🚋 28, Elevador da Glória.
🕐 10am–11:45pm Mon–Fri,
11am–10:45pm Sat. ⬤ public hols.

THE PORTUGUESE WORD *solar* means mansion or manor house and the Solar do Vinho do Porto occupies the ground floor of an 18th-century mansion. The building was once owned by the German architect, Johann Friedrich Ludwig (Ludovice), who built the monastery at Mafra *(see p92)*. Up to 6,000 varieties of port are stored in its cellars, including some rare vintages that date back as far as 1937. Visitors are permitted to try about 300 of these rich fortified wines in the bar. They range from the younger red-coloured ruby port, through the lighter tawny, to the aristocratic vintages from the great shippers of Oporto. Although rather expensive, these ports can be tasted at the bar or in the comfort of armchairs in the club-like sitting room.

Miradouro de São Pedro de Alcântara ❽

Rua de São Pedro de Alcântara. **Map** 7
A2. 🚌 58. 🚋 28, Elevador da Glória.

THE BELVEDERE *(miradouro)* commands a sweeping view of eastern Lisbon, seen across the Baixa. A tiled map, conveniently placed against the balustrade, helps you locate the landmarks in the city below. The panorama extends from the battlements of the Castelo de São Jorge *(see pp38–9)*, clearly seen surrounded by trees on the hill to the southeast, to the 18th-century church of Penha da França in the northwest. The large monastery complex of the Igreja da Graça *(see p37)* is also visible on the hill, and in the distance São Vicente de Fora *(see p35)* is recognizable by the symmetrical towers that flank its white façade.

Benches and ample shade from the trees make this terrace a pleasant stop after the steep walk up Calçada da Glória from the Baixa. Alternatively, the yellow funicular, Elevador da Glória, will drop you off nearby.

The memorial in the garden, erected in 1904, depicts Eduardo Coelho (1835–89), founder of the newspaper *Diário de Notícias*, and below him a ragged paper boy running with copies of the famous

daily. This area was once the centre of the newspaper industry, however the modern printing presses have now moved to more spacious premises west of the city.

The view is most attractive at sunset and by night when the castle is floodlit and the terrace becomes a popular meeting point for young Lisboetas.

Praça do Príncipe Real ❾

Map 4 F1. 🚌 58, 100.

Playing cards in Praça do Príncipe Real

LAID OUT IN 1860 as a prime residential quarter, the square still retains an air of affluence. Smartly painted mansions surround a particularly pleasant park with an open-air café, statuary and some splendid robinia, magnolia and Judas trees. The branches of a huge cedar tree have been trained on a trellis, creating a wide shady spot for the locals who play cards beneath it. On the large square, at No. 26, the eye-catching pink and white Neo-Moorish building with domes and pinnacles is part of Lisbon university.

View across the city to Castelo de São Jorge from Miradouro de São Pedro de Alcântara

Attractive wrought-iron music pavilion in Jardim da Estrela

Palácio de São Bento ⑩

Rua de São Bento. **Map** 4 E2.
📞 01-396 01 41. 🚌 6, 49.
🕐 by appt only.

ALSO KNOWN as the Palácio da Assembleia Nacional, this enormous white Neo-Classical building is the seat of the Portuguese Parliament. It started life at the end of the 16th century as the Benedictine monastery of São Bento. After the dissolution of the religious orders in 1834, the building became the seat of Parliament, known as the Palácio das Cortes. The interior is suitably grandiose with marble pillars and Neo-Classical statues.

Museu Nacional de Arte Antiga ⑪

See pp56–9.

Jardim da Estrela ⑫

Praça da Estrela. **Map** 4 D2. 🚌 9, 20, 22, 38. 🚊 25, 28.

LAID OUT IN the middle of the 19th century, opposite the Basílica da Estrela, the popular gardens are a focal part of the Estrela quarter. Local families congregate here at weekends to feed the ducks and the large carp in the lake, sit at the waterside café or wander among the pleasant flower beds, plants and trees. The formal gardens are planted with neat herbaceous borders and shrubs surrounding plane trees and elms. The central feature of the park is a green wrought-iron bandstand, decorated with elegant filigree, where musicians strike up in the summer months. This was built in 1884 and originally stood on the Passeio Público, before the creation of Avenida da Liberdade *(see p44).*

The English Cemetery to the north of the gardens is best known as the burial place of Henry Fielding (1707–54), the English novelist and playwright who died in Lisbon at the age of 47. The *Journal of a Voyage to Lisbon,* published posthumously in 1775, recounts his last voyage to Portugal made in a fruitless attempt to recover his failing health.

Basílica da Estrela ⑬

Praça da Estrela. **Map** 4 D2. 📞 01-396 09 15. 🚌 9, 20, 22, 38. 🚊 25, 28. 🕐 7:30am–1pm, 3–8pm daily.
🈂 📷

The tomb of the pious Maria I in the Basílica da Estrela

IN THE SECOND half of the 18th century Maria I *(see p105),* daughter of José I, vowed she would build a church if she bore a son and heir to the throne. Her wish was granted and construction of the basilica began in 1779. Her son José, however, died of smallpox two years before the completion of the church in 1790. The huge domed basilica, set on a hill in the west of the city, is one of Lisbon's great landmarks. A simpler version of the basilica at Mafra *(see p92),* this church was built by architects from the Mafra School in late Baroque and Neo-Classical style. The façade is flanked by twin belltowers and decorated with an array of statues of saints and allegorical figures.

The spacious, somewhat awe-inspiring interior, where light streams down from the pierced dome, is clad in grey, pink and yellow marble. The elaborate Empire-style tomb of Queen Maria I, who died in Brazil, lies in the right transept. Locked in a room nearby is Machado de Castro's extraordinary Nativity scene, composed of over 500 cork and terracotta figures. (To see it, ask the sacristan.)

Neo-Classical façade and stairway of Palácio de São Bento

Museu Nacional de Arte Antiga ⓫

Portugal's national art collection is housed in a 17th-century palace that was built for the counts of Alvor. In 1770 it was acquired by the Marquês de Pombal and remained in the possession of his family for over a century. Inaugurated in 1884, the museum is known to locals as the Casa das Janelas Verdes, referring to the former green windows of the palace. In 1940 a modern annexe (including the main façade) was added. This was built on the site of the St Albert Carmelite monastery, which was destroyed in the 1755 earthquake *(see pp20–21)*. The only surviving feature was the chapel, now integrated into the museum.

15th-century wood carving of St George

★ St Jerome
This masterly portrayal of old age by Albrecht Dürer expresses one of the central dilemmas of Renaissance humanism: the ephemeral nature of man (1521).

Gallery Guide

The ground floor contains 14th–19th-century European paintings, as well as some decorative arts and furniture. Oriental and African art, Chinese and Portuguese ceramics and silver, gold and jewellery are on display on the first floor. The top floor is dedicated to Portuguese art and sculpture.

Stairs down to

The Temptations of St Antony by Hieronymus Bosch

St Augustine by Piero della Francesca

The Virgin and Child and Saints
Hans Holbein the Elder's balanced composition of a Sacra Conversazione (1519) is set among majestic Renaissance architecture with saints in detailed contemporary costumes sewing or reading.

Ecce Homo
Painted in the late 15th century by an artist of the Portuguese school, the unusual depiction of the accused Jesus, with the shroud lowered over his eyes, retains an air of dignified calm, despite the crown of thorns, the rope and the specks of blood.

Key to Floorplan

- European art
- Portuguese painting and sculpture
- Portuguese and Chinese ceramics
- Oriental and African art
- Silver, gold and jewellery
- Decorative arts
- Chapel of St Albert
- Temporary exhibitions
- Non-exhibition space

Star Exhibits

★ **St Jerome by Dürer**

★ **Namban Screens**

★ **Adoration of St Vincent by Gonçalves**

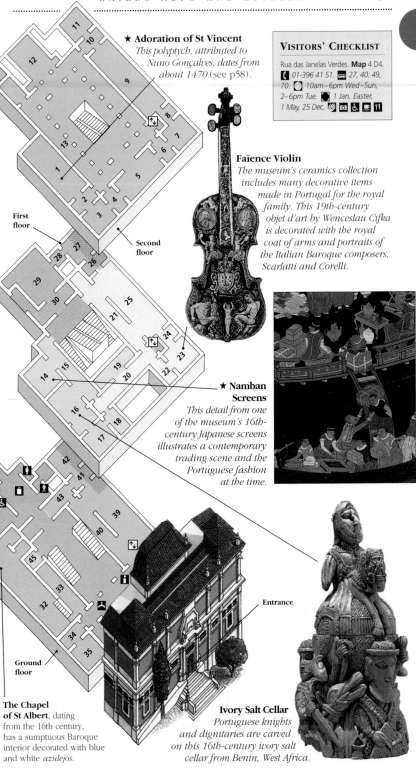

★ **Adoration of St Vincent**
This polyptych, attributed to Nuno Gonçalves, dates from about 1470 (see p58).

VISITORS' CHECKLIST

Rua das Janelas Verdes. **Map** 4 D4.
01-396 41 51. 27, 40, 49, 70. 10am–6pm Wed–Sun, 2–6pm Tue. 1 Jan, Easter, 1 May, 25 Dec.

Faïence Violin
The museum's ceramics collection includes many decorative items made in Portugal for the royal family. This 19th-century objet d'art by Wenceslau Cifka is decorated with the royal coat of arms and portraits of the Italian Baroque composers, Scarlatti and Corelli.

First floor

Second floor

★ **Namban Screens**
This detail from one of the museum's 16th-century Japanese screens illustrates a contemporary trading scene and the Portuguese fashion at the time.

Entrance

Ground floor

The Chapel of St Albert, dating from the 16th century, has a sumptuous Baroque interior decorated with blue and white *azulejos*.

Ivory Salt Cellar
Portuguese knights and dignitaries are carved on this 16th-century ivory salt cellar from Benin, West Africa.

Exploring the Collections of the Museu Nacional de Arte Antiga

T HE MUSEUM has the largest collection of paintings in Portugal and is particularly strong on early religious works by Portuguese artists. The majority of exhibits came from convents and monasteries following the suppression of religious orders in 1834. There are also extensive displays of sculpture, silverware, porcelain and applied arts giving an overview of Portuguese art from the Middle Ages to the 19th century, complemented by many fine European and Oriental pieces. The theme of the discoveries is ever-present, illustrating Portugal's links with Brazil, Africa, India, China and Japan.

EUROPEAN ART

P AINTINGS by European artists, dating from the 14th to the 19th century, are arranged chronologically on the ground floor. Unlike the Portuguese art, most of the works were donated from private collections, contributing to the great diversity of works on display. The first rooms, dedicated to the 14th and 15th centuries, trace the transition from medieval Gothic taste to the aesthetic of the Renaissance.

The painters best represented in the European Art section are 16th-century German and Flemish artists. Notable works are *St Jerome* by Albrecht Dürer (1471–1528), *Salomé* by Lucas Cranach the Elder (1472–1553), *Virgin and Child* by Hans Memling (c.1430–94) and *The Temptations of St Antony* by the great Flemish master of fantasy, Hieronymus Bosch (1450–1516). Of the small number of Italian works, the finest are *St Augustine* by

the Renaissance painter, Piero della Francesca (c.1420–92) and a graceful early altar panel representing the Resurrection by Raphael (1483–1520).

Some Portuguese painters, including Josefa de Óbidos (1631–84) and Gregório Lopes (1490–1550), are also displayed in the galleries of European art.

PORTUGUESE PAINTING AND SCULPTURE

M ANY OF THE EARLIEST works of art are by the Portuguese primitive painters who were influenced by the realistic detail of Flemish artists. There had always been strong trading links between Portugal and Flanders and in the 15th and 16th centuries several painters of Flemish origin, for example Frey Carlos of Évora, set up workshops in Portugal.

Pride of place, however, goes to the São Vicente de Fora polyptych, the most important painting of 15th-century Portuguese art and one that has

ADORATION OF ST VINCENT

Cistercian monks from Alcobaça in central Portugal   **Friar**

Fisherman

become a symbol of national pride in the Age of Discovery. Painted in about 1467–70, and generally believed to be by Nuno Gonçalves, the altarpiece portrays the *Adoration of St Vincent*, patron saint of Portugal, surrounded by dignitaries, knights and monks as well as fishermen and beggars. The accurate portrayal of contemporary figures makes the painting an invaluable historical and social document.

Later works include a 16th-century portrait of the young Dom Sebastião (1557–78) by Cristóvão de Morais and paintings by Neo-Classical artist Domingos António de Sequeira.

The museum's sculpture collection has many Gothic polychrome stone and wood statues of Christ, the Virgin and saints. There are also statues from the 17th century and an 18th-century nativity scene by Machado de Castro in the Chapel of St Albert.

PORTUGUESE AND CHINESE CERAMICS

T HE EXTENSIVE collection of ceramics enables visitors to trace the evolution of Chinese porcelain and Portuguese faïence and to see the influence of oriental designs on

Central panel of *The Temptations of St Antony* by Hieronymus Bosch

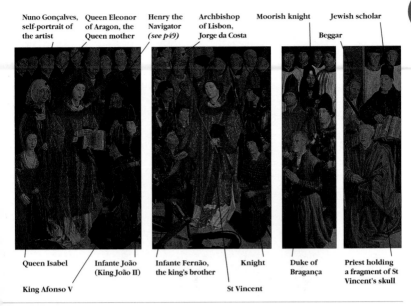

Nuno Gonçalves, self-portrait of the artist

Queen Eleonor of Aragon, the Queen mother

Henry the Navigator *(see p49)*

Archbishop of Lisbon, Jorge da Costa

Moorish knight

Jewish scholar

Beggar

Queen Isabel

Infante João (King João II)

Infante Fernão, the king's brother

Knight

Duke of Bragança

Priest holding a fragment of St Vincent's skull

King Afonso V

St Vincent

Portuguese pieces, and vice versa. From the 16th century Portuguese ceramics show a marked influence of Ming, and conversely the Chinese pieces bear Portuguese motifs such as coats of arms. By the mid-18th century individual potters had begun to develop an increasingly personalized, European style, with popular, rustic designs. The collection also includes ceramics from Italy, Spain and the Netherlands.

Chinese porcelain vase, 16th century

ORIENTAL AND AFRICAN ART

THE COLLECTION of ivories and furniture, with their European motifs, further illustrates the reciprocal influences of Portugal and her colonies. The 16th-century predilection for the exotic gave rise to a huge demand for items such as carved ivory hunting horns from Africa. The fascinating 16th-century Japanese Namban screens show the Portuguese trading in Japan. *Namban-jin* (barbarians from the south) is the name the Japanese gave to the Portuguese.

SILVER, GOLD AND JEWELLERY

AMONG THE MUSEUM'S fine collection of ecclesiastical treasures are King Sancho I's gold cross (1214) and the Belém monstrance (1506). Also on display is the 16th-century Madre de Deus reliquary which allegedly holds a thorn from the crown of Christ. Highlight of the foreign collection is a sumptuous set of rare 18th-century silver tableware. Commissioned by José I from the Paris workshop of Thomas Germain, the 1,200 pieces include intricately decorated tureens, sauce boats and salt cellars. The rich collection of jewels came from the convents, originally donated by members of the nobility and wealthy bourgeoisie on entering the religious orders.

APPLIED ARTS

FURNITURE, tapestries and textiles, liturgical vestments and bishops' mitres are among the wide range of objects on display. The furniture collection

has many examples from the reigns of King João V, King José and Queen Maria I, tracing the progress from Baroque to Neo-Classical styles. Of the foreign furniture, French pieces from the 18th century are the most prominent.

The textiles include 17th-century bedspreads, tapestries, many of Flemish origin, such as the *Baptism of Christ* (16th century), embroidered rugs and Arraiolos carpets.

Gold Madre de Deus reliquary inlaid with precious stones (c.1502)

Belém

Generosity, statue at entrance to Palácio da Ajuda

At the mouth of the River Tagus, where the caravels set sail on their voyages of discovery, Belém is inextricably linked with Portugal's golden age of discovery. When Manuel I came to power in 1495 he reaped the profits of those heady days of expansion, building grandiose monuments and churches that mirrored the spirit of the time. Two of the finest examples of the exuberant and exotic Manueline style of architecture are the Mosteiro dos Jerónimos and the Torre de Belém. Today Belém is a spacious, relatively green suburb with many museums, parks and gardens, as well as an attractive riverside setting with cafés and a promenade. On sunny days there is a distinct seaside feel to the river embankment.

Before the Tagus receded, the monks in the monastery used to look out onto the river and watch the boats set forth. In contrast today several lanes of traffic along the busy Avenida da Índia cut central Belém off from the picturesque waterfront, and silver and yellow trains rattle regularly past.

Sights at a Glance

Museums and Galleries
Museu de Arte Popular [10]
Museu da Marinha [7]
Museu Nacional de Arqueologia [5]
Museu Nacional dos Coches [2]
Planetário Calouste Gulbenkian [6]

Parks and Gardens
Jardim Agrícola Tropical [3]
Jardim Botânico da Ajuda [14]

Churches and Monasteries
Ermida de São Jerónimo [12]
Igreja da Memória [13]
Mosteiro dos Jerónimos pp66–7 [4]

Historic Buildings
Palácio de Belém [1]
Palácio Nacional da Ajuda [15]
Torre de Belém p70 [11]

Monuments
Monument to the Discoveries [9]

Cultural Centres
Centro Cultural de Belém [8]

Key
Street-by-Street: Belém *pp62–3*
🚉 Railway station
⛴ Ferry boarding point
[P] Parking
Railway line

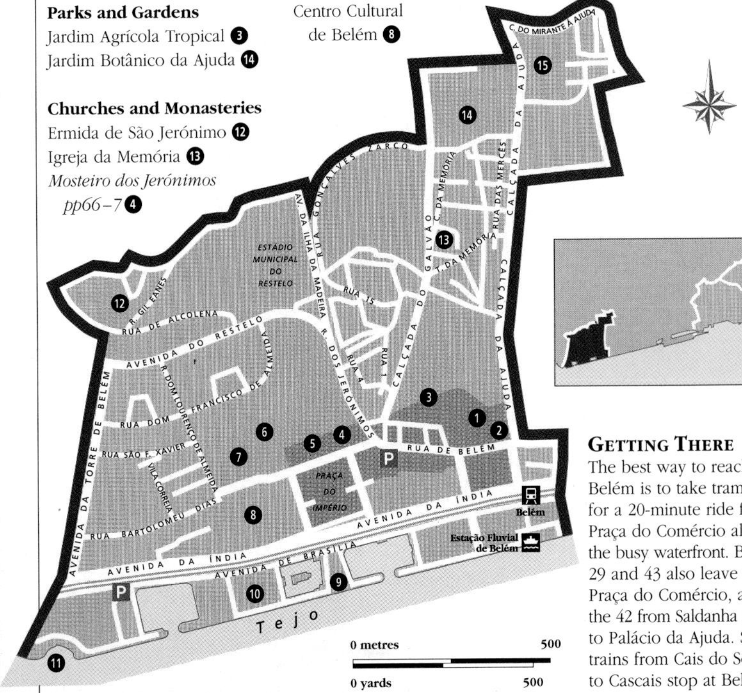

Getting There

The best way to reach Belém is to take tram 15 for a 20-minute ride from Praça do Comércio along the busy waterfront. Buses 29 and 43 also leave from Praça do Comércio, and the 42 from Saldanha goes to Palácio da Ajuda. Slow trains from Cais do Sodré to Cascais stop at Belém.

◁ **Nave of Santa Maria de Belém, the church of the Jerónimos monastery**

Street-by-Street: Belém

PORTUGAL'S FORMER maritime glory, expressed in the imposing, exuberant buildings such as the Jerónimos monastery, is evident all around Belém. In Salazar's *(see p15)* attempted revival of awareness of Portugal's Golden Age, the area along the waterfront, which had silted up since the days of the caravels, was restructured to celebrate the former greatness of the nation. Praça do Império was laid out for the Exhibition of the Portuguese World in 1940 and Praça Afonso de Albuquerque was dedicated to Portugal's first viceroy of India. The royal Palácio de Belém, restored with gardens and a riding school by João V in the 18th century, briefly housed the royal family after the 1755 earthquake.

Stone caravel, Jerónimos monastery

★ Mosteiro dos Jerónimos
Vaulted arcades and richly carved columns adorned with foliage, exotic animals and navigational instruments decorate the Manueline cloister of the Jerónimos monastery ❹

LARGO
DOS
JERÓNIMOS

PRAÇA DO IMPÉRIO

Museu Nacional de Arqueologia
Archaeological finds ranging from an Iron Age gold bracelet to Moorish artefacts are among the interesting exhibits on display ❺

Torre de Belém
(see p70)

STAR SIGHTS

★ **Mosteiro dos Jerónimos**

★ **Museu Nacional dos Coches**

KEY

— — — Suggested route

Praça do Império, an impressive square that opens out in front of the monastery, is lit up on special occasions with a colourful light display in the central fountain.

Rua Vieira Portuense runs along a small park. Its colourful 16th- and 17th-century houses contrast with the typically imposing buildings in Belém.

Jardim Agrícola Tropical

Exotic plants and trees gathered from Portugal's former colonies fill these peaceful gardens that were once part of the Palácio de Belém ❸

LOCATOR MAP
See Lisbon Street Finder maps 1 & 2

Antiga Confeitaria de Belém, a 19th-century café, sells *pastéis de Belém*, rich custard in a flaky pastry cup.

TRAVESSA DOS FERREIROS

T. MARTA PINTO

RUA DE BELÉM

Central Lisbon

RUA VIEIRA PORTUENSE

Palácio de Belém

Also known as the Palácio Cor de Rosa (pink palace) because of its faded pink façade, the 16th-century former royal palace is the official residence of the President of the Republic of Portugal ❶

| 0 metres | 50 |
| 0 yards | 50 |

★ Museu Nacional dos Coches

This 18th-century coach used by the ambassador to Pope Clement XI is part of the collection in the old riding school of the Palácio de Belém ❷

Praça Afonso de Albuquerque is named after the first Portuguese viceroy of India. A Neo-Manueline column in the centre bears his statue, with scenes from his life carved on the base.

Palácio de Belém ❶

Praça Afonso de Albuquerque.
Map 1 C4. 🎧 01-363 71 41. 🚌 14,
28, 43, 49. 🚃 15. 🚊 Belém.
⭕ 3rd Sun (am) of month. 🔲 🚻

BUILT BY the Conde de Aveiras in 1559 before the Tagus had receded, this summer palace once had gardens bordering the river. In the 18th century it was bought by João V, who had acquired vast wealth through gold from Brazil. He radically altered the palace, added a riding school and rendered the interior suitably lavish for his many amorous liaisons.

When the great earthquake struck in 1755 (see pp20–21), the king, José I, and his family were staying here and thus survived the devastation of central Lisbon. Fearing another earth tremor, the royal family temporarily set up camp in tents in the palace grounds and the palace interior was used as a hospital. Today the elegant pink building, which resembles a country estate, is the residence of the President of Portugal.

Pink façade of the Palácio de Belém, home of the President of Portugal

Museu Nacional dos Coches ❷

Praça Afonso de Albuquerque. **Map** 2
D4. 🎧 01-363 80 22. 🚌 14, 28, 43,
49. 🚃 15. 🚊 Belém. ⭕ 10am–6pm
Tue–Sun. ⬤ 1 Jan, Easter, 1 May,
25 Dec. 🔲 🔲 🚻 ground floor only.

THE MUSEUM'S collection of coaches is arguably the finest in Europe. Occupying the east wing of the Palácio de Belém, this was formerly the riding school built by the Italian architect Giacomo Azzolini in 1726. Seated in the upper gallery, the royal family used to watch their beautiful Lusitanian horses performing in the arena. In 1905 the riding school was turned into a museum by King Carlos's wife, Dona Amélia, whose riding cloak is on show.

Made in Portugal, Italy, France, Austria and Spain, the coaches span three centuries and range from the plain to the preposterous. The main gallery, in Louis XVI style with splendid painted ceiling, is the setting for two straight, regimented rows of coaches created for Portuguese royalty.

The collection starts with the comparatively plain 17th-century red leather and wood coach of Philip II of Spain. The coaches become increasingly sumptuous, the interiors are lined with red velvet and gold, the exteriors are profusely carved and decorated with allegories and royal coats of arms. The rows end with three huge Baroque coaches made in Rome for the Portuguese ambassador to the Vatican, Dom Rodrigo Almeida e Menezes, the Marquês de Abrantes. The epitome of pomp and extravagance, but not necessarily of comfort, these 5-tonne carriages are embellished with a plush interior and life-size gilded statues.

The neighbouring gallery has further examples of royal carriages, including two-wheeled cabriolets, landaus and pony-drawn chaises used by young members of the royal family. There is also a 19th-century Lisbon cab, painted black and green, the colours of

Rear view of a coach built in 1716 for the Marquês de Abrantes, the Portuguese ambassador to Pope Clement XI

taxis right up to the 1990s. The 18th-century Eyeglass Chaise, whose black leather hood is pierced by sinister eye-like windows, was made during the era of Pombal *(see p15)* when lavish decoration was discouraged. The upper gallery has a collection of harnesses, court costumes and portraits of members of the royal family.

Jardim Agrícola Tropical **❸**

Calçada do Galvão. **Map** 1 C4.
[01-362 02 10. **▦** 27, 28, 43, 51.
▣ 15. **◯** 10am–5pm Tue–Sun.
● public hols. **▨ ▧ Museu
Tropical ◯** by appt only.

A LSO KNOWN AS the Jardim do Ultramar, this peaceful park with ponds, waterfowl and peacocks, attracts surprisingly few visitors. Laid out at the beginning of this century as the research centre of the Institute for Tropical Sciences, it is more of an arboretum than a flower garden. The emphasis is on rare tropical and subtropical trees and plants, many of them endangered species. Among the striking trees grown here are dragon trees, native to the Canary Islands and Madeira, monkey puzzle trees from South America and a handsome avenue of lofty Washington palms. The oriental garden with its streams, bridges and hibiscus is heralded by a large Chinese-style gateway which represented Macau in the Exhibition of the Portuguese World in 1940 *(see p62)*.

The research buildings and **Museu Tropical** are housed in the Palácio dos Condes da Calheta, an 18th-century mansion whose interior walls are covered with *azulejos* spanning three centuries. The museum has 50,000 dried plant specimens and 2,414 samples of wood.

Mosteiro dos Jerónimos **❹**

See pp66–7.

Washington palms in the Jardim Agrícola Tropical

Museu Nacional de Arqueologia **❺**

Praça do Império. **Map** 1 B4. **[** 01-362 00 00. **▦** 28, 43, 49, 51. **▣** 15.
◯ 10am–6pm Wed–Sun, 2pm–6pm Tue. **●** 1 Jan, Easter, 1 May, 25 Dec.
▨ ▣ ▧

T HE LONG west wing of the Mosteiro dos Jerónimos *(see pp66–7)*, formerly the monks' dormitory, has been a museum since 1893. Reconstructed in the middle of the 19th century, the building is a poor imitation of the Manueline original. The museum houses Portugal's main archaeological research centre and the exhibits, from sites all over the country, include a gold Iron Age bracelet and, Visigothic jewellery found in the Alentejo in southern Portugal,

Visigothic gold buckle, Museu de Arqueologia

Roman ornaments and early 8th-century Moorish artefacts. The main Greco-Roman and Egyptian section is strong on funerary art, featuring figurines, tombstones, masks, terracotta amulets and funeral cones inscribed with hieroglyphics alluding to the solar system. The dimly-lit Room of Treasures has a fine collection of coins, necklaces, bracelets and other jewellery dating from 1800–500 BC, but a frustrating lack of information.

Some of the space is devoted to long-running temporary exhibitions and part of the permanent collection remains in the reserves.

Planetário Calouste Gulbenkian **❻**

Praça do Império. **Map** 1 B4. **[** 01-362 00 02. **▦** 28, 43, 49, 51. **▣** 15.
◯ for shows: 4pm & 5pm Sat & Sun (also school hols: 11am, 3pm & 4:15pm Wed & Thu). Special shows for children 11am Sun. **●** public hols. **▨ ▣ ▧**

F INANCED BY the Gulbenkian Foundation *(see p79)* and built in 1965, this modern building sits incongruously beside the Jerónimos monastery. Inside, the Planetarium recreates the sky at night and reveals the mysteries of the cosmos. There are shows in Portuguese, English and French explaining the movement of the stars and our solar system, as well as presentations on more specialist themes, such as the constellations or the Star of Bethlehem (Belém).

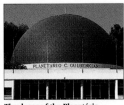

The dome of the Planetário Calouste Gulbenkian

Mosteiro dos Jerónimos ❹

Armillary sphere in the cloister

A MONUMENT TO THE WEALTH of the Age of Discovery *(see pp18–19)*, this monastery is the culmination of Manueline architecture in this period. Commissioned by Manuel I in 1501, soon after Vasco da Gama's return from his historic voyage, it was financed largely by "pepper money", the profits made from the spice trade. Various masterbuilders worked on the building, the most notable of whom was Diogo Boitac, replaced by João de Castilho in 1516. The monastery was entrusted to the Order of St Jerome (Hieronymites) until 1834, when all religious orders were disbanded.

Tomb of Vasco da Gama
The 19th-century tomb of the explorer (see p68) is carved with ropes, armillary spheres and other seafaring symbols.

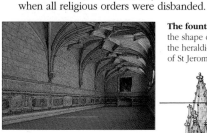

Refectory
The walls of the refectory are tiled with 18th-century azulejos. The panel at the northern end depicts the Feeding of the Five Thousand.

The modern wing, built in 1850 in Neo-Manueline style, houses the Museu Nacional de Arqueologia *(see p65).*

The fountain is in the shape of a lion, the heraldic animal of St Jerome.

The west portal was designed by the French sculptor Nicolau Chanterène.

Entrance to church and cloister

Gallery

View of the Monastery
This 17th-century scene by Felipe Lobo shows women at a fountain in front of the Mosteiro dos Jerónimos.

STAR FEATURES
★ **South Portal**
★ **Cloister**

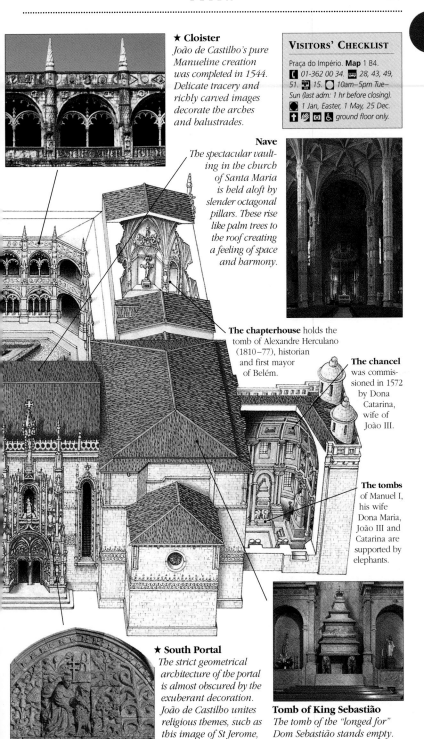

★ Cloister
João de Castilho's pure Manueline creation was completed in 1544. Delicate tracery and richly carved images decorate the arches and balustrades.

VISITORS' CHECKLIST

Praça do Império. **Map** 1 B4.
📞 01-362 00 34. 🚌 28, 43, 49, 51. 🚃 15. ⬤ 10am–5pm Tue–Sun (last adm: 1 hr before closing). ⬤ 1 Jan, Easter, 1 May, 25 Dec. 🚻 📷 📹 ♿ ground floor only.

Nave
The spectacular vaulting in the church of Santa Maria is held aloft by slender octagonal pillars. These rise like palm trees to the roof creating a feeling of space and harmony.

The chapterhouse holds the tomb of Alexandre Herculano (1810–77), historian and first mayor of Belém.

The chancel was commissioned in 1572 by Dona Catarina, wife of João III.

The tombs of Manuel I, his wife Dona Maria, João III and Catarina are supported by elephants.

★ South Portal
The strict geometrical architecture of the portal is almost obscured by the exuberant decoration. João de Castilho unites religious themes, such as this image of St Jerome, with the secular, exalting the kings of Portugal.

Tomb of King Sebastião
The tomb of the "longed for" Dom Sebastião stands empty. The young king never returned from battle in 1578.

Façade of the Museu da Marinha

Museu da Marinha ❼

Praça do Império. **Map** 1 B4. ◖ 01-362 00 19. ▦ 28, 43, 49, 51. ▧ 15. ◷ 10am–6pm (Oct–May: 5pm) Tue–Sun. ◕ public hols. ▨ ▣ ⬥

THE MARITIME MUSEUM was inaugurated in 1962 in the west wing of the Jerónimos monastery (see p66–7). The site was significant since it was here, in the chapel built by Henry the Navigator (see p19), that mariners took mass before embarking on their historic voyages. A hall devoted to the Discoveries illustrates the rapid progress in shipbuilding from the mid-15th century, capitalizing on the experience of the long-distance explorers. Small replicas show the transition from the bark to the lateen-rigged caravel, through the faster square-rigged caravel, to the Portuguese *nau*. Also relating to the Discoveries are navigational instruments, astrolabes and replicas of 16th-century maps showing the world as it was known then. The stone pillars, carved with the Cross of the Knights of Christ, are replicas of the types of *padrão* set up as monuments to Portuguese sovereignty on the lands discovered. Beyond the Hall of Discoveries a series of rooms displaying models of modern Portuguese ships leads on to the Royal Quarters where you can see the exquisitely furnished wood-panelled cabin of King Carlos and Queen Amélia from the royal yacht *Amélia*, built in Scotland in 1900.

The modern, incongruous pavilion opposite houses original royal barges, the most extravagant of which is the royal brig built in 1780 for Maria I. The collection ends with a display of seaplanes, including the *Santa Clara* which made the first crossing of the South Atlantic in 1922.

VASCO DA GAMA (c.1460–1524)

In 1498 Vasco da Gama sailed around the Cape of Good Hope and opened the sea route to India (see pp18–9). Although the Hindu ruler of Calicut, who received him wearing diamond and ruby rings, was not impressed by his humble offerings of cloth and wash basins, da Gama returned to Portugal with a cargo of spices. In 1502 he sailed again to India, establishing Portuguese trade routes in the Indian Ocean. João III nominated him Viceroy of India in 1524, but he died of a fever soon after.

16th-century painting of Vasco da Gama in Goa

Centro Cultural de Belém ❽

Praça do Império. **Map** 1 B5. ◖ 01-361 24 00. ▦ 28, 43, 49, 51. ▧ 15. ◷ 9am–9:45pm daily. ⬥ **Exhibition Centre** ◷ 11am–8pm. ▨ ⬥

THE CONSTRUCTION of a stark modern building directly between the Jerónimos monastery and the Tagus was inevitably controversial. Built in 1990 as the headquarters of the Portuguese presidency of the European Community, the complex opened as a cultural centre in 1993. The emphasis is on music, performing arts and photography, with a large **Exhibition Centre** used for temporary exhibitions. Lecture halls are named after places in Asia visited by the author and adventurer Fernão Mendes Pinto (1510–83).

The centre is somewhat soulless but at weekends it is enlivened by street performers, actors and rollerbladers.

The modern complex of the Centro Cultural de Belém

Monument to the Discoveries ❾

Padrão dos Descobrimentos, Avenida de Brasília. **Map** 1 C5. ◖ 01-301 62 28. ▦ 28, 29, 43, 51. ▧ 15. ◷ 9:30am–6pm Tue–Sun. ◕ public hols. ▨ for lift. ▣

STANDING PROMINENTLY on the Belém waterfront, this massive angular monument, the Padrão dos Descobrimentos, was built in 1960 to mark the 500th anniversary of the death of Henry the Navigator (see p19). The 52-m (170-ft) high monument, commissioned by the Salazar regime, commemorates the mariners, royal patrons and all those who participated in the rapid development of the Portuguese Age

The huge pavement compass in front of the Monument to the Discoveries

Museu de Arte Popular **⓾**

Avenida de Brasília. **Map** 1 B5.
C *01-301 12 82.* **▦** *28, 29, 43, 51.*
▦ *15.* **O** *10am–5pm Tue–Sun.*
● *1 Jan, Easter, 1 May, 25 Dec.* **⬚**

THE DRAB BUILDING on the waterfront, between the Monument to the Discoveries and the Torre de Belém (see p70), houses the museum of Portuguese folk art and traditional handicrafts, opened in 1948. The exhibits, which are arranged by province, include local pottery, agricultural tools, costumes, musical instruments, jewellery and brightly coloured saddles. The display gives a vivid indication of the diversity between the different regions of Portugal. Each area has its speciality such as the colourful ox yokes and ceramic cocks from the Minho and basketware from Trás-os-Montes, both in northern Portugal, and cowbells and terracotta casseroles from the Alentejo and fishing equipment from the Algarve, in the south. Although the labelling on the exhibits is sometimes sparse, if you are planning to travel around Portugal the museum offers an excellent preview to the traditional handicrafts of the various provinces that you will most likely visit.

of Discovery. The monument is designed in the shape of a caravel, with Portugal's coat of arms on the sides and the sword of the Royal House of Avis rising above the entrance. Henry the Navigator stands at the prow with a caravel in hand. In two sloping lines either side of the monument are stone statues of Portuguese heroes linked with the Age of Discovery. On the western face these include Dom Manuel I holding an armillary sphere, the poet Camões with a copy of *Os Lusíadas*, the painter Nuno Gonçalves with a paint pallet as well as famous navigators, cartographers and kings.

On the monument's north side, the huge mariner's compass cut into the paving stone was a present from the Republic of South Africa

in 1960. The central map, dotted with galleons and mermaids, shows the routes of the discoverers in the 15th and 16th centuries. Inside the monument a lift whisks you up to the sixth floor where steps then lead to the top for a splendid panorama of the river and Belém. The basement level is used for temporary exhibitions, but not necessarily related to the Discoveries.

The rather ostentatious Padrão is not to everyone's taste but the setting is undeniably splendid and the caravel design is imaginative. The monument looks particularly dramatic when viewed from the west in the light of the late afternoon sun.

Traditional costume from Trás-os-Montes

EASTERN FACE OF THE MONUMENT TO THE DISCOVERIES

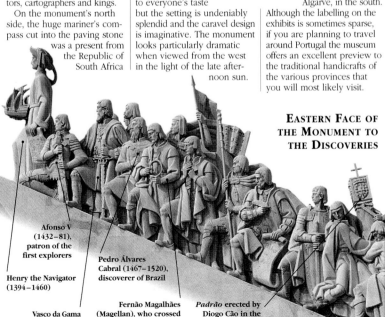

Afonso V (1432–81), patron of the first explorers

Pedro Álvares Cabral (1467–1520), discoverer of Brazil

Henry the Navigator (1394–1460)

Vasco da Gama (1460–1524)

Fernão Magalhães (Magellan), who crossed the Pacific in 1520–21

Padrão erected by Diogo Cão in the Congo in 1482

Torre de Belém ⑪

Arms of Manuel I

COMMISSIONED BY Manuel I, the tower was built as a fortress in the middle of the Tagus in 1515–21. The starting point for the navigators who set out to discover the trade routes, this Manueline gem became a symbol of Portugal's great era of expansion. The real beauty of the tower lies in the decoration of the exterior. Adorned with rope carved in stone, it has openwork balconies, Moorish-style watchtowers and distinctive battlements in the shape of shields. The Gothic interior below the terrace, which served as a storeroom for arms and a prison, is very austere but the private quarters in the tower are worth visiting for the loggia and the panorama.

VISITORS' CHECKLIST

Avenida da India. **Map** 1 A5.
📞 01-362 00 34. 🚌 14, 28, 43, 51. 🚋 15. 🚊 Belém.
🕐 10am–5pm Tue–Sun.
⛔ 1 Jan, Easter, 1 May, 25 Dec.
📷 🔲 ♿ ground floor only.

Renaissance Loggia
The elegant arcaded loggia, inspired by Italian architecture, gives a light touch to the defensive battlements of the tower.

Armillary spheres and nautical rope are symbols of Portugal's seafaring prowess.

Royal coat of arms of Manuel I

Chapel

Battlements are decorated with the cross of the Order of Christ.

Virgin and Child
A statue of Our Lady of Safe Homecoming faces the sea, a symbol of protection for sailors on their voyages of discovery.

Governor's room

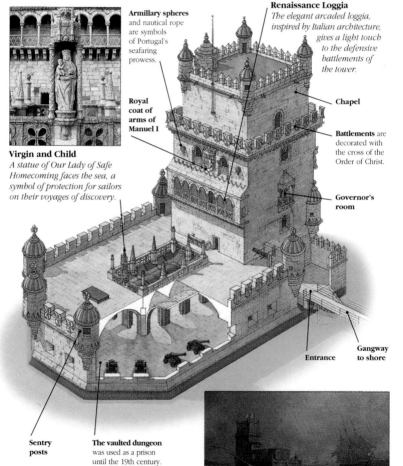

Gangway to shore

Entrance

Sentry posts

The vaulted dungeon was used as a prison until the 19th century.

The Torre de Belém in 1811
This painting of a British ship navigating the Tagus, by JT Serres, shows the tower further from the shore than it is today. Land on the north bank was reclaimed in the 19th century, making the river narrower.

The simple Manueline chapel, Ermida de São Jerónimo

Ermida de São Jerónimo ⑫

Rua Pedro de Covilhã. **Map** 1 A3.
📞 01-301 86 48. 🚌 27, 28, 41.
🕐 by appt only.

ALSO KNOWN AS the Capela de São Jerónimo, this elegant little chapel was constructed in 1514 when Diogo Boitac was working on the Jerónimos monastery (see pp66–7). Although a far simpler building, it is also Manueline in style and may have been built to a design by Boitac. The only decorative elements on the monolithic chapel are the four pinnacles, corner gargoyles and Manueline portal. Perched on a quiet hill above Belém, the chapel has fine views down to the River Tagus and a path from the terrace winds down the hill towards the Torre de Belém.

Igreja da Memória ⑬

Calçada do Galvão, Ajuda. **Map** 1 C3.
📞 01-363 52 95. 🚌 14, 29, 73.
🕐 4–6pm Mon–Sat. 🚹 ♿

BUILT IN 1760, the church was founded by King José I in gratitude for his escape from an assassination plot on this site in 1758. The king was returning from a secret liaison with a lady of the noble Távora family when his carriage was attacked and a bullet hit him in the arm. Pombal (see p15), whose power had now become absolute, used this as an excuse to get rid of his enemies in the Távora family,

accusing them of conspiracy. In 1759 they were savagely tortured and executed. Their deaths are commemorated by a pillar in Beco do Chão Salgado, off Rua de Belém.

The Neo-Classical domed church has a marble-clad interior and a small chapel, on the right, containing the tomb of Pombal. He died at the age of 83, a year after he had been banished from Lisbon.

Jardim Botânico da Ajuda ⑭

Calçada da Ajuda. **Map** 1 C2. 🚌 14, 29, 73. 🚋 18. 🕐 8am–5pm Mon–Fri. 🌑 public hols. ♿ ♿

LAID OUT on two levels by Pombal (see p15) in 1768, these Italian-style gardens provide a pleasant respite from the noisy suburbs of Belém. The entrance, through green wrought-iron gates in a pink wall, is easy to miss. The park comprises tropical trees and geometrical box-hedge gardens surrounding neat flower beds. Notable features are the 400-year-old dragon tree, native of Madeira, and the large and flamboyant 18th-century fountain decorated with writhing serpents, winged fish, sea horses and mythical creatures. A broad, majestic terrace looks out over the lower level of the gardens.

Palácio Nacional da Ajuda ⑮

Largo da Ajuda. **Map** 2 D2. 📞 01-363 70 95. 🚌 42, 60. 🚋 18. 🕐 10am–5pm Thu–Tue. 🌑 1 Jan, Easter, 1 May, 25 Dec. ♿ ♿

THE ROYAL PALACE, destroyed by fire in 1795, was replaced in the early 19th century by the Neo-Classical building you see today. This was left incomplete when the royal family was forced into exile in Brazil during 1807.

The palace only became a permanent residence of the royal family when Luís I became king in 1861 and married an Italian Princess, Maria Pia di Savoia. No expense was spared in furnishing the apartments. The ostentatious rooms are decorated with silk wallpaper, Sèvres porcelain and crystal chandeliers. A prime example of regal excess is the extraordinary Saxe Room, a wedding present to Maria Pia from the King of Saxony, in which every piece of furniture is decorated with Meissen porcelain. On the first floor the huge Banqueting Hall, with crystal chandeliers, silk-covered chairs and an allegory of the birth of João VI on the frescoed ceiling, is truly impressive. At the other end of the palace, Luís I's Neo-Gothic painting studio is a more intimate display of intricately carved furniture.

19th-century throne from the Palácio Nacional da Ajuda

Manicured formal gardens of the Jardim Botânico da Ajuda

FURTHER AFIELD

Azulejo panel from Palácio Fronteira

THE MAJORITY of the outlying sights, which include some of Lisbon's finest museums, are easily accessible by bus or metro from the city centre. A ten-minute walk north from the gardens of the Parque Eduardo VII brings you to Portugal's great cultural complex, the Calouste Gulbenkian Foundation, set in a pleasant park. Few tourists go further north than the Gulbenkian, but the Museu da Cidade on Campo Grande is worth a detour for its fascinating overview of Lisbon's history.

The charming Palácio Fronteira, decorated with splendid tiles, is one of the many villas built for the aristocracy that now overlook the city suburbs. Those interested in tiles will also enjoy the Museu Nacional do Azulejo in the cloisters of the Madre de Deus convent. Visitors with half a day to spare can cross the Tagus to the Cristo Rei monument. Northeast of the city centre, the vast Oceanarium is part of Expo '98, a project that is regenerating the area into a residential and commercial centre.

SIGHTS AT A GLANCE

Museums and Galleries
Centro de Arte Moderna **7**
Museu da Água **9**
Museu Calouste Gulbenkian pp76–9 **6**
Museu da Cidade **12**
Museu Nacional do Azulejo pp82–3 **10**

Modern Architecture
Amoreiras Shopping Centre **3**
Cristo Rei **1**
Ponte 25 de Abril **2**

Historic Architecture
Aqueduto das Águas Livres **14**
Campo Pequeno **8**
Palácio Fronteira **15**
Praça Marquês de Pombal **4**

Parks and Gardens
Parque Eduardo VII **5**
Parque do Monteiro-Mor **16**

Zoos
Jardim Zoológico **13**
Pavilhão dos Oceanos **11**

KEY

▓ Main sightseeing areas

✈ Airport

⚓ Ferry boarding point

▬ Motorway

▬ Major road

═ Minor road

0 kilometres 4

0 miles 2

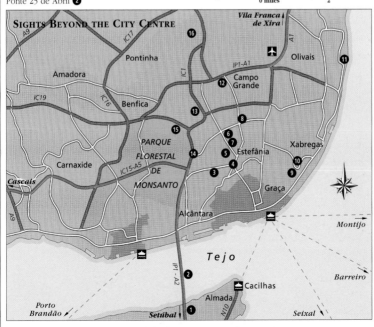

SIGHTS BEYOND THE CITY CENTRE

◁ **Nymph fountain among tropical vegetation inside the Estufa Fria, Parque Eduardo VII**

Cristo Rei ●

Santuário Nacional do Cristo Rei, Alto do Pragal, Almada. █ 01-275 10 00. ▤ from Praça do Comércio & Cais do Sodré to Cacilhas then ▤ 101. **Lift** ◻ 9am–6:30pm daily. ▨

MODELLED ON the more famous Cristo Redentor in Rio de Janeiro, this giant-sized statue stands with arms outstretched on the south bank of the Tagus. The 28 m (92 ft) tall figure of Christ, mounted on a huge pedestal, was built by Francisco Franco in 1949–59 at the instigation of Prime Minister Salazar.

You can see the monument from various viewpoints in the city, but it is fun to take a ferry to the Outra Banda (the other bank), then a bus or taxi to the monument. (Rush hour is best avoided.) A lift, plus some steps, takes you up 82 m (269 ft) to the top of the pedestal, affording fine views of the city and river.

Ponte 25 de Abril ●

Map 3 A5. ▤ 52, 53.

ORIGINALLY CALLED the Ponte Salazar after the dictator who had it built in 1966, Lisbon's suspension bridge was renamed (like many other

The towering monument of Cristo Rei overlooking the Tagus

monuments) to commemorate the revolution of 25 April 1974 which restored democracy to Portugal (see p15).

Inspired by San Francisco's Golden Gate in the United States, this steel construction stretches for 2 km (1 mile). Work currently being done

will add a new tier under the bridge for a much-needed railway across the Tagus. The bridge is notorious for traffic congestion, particularly at weekends but the problem should be partly resolved by the construction of the 12-km (7-mile) Vasco da Gama bridge. Spanning the river from Montijo to Sacavém, north of the Expo site, this new bridge is due to be completed in 1998.

Amoreiras Shopping Centre ●

Avenida Engenheiro Duarte Pacheco. **Map** 5 A5. █ 01-381 02 00. Ⓜ Rotunda. ▤ 11, 23, 53. ◻ 10am–11pm daily. ● 25 Dec. ♿

IN THE 18TH CENTURY, the Marquês de Pombal (see p15) planted mulberry trees (amoreiras) on the western edge of the city to create food for silk worms. Hence the name of the futuristic shopping centre that was built here in 1985. This massive complex, with pink and blue towers, houses 370 shops, ten cinemas, and numerous cafés. An incongruous feature of Lisbon, it nevertheless manages to draw the crowds, particularly the young, and has taken many shoppers away from the more traditional quarters of the city.

Ponte 25 de Abril linking central Lisbon with the Outra Banda, the south bank of the Tagus

Tropical plants in the Estufa Quente glasshouse, Parque Eduardo VII

Praça Marquês de Pombal ❹

Map 5 C5. **M** *Rotunda.* **🚌** *11, 23, 36, 101 & many other routes.*

AT THE TOP of the Avenida da Liberdade *(see p44)*, traffic thunders round the "Rotunda" (roundabout), as the praça is also known. At the centre rises the lofty monument to Pombal, unveiled in 1934. The despotic statesman, who virtually ruled Portugal from 1750–77, stands on the top of the column, his hand on a lion (symbol of power) and his eyes directed down to the Baixa, whose creation he masterminded *(see p15)*.

Allegorical images depicting Pombal's political, educational and agricultural reforms decorate the base of the monument. Standing figures represent Coimbra University where he introduced a new Faculty of Science. Although greatly feared, this dynamic politician propelled the country into the Age of Enlightenment. Broken blocks of stone at the foot of the monument and tidal waves flooding the city are an allegory of the destruction caused by the 1755 earthquake.

The sculptures on the pedestal and the inscriptions relating to Pombal's achievements can be seen by taking the underpass into the centre of the square. This also leads to the Rotunda metro station and the well-tended Parque Eduardo VII that extends northwards behind the square. The paving stones around the Rotunda are decorated with a mosaic of Lisbon's coat of arms. Similar patterns in small black and white cobbles decorate many of the city's streets and squares.

Detail representing agricultural toil on the base of the monument in Praça Marquês de Pombal

Parque Eduardo VII ❺

Praça Marquês de Pombal. **Map** 5 B4. **📞** *01-385 04 08.* **M** *Rotunda.* **🚌** *2, 11, 22, 36.* **Estufa Fria** **🕘** *9am–6pm (Oct–Feb: 5pm) daily.* **⬤** *1 Jan, 25 Apr, 1 May, 25 Dec.* 🎫

THE LARGEST PARK in central Lisbon was named in honour of King Edward VII of England who came to Lisbon in 1902 to reaffirm the Anglo-Portuguese alliance. The wide grassy slope, that extends for 25 hectares (62 acres), was laid out as a continuation of Avenida da Liberdade *(see p44)* at the beginning of the 20th century. Neatly clipped box hedging, flanked by mosaic patterned walkways, stretches uphill from the Praça Marquês de Pombal to a belvedere at the top. From here there are fine views of the city and the distant hills on the far side of the Tagus. On clear days it is possible to see as far as the Serra da Arrábida *(see p107)*.

Located at the northwest corner, the most inspiring feature of this rather monotonous park is the jungle-like **Estufa Fria**, or greenhouse, where exotic plants, streams and waterfalls provide an oasis from the city streets. There are in fact two greenhouses: in the Estufa Fria (cold greenhouse), palms push through the slatted bamboo roof and paths wind through a forest of ferns, fuchsias, flowering shrubs and banana trees; the warmer Estufa Quente, or hot-house, is a glassed-over garden with lush plants, waterlily ponds and cacti, as well as tropical birds in cages.

Near the estufas a shallow pond with large carp and a play area in the shape of a galleon are popular with children. On the east side the **Pavilhão Carlos Lopes**, named after the winner of the 1984 Olympic marathon, is now a venue for concerts and conferences. The dazzling white and ochre façade is decorated with a series of modern tiled scenes by *azulejo* artist, Jorge Colaço, mainly of Portuguese battles. A pleasant waterside café lies to the north of the pavilion.

Museu Calouste Gulbenkian ❻

THANKS TO A WEALTHY Armenian oil magnate, Calouste Gulbenkian *(see p 79)*, with wide-ranging tastes and an eye for a masterpiece, the museum has one of the finest collections of art in Europe. Inaugurated in 1969, the purpose-built museum was created as part of the charitable institution bequeathed to Portugal by the multimillionaire. The design of the building, set in a spacious park allowing natural light to fill some of the rooms, was devised to create the best layout for the founder's varied collection.

Mustard Barrel
This 18th-century silver mustard barrel was made in France by Antoine Sébastien Durand.

Lalique Corsage Ornament
The sinuous curves of the gold and enamel snakes are typical of René Lalique's Art Nouveau jewellery.

★ Diana
This fine marble statue (1780) by the French sculptor Jean-Antoine Houdon, was once owned by Catherine the Great of Russia but was considered too obscene to exhibit. The graceful Diana, goddess of the hunt, stands with a bow and arrow in hand.

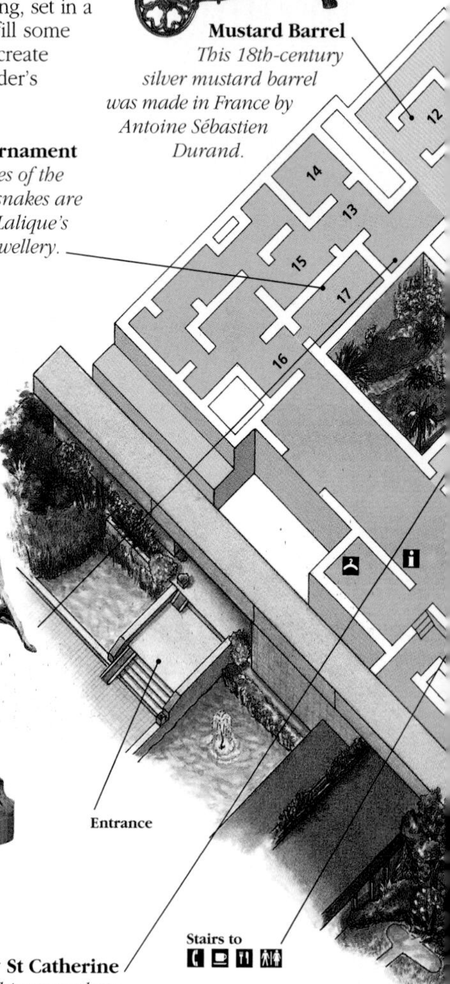

Entrance

Stairs to

★ St Catherine
This serene bust of St Catherine was painted by the Flemish artist Rogier Van der Weyden (1400–64). The thin strip of landscape on the left of the wooden panel brings light and depth to the still portrait.

STAR EXHIBITS

★ **Portrait of an Old Man by Rembrandt**

★ **Diana by Houdon**

★ **St Catherine by Van der Weyden**

★ Portrait of an Old Man
Rembrandt was a master of light and shade. In this expressive portrait, dated 1645, the fragile countenance of the old man is contrasted with the strong and dramatic lighting.

Renaissance art

Vase of a Hundred Birds
The enamel decoration that adorns this Chinese porcelain vase is known as Famille Verte. *This type of elaborate design is characteristic of the Ch'ing dynasty during the reign of the Emperor K'ang Hsi (1662–1722).*

GALLERY GUIDE
The galleries are laid out both chronologically and geographically, the first section (rooms 1–6) dedicated to Classical and Oriental art, the second section (rooms 7–17) housing the European collection of paintings, sculpture, furniture, silverware and jewellery.

Armenian art

Persian faïence

Egyptian Bronze Cat
This bronze of a cat feeding her kittens dates from the Saite Period (8th century BC). Other stunning Egyptian pieces include a gilded mask of a mummy.

Turkish Faïence Plate
The factories at Iznik in Turkey produced some of the most beautiful jugs, plates and vases of the Islamic world, including this 17th-century deep plate decorated with stylized animal forms.

KEY TO FLOORPLAN

⬜	Egyptian, Classical and Mesopotamian art
⬜	Oriental Islamic art
⬜	Far Eastern art
⬜	European art (14th–17th centuries)
⬜	French 18th-century decorative arts
⬜	European art (18th–19th centuries)
⬜	Lalique collection
⬛	Non-exhibition space

Exploring the Gulbenkian Collection

Housing calouste gulbenkian's unique collection of art, the museum ranks with the Museu de Arte Antiga *(see pp56–9)* as the finest in Lisbon. The exhibits, which span over 4,000 years from ancient Egyptian statuettes, through translucent Islamic glassware, to Art Nouveau brooches, are displayed in spacious and well-lit galleries, many overlooking the gardens or courtyards. The museum is quite small, however each individual work of art, from the magnificent pieces that make up the rich display of Oriental and Islamic art, to the selection of European paintings and furniture, is worthy of attention.

Late 16th-century Persian faïence tile from the School of Isfahan

EGYPTIAN, CLASSICAL AND MESOPOTAMIAN ART

Priceless treasures chart the evolution of Egyptian art from the Old Kingdom (c.2700 BC) to the Roman Period (1st century BC). The exhibits range from an alabaster bowl of the 3rd Dynasty to a surprisingly modern-looking blue terracotta torso of a statuette of *Venus Anadyomene* from the Roman period.

Outstanding pieces in the Classical art section are a magnificent red-figure Greek vase and 11 Roman medallions, found in Egypt. These are believed to have been struck to commemorate the athletic games held in Macedonia in AD 242 in honour of Alexander the Great. In the Mesopotamian art section the large Assyrian

5th-century BC Greek vase

alabaster bas-relief represents the winged genius of Spring, carrying a container of sacred water (9th century BC).

ORIENTAL ISLAMIC ART

Being armenian, Calouste Gulbenkian had a keen interest in art from the Near and Middle East. The Oriental Islamic gallery has a fine collection of Persian and Turkish carpets, textiles, costumes and ceramics. In the section overlooking the courtyard, the Syrian mosque lamps and bottles commissioned by princes and sultans, are beautifully decorated with coloured enamel on glass. The Armenian section has some exquisite illustrated manuscripts from the 16th to 18th centuries, produced by Armenian refugees in Istanbul, Persia and the Crimea.

FAR EASTERN ART

Calouste gulbenkian acquired a large collection of Chinese porcelain between 1910 and 1930. One of the rarest pieces is the small blue-glazed bowl from the Yüan Dynasty (1279–1368), on the right as you go into the gallery. The majority of exhibits, however, are the later, more exuberantly decorated *famille verte* porcelain and the K'ang Hsi biscuitware of the 17th and 18th centuries. Further exhibits from the Far East are translucent Chinese jades and other semi-precious stones, Japanese prints, brocaded silk hangings and bound books, and lacquerwork.

EUROPEAN ART (14TH–17TH CENTURIES)

Illuminated manuscripts, rare printed books and medieval ivories introduce the section on Western art. The delicately sculpted 14th-century ivory diptychs and triptychs, made in France, show scenes from the lives of Christ and the Virgin.

The collection of early European paintings starts with panels of *St Joseph* and *St Catherine* by Rogier van der Weyden, leading painter of the mid-15th century in Flanders. Italian Renaissance painting is represented by Cima da Conegliano's *Sacra Conversazione* from the late 15th century and Domenico Ghirlandaio's *Portrait of a Young Woman* (1485).

The collection progresses to Flemish and Dutch works of the 17th century, including two works by Rembrandt: *Portrait of an Old Man* (1645),

French ivory triptych of
Scenes from the Life of the Virgin **(14th century)**

a masterpiece of psychological penetration, and *Alexander the Great* (1660), said to have been modelled on Rembrandt's son, Titus, and previously thought to have portrayed the Greek goddess Pallas Athena. Rubens is represented by three paintings, the most remarkable of which is the *Portrait of Hélène Fourment* (1630), the artist's second wife.

The gallery beyond the Dutch and Flemish paintings has tapestries and textiles from Italy and Flanders, Italian ceramics, rare 15th-century medallions and sculpture.

View of the Molo with the Ducal Palace (1790) by Francesco Guardi

FRENCH 18TH-CENTURY DECORATIVE ARTS

SOME REMARKABLY elaborate Louis XV and Louis XVI pieces, many commissioned by royalty, feature in the collection of French 18th-century furniture. The exhibits, many of them embellished with laquer panels, ebony and bronze, are grouped together according to historical style with Beauvais and "chinoiserie" Aubusson tapestries decorating the walls.

The French silverware from the same period, much of which once adorned the dining tables of Russian palaces, includes lavishly decorated soup tureens, salt-cellars and platters.

Louis XV chest of drawers inlaid with ebony and bronze

EUROPEAN ART (18TH–19TH CENTURIES)

THE ART of the 18th century is dominated by French painters, including Watteau (1684–1721), Fragonard (1732–1806) and Boucher (1703–70). The most celebrated piece of sculpture is a statue of *Diana* by Jean-Antoine Houdon. Commissioned in 1780 by the Duke of Saxe-Gotha for his

gardens, it became one of the principal exhibits in the Hermitage in Russia during the 19th and early 20th centuries.

One whole room is devoted to views of Venice by the 18th-century Venetian painter Francesco Guardi, and a small collection of British art includes works by leading 18th-century portraitists, such as Gainsborough's *Portrait of Mrs Lowndes-Stone* (c.1775) and Romney's *Portrait of Mrs Constable* (1787). There are also two stormy seascapes by JMW Turner (1775–1851). French 19th-century landscape painting is well represented here, reflecting Gulbenkian's preference for naturalism, with works by the Barbizon school, the Realists and the Impressionists. The best-known paintings in the section, however, are probably Manet's *Boy with Cherries*, painted in about 1858 at the beginning of the artist's career, and *Boy Blowing*

Bubbles, painted about 1867. Renoir's *Portrait of Madame Claude Monet* was painted in about 1872 when the artist was staying with Monet at his country home in Argenteuil, in the outskirts of Paris.

LALIQUE COLLECTION

THE TOUR of the museum ends with an entire room filled with the flamboyant creations of French Art Nouveau jeweller, René Lalique (1860–1945). Gulbenkian was a close friend of Lalique's and he acquired many of the pieces of jewellery, glassware and ivory on display here directly from the artist. Inlaid with semi-precious stones and covered with enamel or gold leaf, the brooches, necklaces, vases and combs are decorated with the dragonfly, peacock or sensual female nude motifs characteristic of Art Nouveau.

CALOUSTE GULBENKIAN

Born in Scutari (Turkey) in 1869, Gulbenkian started his art collection at the age of 14 when he bought some ancient coins in a bazaar. In 1928 he was granted a 5 per cent stake in four major oil companies, including BP and Shell, in thanks for his part in the transfer of the assets of the Iraq Petroleum Company to those four companies. He thereby earned himself the nickname of "Mr Five Percent". With the wealth he accumulated, Gulbenkian was able to indulge his passion for fine works of art. During World War II, he went to live in neutral Portugal and, on his death in 1955, bequeathed his estate to the Portuguese in the form of a charitable trust. The Foundation supports numerous cultural activities and has its own orchestra, libraries, ballet company and concert halls.

Henry Moore sculpture in garden of the Centro de Arte Moderna

Centro de Arte Moderna ❼

Rua Dr Nicolau de Bettencourt.
Map 5 B3. **[C** 01-795 02 41. **M** São
Sebastião. **🚌** 41, 46. **◯** Jun–Sep:
10am–5pm Tue, Thu, Fri & Sun, 2–
7:30pm Wed & Sat; Oct–May: 10am–
5pm Tue–Sun. **◐** public hols. **🖼 &**

THE MODERN ART MUSEUM lies
across the gardens from the
Calouste Gulbenkian museum
and is part of the same cultural foundation *(see p59)*.
The permanent collection
housed in the centre features
paintings and sculpture by
Portuguese artists from the turn
of the century to the present

day. The most famous painting
is the striking portrait of the
poet Fernando Pessoa in the
Café Irmãos Unidos (1964) by
José de Almada Negreiros
(1893–1970), a main exponent
of Portuguese Modernism. Also
of interest are paintings by
Eduardo Viana (1881–1967),
Amadeo de Sousa Cardoso
(1887–1910), as well as contemporary artists such as Paula
Rego, Rui Sanches, Graça
Morais and Teresa Magalhães.
The museum is light and
spacious with pleasant gardens
and a cafeteria which attracts
very long queues at weekends.

Campo Pequeno ❽

Map 5 C1. **M** Campo Pequeno.
🚌 22, 45. **Bullring [C** 01-793 24 42.
◯ Easter–Oct: for bullfights. **🖼 &**

THIS SQUARE is dominated by
the red-brick Neo-Moorish
bullring built in the late 19th
century. A large building,
accommodating up to 9,000
spectators, its keyhole-shaped
windows and double cupolas
decorated with a crescent
moon evoke Moorish-style
architecture. Bullfights take
place once or twice a week in

season. During the rest of the
year the bullring is occasionally used for concerts and the
annual Christmas circus.

Renovated 19th-century steam pump in the Museu da Água

Museu da Água ❾

Rua do Alviela 12. **[C** 01-813 55 22.
🚌 35, 104, 105, 107. **◯** 10am–
12:30pm, 2–5pm Tue–Sat. **◐** public
hols. **🖼 📷**

DEDICATED TO the history of
Lisbon's water supply, this
small but informative museum
was imaginatively created
around the city's first steam
pumping station. It commemorates Manuel da Maia, the
18th-century engineer who
masterminded the Águas Livres
aqueduct *(see p84)*. The excellent layout of the museum
earned it the Council of Europe
Museum Prize in 1990.
Pride of place goes to four
lovingly preserved steam
engines, one of which still
functions (by electricity) and
can be switched on for visitors.
The development of technology relating to the city's water
supply is documented with
photographs. Particularly interesting are the sections on the
Águas Livres aqueduct and the
Alfama's 17th-century Chafariz
d'El Rei, one of Lisbon's first
fountains. Locals used to queue
at one of six founts, depending on their social status.

Museu Nacional do Azulejo ❿

See pp82–3.

Neo-Moorish façade of the bullring in Campo Pequeno

Pavilhão dos Oceanos ⓫

Doca das Olivais. 🇨 01-831 98 98.
🅼 Oriente. 🚍 18, 28, 50, 82.
🚆 Gare do Oriente. 🅾 10am–8pm
daily from 22 May 1998. 🈂 🅶

ON THE BANKS of the Tagus, centrally located within the Expo complex, this huge and innovative Ocean Pavilion is the largest in Europe and the second biggest in the world. Built for Expo '98, the pavilion illustrates the environmental theme of "The Oceans: A Heritage for the Future". It was conceived by an American architect, Peter Chermayeff, to enhance public awareness of the diversity of the oceans' vast natural resources and to encourage mankind's responsibility to preserve the seas for future generations.

The central feature is the gigantic aquarium, the "Open Tank", with a volume of water equivalent to that of four Olympic swimming pools. Representing the open ocean, this features the fauna of the high seas, from shoals of sardines to sharks. Around the main tank four smaller aquariums reconstruct the eco-systems of the Atlantic, Antarctic, Pacific and Indian oceans. Each one features fauna and flora specific to the ocean, from seals in the Antarctic to the coral reefs of the Indian Ocean.

Museu da Cidade ⓬

Campo Grande 245. 🇨 01-759 16 17.
🅼 Campo Grande. 🚍 1, 7, 36, 101.
🅾 10am–1pm, 2–6pm Tue–Sun.
⬤ public hols. 🈂 🅶

PALÁCIO PIMENTA was allegedly commissioned by João V (see p17) for his mistress Madre Paula, a nun from the nearby convent at Odivelas. When the mansion was built, in the middle of the 18th century, it occupied a peaceful rural site outside the capital. Nowadays it has to contend

Original 18th-century tiled kitchen in the Museu da Cidade

with the teeming traffic of Campo Grande and the city's main east-west flyover nearby. The house itself, however, still retains its period charm, and the city museum, established here in 1979, is one of the most interesting in Lisbon.

The displays follow the development of the city, from prehistoric times, through the Romans, Visigoths and Moors, traced by means of tiles, drawings, paintings, models and historical documents. Visits also take you through the former living quarters of the mansion, including the kitchen, decorated with blue and white tile panels of fish, flowers and hanging game. Other rooms contain period furniture, paintings and toys. A collection of 18th-century ceramics includes intricately modelled statuettes, tureens and plates made at the royal china factory in Rato.

Some of the most fascinating exhibits are those depicting the city before the earthquake of 1755, including a highly detailed model made in the 1950s and

18th-century Indian toy, Museu da Cidade

an impressive 17th-century oil painting by Dirk Stoop (1610–86) of *Terreiro do Paço*, as Praça do Comércio was known then (see p47). One room is devoted to the Águas Livres aqueduct (see p84) with detailed architectural plans for its construction as well as prints and watercolours of the completed aqueduct by foreign and Portuguese artists.

The earthquake theme is resumed with pictures of the city amid the devastation and various plans for its reconstruction. The museum brings you into the 20th century with a large colour poster celebrating the Revolution of 1910 and the proclamation of the new republic (see p15). Several other exhibits depict life and customs in 20th-century Lisbon, including an evocative painting of *O Fado* (1910) by José Malhôa (see p143).

Detail of Dirk Stoop's 17th-century view of the Terreiro do Paço, Museu da Cidade

Museu Nacional do Azulejo ⑩

Pelican on the Manueline portal

D ONA LEONOR, widow of King João II, founded the Convento da Madre de Deus in 1509. Originally built in Manueline style, the church was restored under João III using simple Renaissance designs. The striking Baroque decoration was added by João V.

The convent cloisters provide a stunning setting for the National Tile Museum. Decorative panels, individual tiles and photographs trace the evolution of tile-making from its introduction by the Moors, through Spanish influence and the development of Portugal's own style up to the present day.

Panorama of Lisbon
A striking 18th-century panel, along one wall of the cloister, depicts Lisbon before the 1755 earthquake (see pp20–21). This detail shows the royal palace on Terreiro do Paço.

Hunting Scene
Artisans rather than artists began to decorate tiles in the 17th century. This detail shows a naive representation of a hunt.

First floor

Ground floor

KEY TO FLOORPLAN

▦	Moorish tiles
▦	16th-century tiles
▢	17th-century tiles
▦	18th-century tiles
▦	19th-century tiles
▦	20th-century tiles
▦	Temporary exhibition space
▦	Non-exhibition space

STAR FEATURES

★ **Madre de Deus**

★ **Manueline Cloister**

★ **Nossa Senhora da Vida**

★ **Nossa Senhora da Vida**
This detail showing St John is part of a fine 16th-century maiolica altarpiece. The central panel of the huge work depicts The Adoration of the Shepherds.

Tiles from the 17th century with oriental influences are displayed here.

Café Tiles
The walls of the restaurant are lined with 20th-century tiles showing hanging game, including wild boar, pheasant and sausages.

VISITORS' CHECKLIST

Rua da Madre de Deus 4. 01-
814 77 47. 18, 42, 104, 105.
2–6pm Tue, 10am–6pm
Wed–Sun (last adm: 30 mins
before closing). 1 Jan, Easter,
1 May, 25 Dec.

Moorish Tiles
Bold, geometric designs were characteristic of Moorish azulejo patterns. These 15th-century tiles, decorated with stylized animal motifs, were probably made by Moorish artisans in Seville.

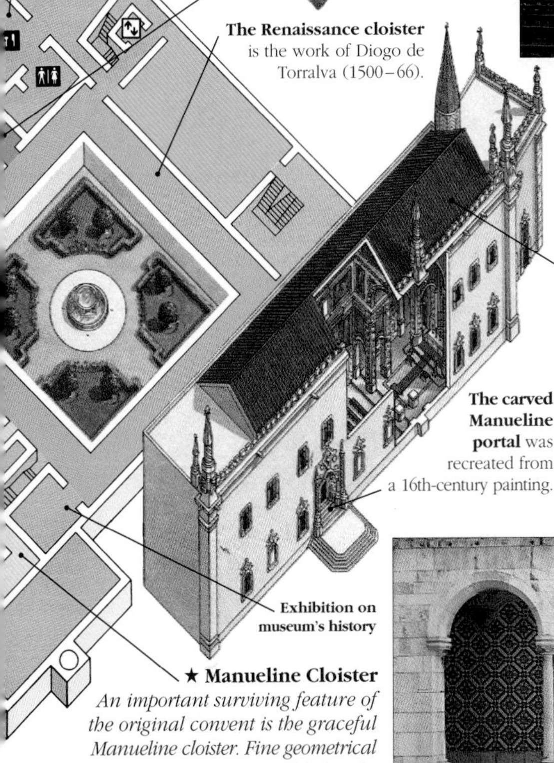

Entrance

The Renaissance cloister
is the work of Diogo de
Torralva (1500–66).

★ **Madre de Deus**
Completed in the mid-16th century, it was not until two centuries later, under João V, that the church of Madre de Deus acquired its ornate decoration. The sumptuous Rococo altarpiece was added after the earthquake of 1755.

GALLERY GUIDE
The rooms around the central cloister are arranged chronologically, from the Moorish tiles near the entrance to the 20th-century tiles upstairs. A room on the ground floor explains the history of the museum and tile-making techniques.

**The carved
Manueline
portal** was
recreated from
a 16th-century painting.

**Exhibition on
museum's history**

★ **Manueline Cloister**
An important surviving feature of the original convent is the graceful Manueline cloister. Fine geometrical patterned tiles were added to the cloister walls in the 17th century.

Jardim Zoológico ⓭

Estrada de Benfica 158–60. **℡** *01-726 93 49*. **Ⓜ** *Sete-Rios*. **🚌** *16, 34, 54, 68*. **◯** *9am–6pm (Apr–Sep: 8pm) daily*. 🅿️ 🎦

T HE GARDENS of the Jardim Zoológico are as much a feature as the actual zoo, and some of the plants look a good deal happier than the animals. Opened in 1905, some cages and aviaries still date from this time, although plans are afoot to revamp the park and improve the conditions for the inmates. The most bizarre feature is the dogs' cemetery, complete with tombstones and flowers. Current attractions of the zoo include a cable car which tours the park, a reptile house and dolphin shows. The area is divided into four zones and the admission charge is based on how many you visit.

Dolphins performing in the aquarium of the Jardim Zoológico

Aqueduto das Águas Livres ⓮

Calçada da Quintinha. **℡** *01-813 55 22*. **🚌** *2, 58, 74*. **◯** *for guided tours by appt*. **Mãe d'Água das Amoreiras**, Praça das Amoreiras. **◯** *for exhibitions*.

C ONSIDERED THE most beautiful sight in Lisbon at the turn of the century, the impressive structure of the Aqueduto das Águas Livres looms over the Alcântara valley to the northwest of the city. The construction of an aqueduct to bring fresh water to the city gave João V *(see p17)* an ideal opportunity to indulge his passion for grandiose building schemes, as the only area of Lisbon with fresh drinking water was the Alfama. A tax on meat, wine, olive oil and other comestibles funded the project, and although not complete until the 19th century, it was already supplying the city with water by 1748. The main pipeline measures 19 km (12 miles), but the total length, including all the secondary channels, is 58 km (36 miles). The most visible part of this imposing structure are the 14 arches that stride across the Alcântara valley, the tallest of which rise to a spectacular 65 m (213 ft) above the city.

The public walkway along the aqueduct, once a pleasant promenade, has been closed since 1853. This is partly due to Diogo Alves, the infamous robber who threw his victims over the edge. Today, it is possible to take a lively, informative guided tour over the Alcântara arches. There are also occasional tours of the Mãe d'Água reservoir and trips to the Mãe d'Água springs, the source of the water supply. These tours can be irregular, so it is best to contact the Museu da Água *(see p80)* for details of the trips on offer.

At the end of the aqueduct, the **Mãe d'Água das Amoreiras** is a castle-like building which once served as a reservoir for the water supplied from the aqueduct. The original design of 1745 was by the Hungarian architect, Carlos Mardel, who worked under Pombal *(see pp20–21)* in the rebuilding of the Baixa. Completed in 1834, it became a popular meeting place and acquired a reputation as the rendezvous for kings and their mistresses. Today the 5-m (16-ft) thick walls, surrounding the water-filled basin, are used to display temporary exhibitions of art by local artists.

Imposing arches of the Aqueduto das Águas Livres spanning the Alcântara valley

Palácio Fronteira ⑮

Largo São Domingos de Benfica 1.
📞 01-778 20 23. 🅼 Sete-Rios.
🚌 72. 🚉 Benfica. ◯ 10:30am–1pm
(Oct–May: 11am–1pm) Mon–Sat.
🎫 for palace. � public hols. ⬚ ◯

THIS DELIGHTFUL country
manor house was built as
a hunting pavilion for João de
Mascarenhas, the first Marquês
de Fronteira, in 1640. Although
skyscrapers are visible in the
distance, it still occupies a
quiet rural spot, bordering the
wooded Parque Florestal de
Monsanto. Both house and
garden have striking *azulejo*
decoration whose subjects
range from battle scenes to
trumpet-blowing monkeys.

Although the palace is still
occupied by the 12th Marquis,
some of the living rooms and
the library, as well
as the formal gar-
dens, are included
in the tour. The
Battles Room has
lively tiled panels
depicting scenes
of the War of
Restoration
(1640–1668), with
a detail of João de
Fronteira fighting
a Spanish general.
It was his loyalty to
Pedro II during this
war that earned him the title
of Marquis. Interesting compar-
isons can be made between
these naive 17th-century Portuguese tiles and the Delft ones
from the same period in the
dining room, depicting natur-
alistic scenes. The dining room
is also decorated with frescoed
panels and portraits of Portuguese nobility by artists such
as Domingos António de
Sequeira (1768–1837).

The late 16th-century chapel
is the oldest part of the house.
The façade is adorned with
stones, shells, broken glass and
bits of china. These fragments
of crockery are believed to
have been used at the feast
inaugurating the palace and
then smashed to ensure no one
else could sup off the same set.
Visits to the **garden** start at the
chapel terrace, where tiled
niches are decorated with
figures personifying the arts
and mythological creatures.

Tiled terrace leading to the chapel of the Palácio Fronteira

**Bust of João I in gardens
of Palácio Fronteira**

In the formal Italian garden the
immaculate box hedges are
cut into shapes to represent
the seasons of the year. To
one end, tiled
scenes of dashing
knights on horse-
back, representing
ancestors of the
Fronteira family,
are reflected in the
waters of a large
tank. On either
side of the water,
a grand staircase
leads to a terrace
above. Here,
decorative niches
contain the busts
of Portuguese kings and colourful majolica reliefs adorn
the arcades. More blue and
white tiled scenes, realistic and
allegorical, decorate the wall
at the far end of the garden.

**Entrance to the theatre museum
in Parque do Monteiro-Mor**

Parque do Monteiro-Mor ⑯

Largo Júlio Castilho. 📞 01-759 03 18.
🅼 Campo Grande. 🚌 3, 7, 36.
Park ◯ 10am–6pm Tue–Sun.
◯ 1 Jan, Easter, 1 May, 25 Dec.
Museu Nacional do Traje ◯ 10am–
6pm Tue–Sun. **Museu Nacional do
Teatro** ◯ 10am–6pm Wed–Sun,
2–6pm Tue. 🎫 combined ticket for
park & museums. ◯ ♿

MONTEIRO-MOR PARK was
sold to the state in 1975
and the 18th-century palace
buildings were converted to
museums. Relatively few
visitors come here because
of the distance from the city
centre, but the gardens are
attractive and rather more
romantic than the manicured
box-hedge gardens so typical
of Lisbon. Much of the land
is wooded, though the area
around the museums has
gardens with flowering shrubs,
duck ponds and tropical trees.

The rather old-fashioned
Museu Nacional do Traje
(costume museum) has a
varied collection of costumes
worn by musicians, politicians,
poets, aristocrats and soldiers.

The **Museu Nacional do
Teatro** has two buildings, one
devoted to temporary exhibitions, the other containing a
very small permanent collection. Photographs, posters
and cartoons feature famous
20th-century Portuguese actors
and one section is devoted to
Amália Rodrigues, the famous
fado singer (*see pp142–3*).

View across the rooftops of Sintra to the town hall ▷

THE LISBON COAST

THE LISBON COAST

WITHIN AN HOUR'S DRIVE *northwest of Lisbon you can reach the rocky Atlantic coast, the wooded slopes of Sintra or countryside dotted with villas and royal palaces. South of Lisbon you can enjoy the sandy beaches and fishing towns along the coast or explore the lagoons of the Tagus and Sado river estuaries.*

Traders and invaders, from the Phoenicians to the Spanish, have left their mark in this region, in particular the Moors whose forts and castles, rebuilt many times over the centuries, can be found all along this coast. After Lisbon became the capital in 1256, Portuguese kings and nobles built summer palaces and villas in the countryside west of the city, particularly on the cool, green heights of the Serra de Sintra.

Across the Tagus, the less fashionable southern shore (Outra Banda) could be reached only by ferry, until the suspension bridge was built in 1966. Now, the long sandy beaches of the Costa da Caparica, the coast around the fishing town of Sesimbra and even the remote Tróia peninsula have become popular resorts during the summer months. Fortunately, large stretches of coast and unspoilt countryside are being protected as conservation areas and nature reserves.

Despite the region's rapid urbanization, small fishing and farming communities still flourish. Lively fish markets offer a huge variety of fresh fish and seafood; Colares and Palmela are noted for their wine; flocks of sheep still roam the unspoilt Serra da Arrábida, providing milk for Azeitão cheese; and rice is the main crop in the Sado estuary. Traditional industries also survive, such as salt panning near Alcochete and marble quarries at Pero Pinheiro.

Though the sea is cold and often rough, especially on west-facing coasts, the beaches are among the cleanest in Europe. As well as surfing, fishing and scuba diving, the region provides splendid golf courses, horse riding facilities and a Formula 1 motor-racing track. Arts and entertainment range from music and cinema festivals to bullfights and country fairs where regional crafts, such as hand-painted pottery and baskets, are on display.

Tiled façades of houses in Alcochete, an attractive town on the Tagus estuary

◁ Brightly painted fishing boats moored in the harbour at Sesimbra

Exploring the Lisbon Coast

NORTH OF THE TAGUS, the beautiful hilltown of Sintra is dotted with historic palaces and surrounded by wooded hills, at times enveloped in an eerie sea mist. On the coast, cosmopolitan Cascais and the traditional fishing town of Ericeira are both excellent bases from which to explore the rocky coastline and surrounding countryside. South of the Tagus, the Serra da Arrábida and the rugged coast around Cabo Espichel can be visited from the small port of Sesimbra. Inland, the nature reserves of the Tagus and Sado estuaries offer a quiet retreat.

SIGHTS AT A GLANCE

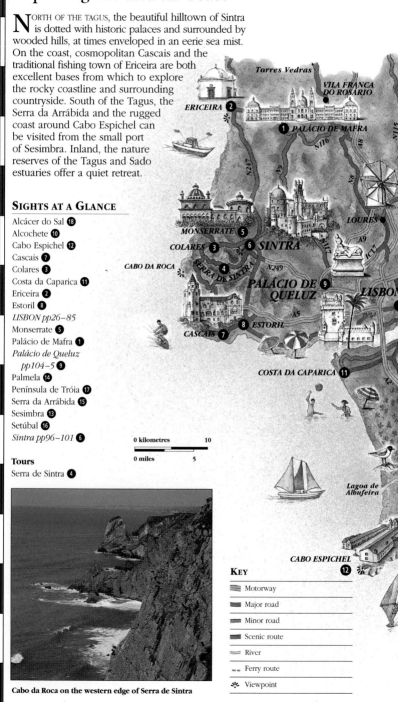

Torres Vedras

VILA FRANCA DO ROSÁRIO

ERICEIRA 2

1 PALÁCIO DE MAFRA

N116

N8

MONSERRATE 5

COLARES 3

CABO DA ROCA

6 SINTRA

LOURES

SERRA DE SINTRA

N249

4

PALÁCIO DE QUELUZ 9

LISBON

CASCAIS 7

8 ESTORIL

A5

COSTA DA CAPARICA 11

A2

Lagoa de Albufeira

CABO ESPICHEL 12

0 kilometres 10

0 miles 5

Cabo da Roca on the western edge of Serra de Sintra

KEY

▨	Motorway
▨	Major road
▨	Minor road
▨	Scenic route
▨	River
--	Ferry route
☆	Viewpoint

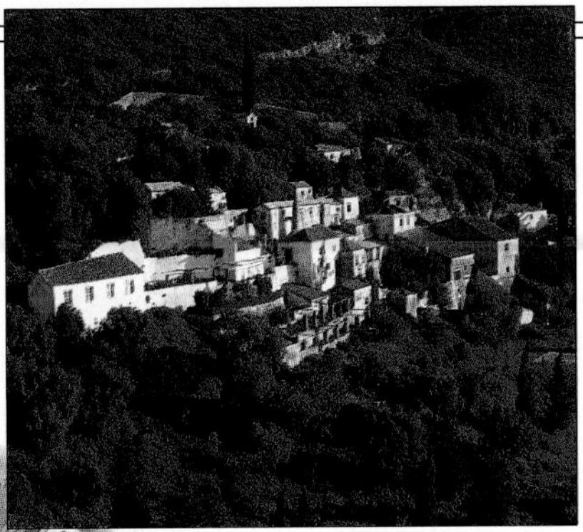

Convento da Arrábida in the hills of the Serra da Arrábida

GETTING AROUND

Motorways give quick access from Lisbon to Sintra, Estoril, Palmela and Setúbal. Main roads are generally well signposted and surfaced, though traffic congestion can be a problem, particularly at weekends and holidays. Watch out for potholes on smaller roads. Fast, frequent trains run west from Lisbon's Cais do Sodré station to Estoril and Cascais, and from Rossio station to Queluz and Sintra. For trains south to Setúbal, Alcácer do Sal and beyond, take a ferry to Barreiro on the southern bank of the Tagus. There are good bus services to all parts of the region, most of which leave from Lisbon's Praça de Espanha.

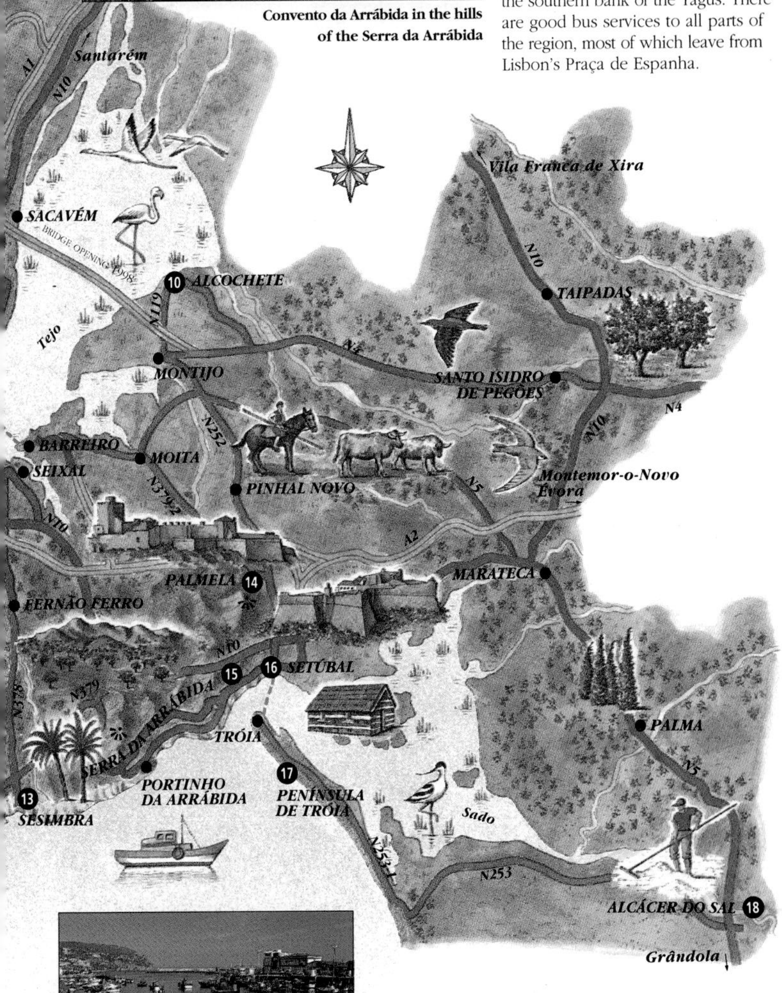
A1
N10
Santarém
Vila Franca de Xira
SACAVÉM
BRIDGE OPENING 1998
10 ALCOCHETE
N119
Tejo
N10
TAIPADAS
N4
MONTIJO
SANTO ISIDRO DE PEGÕES
N4
N252
N10
BARREIRO
MOITA
SEIXAL
N379-2
PINHAL NOVO
N5
Montemor-o-Novo
Évora
N10
A2
MARATECA
PALMELA 14
FERNÃO FERRO
N10
15
16 SETÚBAL
N379
N378
SERRA DA ARRÁBIDA
TRÓIA
PALMA
N5
13
SESIMBRA
PORTINHO DA ARRÁBIDA
17
PENÍNSULA DE TRÓIA
Sado
N253-1
N253
ALCÁCER DO SAL 18
Grândola

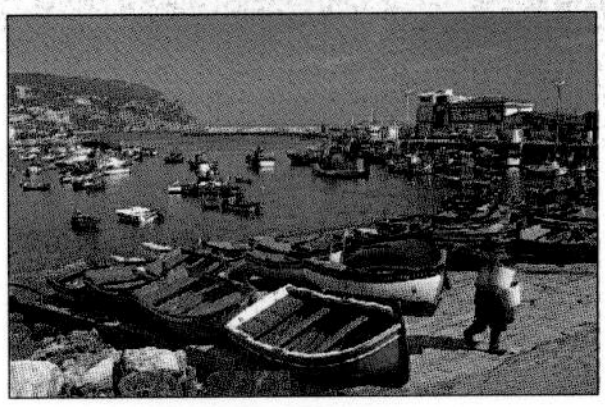

Fishing boats in the harbour at Sesimbra

SEE ALSO

• *Where to Stay* pp118–9

• *Where to Eat* pp132–33

The stunning library in the Palácio de Mafra, paved with chequered marble

Palácio de Mafra ❶

Road map B5. Terreiro de Dom João V, Mafra. ☎ 061-81 18 88. ⬛ from Lisbon. ◯ 10am–1pm, 2–5:30pm Wed–Mon. ● Easter, 1 May, 25 Dec. 🏛 📷 📹 compulsory.

THIS MASSIVE BAROQUE palace and monastery dwarfs the small town of Mafra. It was built during the reign of João V, Portugal's most extravagant monarch and began with a vow by the young king to build a new monastery and basilica, supposedly in return for an heir (but more likely, to atone for his well-known sexual excesses). Work began in 1717 on a modest project to house 13 Franciscan friars but, as the wealth began to pour into the royal coffers from Brazil, the king and his Italian-trained architect, Johann Friedrich Ludwig (1670–1752), made ever more extravagant plans. No expense was spared:

52,000 men were employed and the finished project eventually housed not 13, but 330 friars, a royal palace and one of the finest libraries in Europe, decorated with precious marble, exotic wood and countless works of art. The magnificent basilica was consecrated on the king's 41st birthday, 22 October 1730, with festivities lasting for eight days.

The palace was never a favourite with the members of the royal family, except for those who enjoyed hunting deer and wild boar in the adjoining *tapada* (hunting reserve). Most of the finest furniture and art works were taken to Brazil when the royal family escaped the French invasion in 1807. The monastery was abandoned in 1834 following the dissolution of all religious orders, and the palace itself was finally abandoned in 1910, when the last Portuguese king, Manuel II, escaped from here to the Royal Yacht anchored off Ericeira.

Allow at least an hour for the lengthy tour which starts in the rooms of the monastery, through the pharmacy, with

fine old medicine jars and some alarming medical instruments, to the hospital, where 16 patients in private cubicles could see and hear mass in the adjoining chapel without leaving their beds.

Upstairs, the sumptuous palace state rooms extend across the whole of the monumental west façade, with the King's apartments at one end and the Queen's apartments at the other, a staggering 232 m (760 ft) apart. Halfway between the two, the long, imposing façade is relieved by the twin towers of the domed basilica. The interior of the church is decorated in contrasting colours of marble and furnished with six early 19th-century organs. Fine Baroque sculptures, executed by members of the Mafra School of Sculpture, adorn the atrium of the basilica. Begun by José I in 1754, many renowned Portuguese and foreign artists trained in the school under the directorship of the Italian sculptor Alessandro Giusti (1715–99). Further on, the Sala da Caça has a grotesque collection of hunting trophies and boars' heads.

Mafra's greatest treasure, however, is its magnificent library, which has a patterned marble floor, Rococo-style wooden bookcases, and a collection of over 40,000 books in gold embossed leather bindings, which includes a prized first edition of *Os Lusíadas* (1572) by the celebrated Portuguese poet, Luís de Camões (1524–80).

Statue of St Bruno in the atrium of Mafra's basilica

ENVIRONS: Once a week, on Thursday mornings, the small country town of **Malveira**, 10 km (6 miles) east of Mafra, has the region's biggest market, selling clothes and household goods as well as food.

At the village of **Sobreiro**, 6 km (4 miles) west of Mafra, Zé Franco's model village is complete with houses, farms, a waterfall and working windmill, all in minute detail.

The king's bedroom in the Royal Palace

Tractor pulling a fishing boat out of the sea at Ericeira

Ericeira ❷

Road map B5. 👤 *4,500.* 🚌
ℹ️ *Rua Mendes Leal (061-631 22).*
🎪 *daily.*

Ericeira is an old fishing village which keeps its traditions despite an ever-increasing influx of summer visitors, from Lisbon and abroad, who enjoy the bracing climate, clean, sandy beaches and fresh seafood. In July and August, when the population leaps to 30,000, pavement cafés, restaurants and bars around the tree-lined Praça da República are buzzing late into the night. Red flags warn when swimming is dangerous: alternative attractions include a crazy golf course in Santa Marta park and an interesting local history museum, the **Museu da Ericeira**, exhibiting model boats and traditional regional fishing equipment.

The unspoilt old town, a maze of whitewashed houses and narrow, cobbled streets, is perched high above the ocean. From Largo das Ribas, at the top of a 30-m (100-ft) stone-faced cliff, there is a bird's-eye view over the busy fishing harbour below, where tractors have replaced the oxen that once hauled the boats out of reach of the tide. On 16 August, the annual fishermen's festival is celebrated with a candlelit procession to the harbour at the foot of the cliffs for the blessing of the boats.

On 5 October 1910, Manuel II, the last king of Portugal *(see p17)*, finally sailed into exile from Ericeira as the Republic was declared in Lisbon; a tiled panel in the fishermen's chapel of Santo António above the harbour records the event. The banished king settled in Twickenham, southwest London, where he died in 1932.

🏛 Museu da Ericeira
Largo da Misericórdia. 📞 *061-625 36.*
🕐 *Jun–Sep: Tue–Sun; Oct–May: Mon–Sat (pm only).* ⬛ *1 Jan, 25 Dec.* 🎫

Colares ❸

Road map B5. 👤 *6,500.* 🚌
ℹ️ *Cabo da Roca, 6 km (4 miles) SW (01-928 00 81).*

On the lower slopes of the Serra de Sintra, this lovely village faces towards the sea over a green valley, the Várzea de Colares. A leafy avenue winds its way up to the quiet village, full of beautiful flowers, pine and chestnut trees. The vineyards here produce the famous Colares wine, notably a robust, velvety red. The old vines grow in a sandy soil, with their roots set deep below in clay; these were the only vines in Europe to survive the disastrous phylloxera epidemic brought into Europe from America in the late 19th century with the first viticultural exchanges. The insect, which destroyed vineyards all over Europe by eating the tender roots, could not penetrate the dense sandy soil of the Atlantic coast and thus spared the vines around Colares. Wine can be sampled at the Adega Regional de Colares on Alameda de Coronel Linhares de Lima.

Environs: There are several popular beach resorts west of Colares. From the village of Banzão you can ride 3 km (2 miles) to **Praia das Maçãs** on the old tramway, which opened in 1910 and still runs in the summer months from 1 July to 30 September. Just north of Praia das Maçãs is the picturesque village of **Azenhas do Mar**, clinging to the cliffs; just to the south is the larger resort of **Praia Grande**. Both have natural swimming pools cut into the rocks, which are filled by seawater at high tide. The unspoilt **Praia da Adraga**, 1 km (half a mile) further south, has a delightful beach café. In the evenings and off-season, fishermen set up their rods and lines to catch bass, bream and flat fish that swim in on the high tide.

Natural rock pool at Azenhas do Mar, near Colares

Serra de Sintra Tour ❹

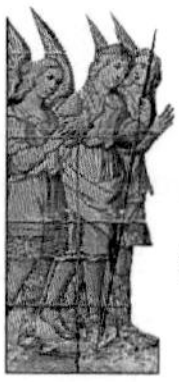

Tiled angels, Peninha chapel

This round trip from Sintra follows a dramatic route over the top of the wooded Serra. The first part is a challenging drive with hazardous hairpin bends on steep, narrow roads that are at times poorly surfaced. It passes through dense forest and a surreal landscape of giant moss-covered boulders, with breathtaking views over the Atlantic coast, the Tagus estuary and beyond. After dropping down to the rugged, windswept coast, the route returns along small country roads passing through hill villages and large estates on the cool, green northern slopes of the Serra de Sintra.

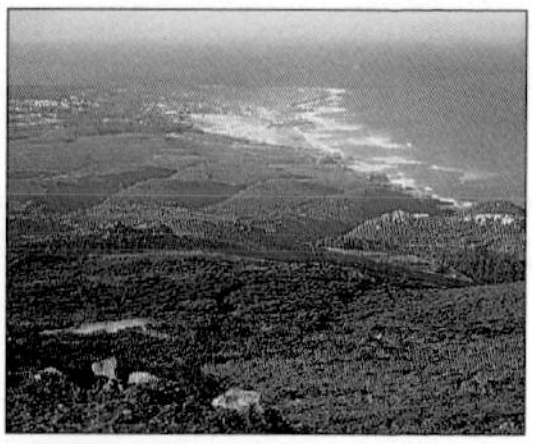

Atlantic coastline seen from Peninha

Colares ⑥
The village of Colares rests on the lower slopes of the wooded Serra, surrounded by gardens and vineyards *(see p93)*.

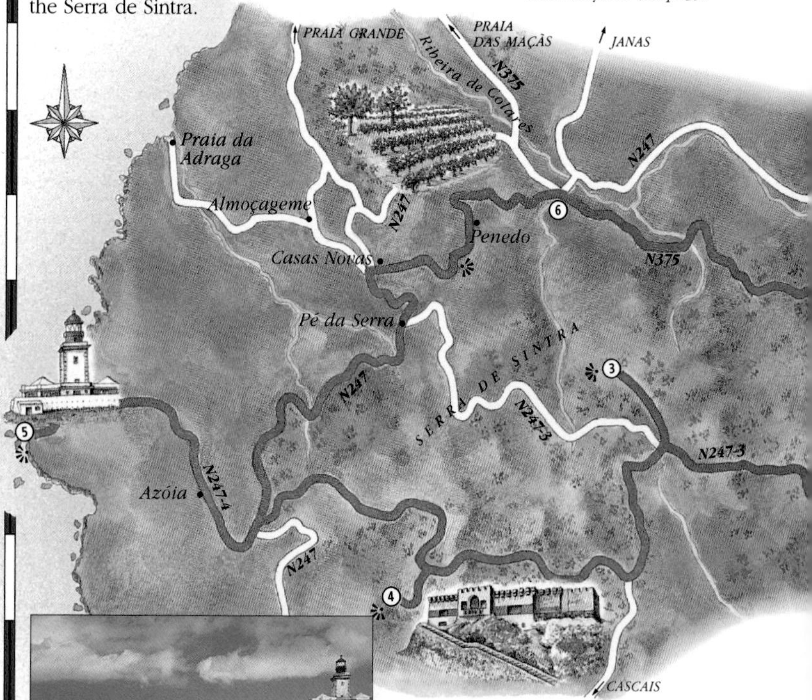

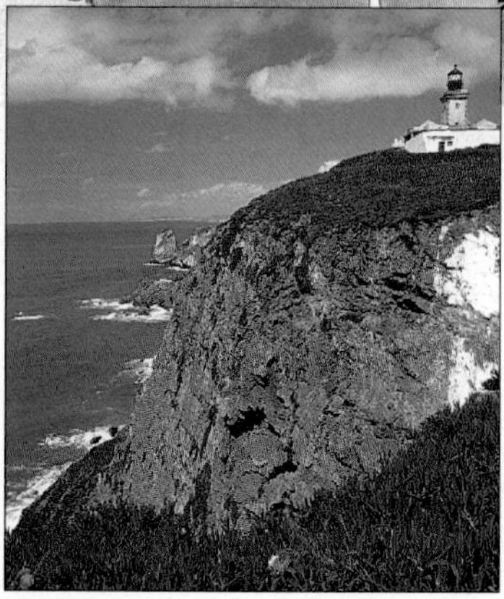

Peninha ④
This 490-m (1,600-ft) high peak affords stunning views towards the coast. A 17th-century chapel decorated with *azulejo* panels is perched high on the grey rocks.

0 kilometres 2
0 miles 1

Cabo da Roca ⑤
A lighthouse at the top of an impressive cliff, 140 m (459 ft) high, marks the most westerly point of the European mainland.

Key

- Tour route
- Other roads
- ☀ Viewpoint

Seteais ⑧
The elegant, pink palace, now a luxury hotel and restaurant *(see p113 & p119)*, was built in the 18th century for the Dutch Consul, Daniel Gildemeester.

Monserrate ⑦
The cool, overgrown forest park and elaborate 19th-century palace epitomize the romanticism of Sintra.

Sintra ①
From the centre of the old town the road winds steeply upwards past magnificent *quintas* (country estates) hidden among the trees.

Parque da Pena ②
This huge, exotic park can be explored on foot *(see p97)*. It is also possible to drive as far as Cruz Alta, the highest point of the Serra de Sintra.

Convento dos Capuchos ③
Two huge boulders guard the entrance to this remote Franciscan monastery, founded in 1560, where the monks lived in tiny rock-hewn cells lined with cork. There are stunning views of the coast from the hill above this austere, rocky hideaway.

Palace of Monserrate

Monserrate ❺

Road Map B5. Estrada de Monserrate. 01-923 12 01. to Sintra then taxi. 9am–7:30pm (Oct–Mar: 5pm) daily. 1 Jan, Easter, 1 May, 25 Dec.

THE WILD, ROMANTIC garden of this once magnificent estate is a jungle of exotic trees and flowering shrubs. Among the sub-tropical foliage and valley of tree ferns, the visitor will come across a waterfall, a small lake and a ruined chapel tangled in the roots of a giant *Ficus* tree. Its history dates back to the Moors, but it takes its name from a small 16th-century chapel dedicated to Our Lady of Montserrat in Catalonia, Spain. The gardens were landscaped in the late 18th century by a wealthy young Englishman, the eccentric aesthete William Beckford. They were later immortalized by Lord Byron in *Childe Harold's Pilgrimage* (1812).

In 1856, the abandoned estate was bought by another Englishman, Sir Francis Cook, who built a fantastic Moorish-style palace (which now stands eerily empty) and transformed the gardens with a large sweeping lawn, camellias and sub-tropical trees from all over the world. These include the giant *Metrosideros* (Australian Christmas tree, covered in a blaze of red flowers in July), the native *Arbutus* (known as the strawberry tree because of its juicy red berries), from which the *medronheira* firewater drink is distilled, and cork oak, with small ferns growing on its bark.

The Friends of Monserrate is an organization that has been set up to help restore the sadly neglected house and gardens to their former glory.

Sintra

Visiting the sights of Sintra by horse-drawn carriage

SINTRA'S STUNNING setting on the north slopes of the granite Serra, among wooded ravines and fresh water springs, made it a favourite summer retreat for the kings of Portugal. The tall conical chimneys of the Palácio Nacional de Sintra *(see pp98–9)* and the fabulous Palácio da Pena *(see pp100–101)*, eerily impressive on its peak when the Serra is blanketed in mist, are unmistakable landmarks.

Today, the town (recognized as a UNESCO World Heritage site in 1995) draws thousands of visitors all through the year. Even so, there are many quiet walks in the wooded hills around the town, especially beautiful in the long, cool evenings of the summer months.

Fonte Mourisca on Volta do Duche

Exploring Sintra

Present-day Sintra is in three parts, Sintra Vila, Estefânia and São Pedro, joined by a confusing maze of winding roads scattered over the surrounding hills. In the pretty cobbled streets of the old town, Sintra Vila, which is centred on the **Palácio Nacional de Sintra**, are the museums and beautifully tiled **post office**. The curving **Volta do Duche** leads from the old town, past the lush **Parque da Liberdade**, north to the Estefânia district and the striking Neo-Gothic **Câmara Municipal** (Town Hall). To the south and east, the hilly village of São Pedro

spreads over the slopes of the Serra. The fortnightly Sunday **market** here extends across the broad market square and along Rua 1º de Dezembro.

Exploring Sintra on foot involves a lot of walking and climbing up and down its steep hills. For a more leisurely tour, take one of the horse and carriage rides around the town. The **Miradouro da Vigia** in São Pedro offers impressive views, as does the cosy **Casa de Sapa** café, where you can sample *queijadas*, the local sweet speciality *(see p135)*.

The numerous fountains dotted around the town are not just ornamental – the locals also fill their bottles here with the fresh spring drinking water. Two of the most striking are the elaborately tiled **Fonte Mourisca** (Arab Fountain), so-called for its Neo-Moorish decoration and geometrical tile patterns, and the **Fonte da Sabuga**, where the water spouts from two breasts.

Toy Alfa Romeo, Museu do Brinquedo

🏛 Museu do Brinquedo

Largo Latino Coelho. 【 01-924 21 71. ◯ Tue–Sun. 🎫 ♿

This small, bright museum is bursting at the seams with a fine collection of toys from all over the world, including model planes, cars and trains, battalions of toy soldiers, dolls and dolls' houses, tin toys and curious clockwork models of cars and soldiers. The museum is fun for a rainy day, particularly for nostalgic adults.

🏛 Museu Regional

Praça da República 23. 【 01-924 05 91. ◯ Mon–Fri (also: Sat & Sun pm). ● Carnaval, 1 May, 22 Dec–2 Jan.
Sintra's regional museum is on two floors. The Art Gallery, used for temporary exhibitions, houses a small permanent collection of paintings and old prints showing views of Sintra, including two early views of Palácio da Pena in the 1860s. The Archaeological Museum upstairs has cases filled with finds from the surrounding area, from Neolithic axes to Roman amphorae and mosaics.

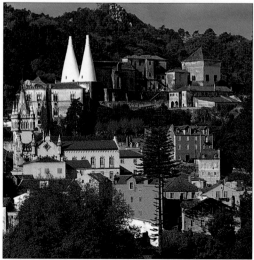

Chimneys of the Palácio Nacional de Sintra above the old town

♜ Castelo dos Mouros

Estrada da Pena. ☎ *01-923 51 16.*
○ *daily.* ● *1 Jan, 25 Dec.*

Standing above the old town, like a sentinel, the ramparts of the 8th-century Moorish castle, conquered by Afonso Henriques in 1147, snake over the top of the Serra. On a fine day, there are breathtaking views from the castle walls over the old town to Palácio da Pena, on a neighbouring peak, and far along the coast. Hidden inside the walls are a ruined chapel and an ancient Moorish cistern. For walkers, a steep footpath threads up through wooded slopes from the 12th-century church of **Santa Maria**. Follow the signs to a dark green swing gate where the footpath begins. The monogram "DFII" carved on the gateway is a reminder that the castle walls were restored by Fernando II *(see p101)* in the 19th century.

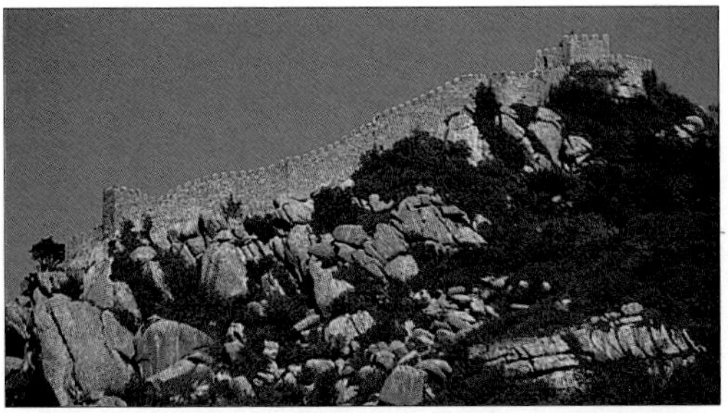

Battlements of the Castelo dos Mouros perched on the slopes of the Serra

Visitors' Checklist

Road map B5. 👥 *23,000.*
🚉 🚌 *Avenida Dr Miguel Bombarda.* ℹ *Praça da República 23 (01-923 11 57).* 🛒 *2nd & 4th Sun of month in São Pedro.*
🎭 *Festival de Música (Jun–Sep).*

🍁 Parque da Pena

Estrada da Pena. ☎ *01-924 08 73.*
○ *daily.* ● *1 Jan, 25 Dec.* ♿

A huge park surrounds the Palácio da Pena where footpaths wind among a lush vegetation of exotic trees and shrubs. Hidden among the foliage are gazebos, follies and fountains, and a Romantic chalet built by Fernando II for his mistress in 1869. Cruz Alta, the highest point of the Serra at 530 m (1,740 ft), commands spectacular views of the Serra and surrounding plain. On a nearby crag stands the statue of Baron Von Eschwege, architect of the palace and park.

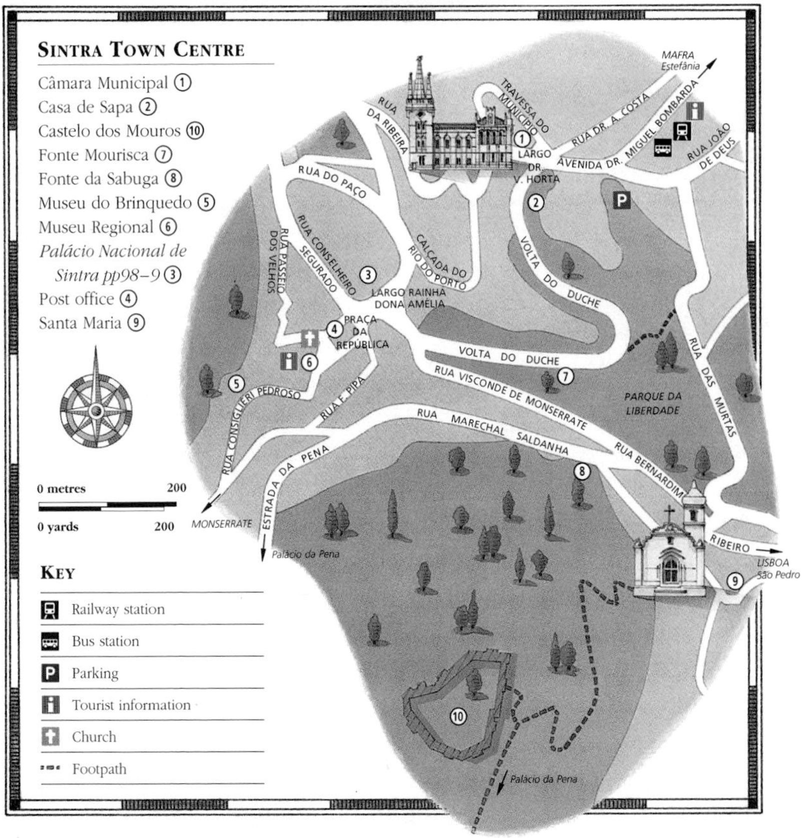
SINTRA TOWN CENTRE
Câmara Municipal ①
Casa de Sapa ②
Castelo dos Mouros ⑩
Fonte Mourisca ⑦
Fonte da Sabuga ⑧
Museu do Brinquedo ⑤
Museu Regional ⑥
Palácio Nacional de Sintra pp98–9 ③
Post office ④
Santa Maria ⑨
0 metres 200
0 yards 200
KEY
Railway station
Bus station
Parking
Tourist information
Church
Footpath
MAFRA
Estefânia
TRAVESSA DO MUNICÍPIO
RUA DA RIBEIRA
RUA DR. A. COSTA
RUA DO PAÇO
LARGO DR. V. HORTA
AVENIDA DR. MIGUEL BOMBARDA
RUA JOÃO DE DEUS
RUA PASSEIO DOS VELHOS
RUA CONSELHEIRO SEGURADO
CALÇADA DO RIO DO PORTO
VOLTA DO DUCHE
LARGO RAINHA DONA AMÉLIA
PRAÇA DA REPÚBLICA
RUA VISCONDE DE MONSERRATE
RUA CONSIGLIERI PEDROSO
RUA F. PIPA
RUA MARECHAL SALDANHA
PARQUE DA LIBERDADE
RUA DAS MURTAS
RUA BERNARDIM RIBEIRO
ESTRADA DA PENA
MONSERRATE
Palácio da Pena
LISBOA
São Pedro

Palácio Nacional de Sintra

Swan panel, Sala dos Cisnes

A T THE HEART of the old town of Sintra (Sintra Vila), a pair of strange conical chimneys rises high above the Royal Palace. The main part of the palace, including the central block with its plain Gothic façade and the large kitchens beneath the chimneys, was built by João I in the late 14th century, on a site once occupied by the Moorish rulers. The Paço Real, as it is also known, became the favourite summer retreat for the court, and continued as a residence for Portuguese royalty until the 1880s. Additions to the building by the wealthy Manuel I, in the early 16th century, echo the Moorish style. Gradual rebuilding of the palace has resulted in a fascinating amalgamation of various different styles.

★ **Sala das Pegas**

It is said that King João I had the ceiling panels painted as a rebuke to the court women for indulging in idle gossip like chattering magpies (pegas).

The Torre da Meca has dovecotes below the cornice decorated with armillary spheres and nautical rope.

The Sala das Galés (galleons) houses temporary exhibitions.

★ **Sala dos Brasões**

The domed ceiling of this majestic room is decorated with stags holding the coats of arms (brasões) of 74 noble Portuguese families. The lower walls are lined with 18th-century Delft-like tiled panels.

Jardim da Preta, a walled garden

Sala de Dom Sebastião, the audience chamber

TIMELINE

			1495–1521 Reign of Manuel I; major restoration and Manueline additions	1683 Afonso VI dies after being imprisoned here for nine years by brother Pedro II	1755 Parts of palace damaged in great earthquake *(see pp20–21)*
10th century Palace becomes residence of Moorish governor	**1281** King Dinis orders restoration of the Palácio de Oliva (as it was then known)				
800	**1000**	**1200**	**1400**	**1600**	**1800**
	1147 Christian reconquest; Afonso Henriques takes over palace	**1385** João I orders complete rebuilding of central buildings and kitchens		**1880s** Maria Pia (grandmother of Manuel II) is last royal resident	
8th century First palace established by Moors		*Siren, Sala das Sereias (c.1660)*		**1910** Palace becomes a national monument	

★ **Sala dos Cisnes**
The magnificent ceiling of the former banqueting hall, painted in the 17th century, is divided into octagonal panels decorated with swans (cisnes).

The Sala dos Árabes
is decorated with
fine *azulejos*.

**Sala das
Sereias**
*Intricate
Arabesque
designs on
16th-century
tiles frame
the door of
the Room
of the Sirens.*

The kitchens, beneath the
huge conical chimneys,
have spits and utensils
once used for pre-
paring royal
banquets.

Entrance

Sala dos Archeiros,
the entrance hall

Manuel I added the
ajimece windows, a distinctive
Moorish design with a slender
column dividing two arches.

Chapel
*Symmetrical Moorish
patterns decorate the
original 14th-century
chestnut and oak ceiling
and the mosaic floor of
the private chapel.*

STAR FEATURES

★ **Sala dos Brasões**

★ **Sala dos Cisnes**

★ **Sala das Pegas**

Sintra: Palácio da Pena

Triton Arch

O N THE HIGHEST PEAKS of the Serra de Sintra stands the spectacular palace of Pena, an eclectic medley of architectural styles built in the 19th century for the husband of the young Queen Maria II, Ferdinand Saxe-Coburg-Gotha. It stands over the ruins of a Hieronymite monastery founded here in the 15th century on the site of the chapel of Nossa Senhora da Pena. Ferdinand appointed a German architect, Baron Von Eschwege, to build his summer palace filled with oddities from all over the world and surrounded by a park. With the declaration of the Republic in 1910, the palace became a museum, preserved as it was when the royal family lived here. Allow at least an hour and a half to visit this enchanting place.

Entrance Arch
A studded archway with crenellated turrets greets the visitor at the entrance to the palace. The palace buildings are painted the original daffodil yellow and strawberry pink.

Manuel II's Bedroom
The oval-shaped room is decorated with bright red walls and stuccoed ceiling. A portrait of Manuel II, the last king of Portugal, hangs above the fireplace.

In the kitchen the copper pots and utensils still hang around the iron stove. The dinner service bears the coat of arms of Ferdinand II.

★ Ballroom
The spacious ball-room is sumptuously furnished with German stained-glass windows, precious Oriental porcelain and four lifesize turbaned torch-bearers holding giant candelabra.

★ Arab Room
Marvellous trompe-l'oeil frescoes cover the walls and ceiling of the Arab Room, one of the loveliest in the palace. The Orient was a great inspiration to Romanticism.

★ Chapel Altarpiece
The impressive 16th-century alabaster and marble retable was sculpted by Nicolau Chanterène. Each niche portrays a scene of the life of Christ, from the manger to the Ascension.

The Triton Arch is encrusted with Neo-Manueline decoration and is guarded by a fierce sea monster.

The cloister, decorated with colourful patterned tiles, is part of the original monastery buildings.

Entrance

FERDINAND: KING CONSORT

Ferdinand was known in Portugal as Dom Fernando II, the "artist" king. Like his cousin Prince Albert, who married the English Queen Victoria, he loved art, nature and the new inventions of the time. He was himself a watercolour painter. Ferdinand enthusiastically adopted his new country and devoted his life to patronizing the arts. In 1869, 16 years after the death of Maria II, Ferdinand married his mistress, the opera singer Countess Edla. His lifelong dream of building the extravagant palace at Pena was completed in 1885, the year he died.

STAR FEATURES

★ Arab Room

★ Ballroom

★ Chapel Altarpiece

Outdoor café in the popular holiday resort of Cascais

Cascais **⊘**

Road map B5. 🚶 *30,000.* 🚊 🚌
ℹ️ *Rua Visconde da Luz 14 (01-486 82 04).* ⛱️ *Wed.*

A FAVOURED HARBOUR since prehistoric times, Cascais stands in a sheltered, sandy bay at the mouth of the River Tagus, once heavily defended against invaders. It became a fashionable resort in the 1870s, when Luís I converted the 17th-century citadel on the southwest corner of the bay into a summer palace. Part of this is now the President of Portugal's summer residence.

Sea bathing became popular at the turn of the century and wealthy families built splendid holiday villas here. Nowadays it is a busy cosmopolitan resort, with fashionable shops in the pleasant pedestrian streets of the old town. Fishing is still an important activity, and the day's catch is auctioned near the harbour in the afternoon.

The **Museu-Biblioteca** in Gandarinha Park was once the palatial residence of the Conde de Castro Guimarães. Superbly sited on a small creek where the sea sweeps in at high tide, the house was built in 1892, when Cascais was at the height of fashion. The count and his wife died without children in the 1920s, and the house with its eclectic collection of Indo-Portuguese furniture, paintings, *azulejos,* porcelain and valuable books, was left to the State. The prize exhibit in the library is a rare 16th-century illustrated book by Duarte Galvão (1455–1517), *Chronicles of Dom Afonso Henriques.* One of the hand-painted illustrations which purports to show the siege of Lisbon by Dom Afonso in 1147, depicts 16th-century Lisbon in minute detail.

On a smaller scale, the **Museu do Mar** focuses on the life and history of Cascais with some fascinating old photographs, painted panoramas and finds from local shipwrecks.

Nearby, the church of **Nossa Senhora da Assunção** is decorated with paintings by Josefa de Óbidos (1631–84).

🏛 **Museu-Biblioteca**
Avenida Rei Humberto de Itália. 📞 *01-484 08 61.* **Museum** ◻ *Tue–Sun.* 🈲
Library ◻ *Mon–Fri.* ● *public hols.*

🏛 **Museu do Mar**
Rua Júlio Pereira de Mello. 📞 *01-484 08 61.* ◻ *Tue–Sun.* ● *public hols.* 🈲

ENVIRONS: At **Boca do Inferno** (Mouth of Hell), about 3 km (2 miles) west on the coast road, the sea rushes into clefts and caves in the rocks making an ominous booming sound and sending up spectacular spray in rough weather. The place is almost obscured by a roadside market and cafés but a small platform gives a good view of the rocky arch with the sea roaring in below.

The magnificent sandy beach of **Guincho**, 10 km (6 miles) further west, is backed by sand dunes with clumps of umbrella pines, and a small fort (now a luxury hotel) stands perched on the rocks above the sea. Atlantic breakers rolling in make this a paradise for experienced windsurfers and surfers, though beware of the strong undercurrent.

Spectacular view of the weatherbeaten coastline at Boca do Inferno, near Cascais

Estoril **⊙**

Road map B5. 🚶 *40,000.* 🚊 🚌
ℹ️ *Arcadas do Parque (01-466 38 13).*

E STORIL HAS THE AIR of a once prosperous resort, as indeed it was. Exiled royalty, including Italy's last king, Umberto II, Juan de Borbón of Spain, Karl I, the last Austro-Hungarian emperor and King Carol of Romania, settled here, and it grew from a small spa village into an elegant town, popular as a smart conference venue.

The proximity to Lisbon, the mild climate and its fame as a haunt of aristocrats have long attracted both summer and winter visitors to this "Portuguese Riviera". Today, grand villas, modern apartments and five-star hotels line the coast, following the long, breezy promenade behind the sandy beach that links Estoril with the town of Cascais, 3 km (2 miles) to the west.

Sandy beach and promenade along the bay of Estoril

Impressively sited at the top of the central park, the casino is flanked with tall, majestic date palms. Other entertainments include several superb golf courses, sailing and horse riding. In September, the drone of Formula 1 motor racing cars at the nearby Autodromo echoes round the hills.

Palácio de Queluz **9**

See pp104–5.

Alcochete **10**

Road map C5. 🏠 *13,000.* 🚌 ❚ *Largo da Misericórdia (01-234 26 31).*

THIS DELIGHTFUL old town overlooks the wide Tagus estuary from the southern shore. Salt has long been one of the main industries here, and saltpans can still be seen to the north and south of the town, while in the town centre a large statue of a muscular salt worker has the inscription: "Do Sal a Revolta e a Esperança" (From Salt to Rebellion and Hope). On the outskirts of town, is a statue of Manuel I (*see p16*), who was born here on 1 June 1469 and granted the town a Royal Charter in 1515.

Statue of a salt worker in Alcochete (1985)

ENVIRONS: The **Reserva Natural do Estuário do Tejo** covers a vast area of estuary water, salt marshes and small islands around Alcochete and is a very important breeding ground for water birds. Particularly interesting are the flocks of flamingos that gather here during the autumn and spring migration, en route from colonies such as the Camargue in France and Fuente de Piedra in Spain. Boat trips are available to see the birdlife and wildlife of the estuary, which includes wild bulls and horses.

🦅 **Reserva Natural do Estuário do Tejo**
Avenida dos Combatentes da Grande Guerra 1. 📞 *01-234 17 42.* 📷

Pilgrims' lodgings, Cabo Espichel

Costa da Caparica **11**

Road map B5. 🏠 *40,000.* 🚌 *to Cacilhas or Trafaria then bus.* ❚ *Av. da República 18 (01-290 00 71).*

LONG SANDY beaches, backed by sand dunes, have made this a popular holiday resort for Lisboetas who come here to swim, sunbathe and enjoy the seafood restaurants and beach cafés. A railway, with open carriages, runs for 10 km (6 miles) along the coast during the summer months. The first beaches reached from the city are popular with families with children, while the furthest beaches suit those seeking quiet isolation. Further south, sheltered by pine forests, **Lagoa do Albufeira** is a peaceful windsurfing centre and camp site.

Cabo Espichel **12**

Road map B5. 🚌 *from Sesimbra.*

SHEER CLIFFS DROP straight into the sea at this windswept promontory where the land ends dramatically. The Romans named it Promontorium Barbaricum, alluding to its dangerous location, and a lighthouse warns sailors of the treacherous rocks below. Stunning views of the ocean and the coast can be enjoyed from this bleak outcrop of land but beware of the strong gusts of wind on the cliff edge.

In this desolate setting stands the impressive **Santuário de Nossa Senhora do Cabo**, a late 17th-century church with its back to the sea. On either side of the church a long line of pilgrims' lodgings facing inwards form an open courtyard. Baroque paintings, ex votos and a frescoed ceiling decorate the interior of the church which otherwise stands abandoned and derelict. Behind the church is a domed chapel tiled with blue and white *azulejo* panels depicting fishing scenes.

The site became a popular place of pilgrimage in the 13th century when a local man had a vision of the Madonna rising from the sea on a mule. Legend has it that the tracks of the mule can be seen embedded in the rock. The large footprints, on Praia dos Lagosteiros below the church, are actually believed to be fossilized dinosaur tracks.

Spring flowers by the saltpans of the Tagus estuary near Alcochete

Palácio de Queluz ⑨

A sphinx in the gardens

IN 1747, PEDRO, younger son of João V, commissioned Mateus Vicente to transform his 17th-century hunting lodge into a Rococo summer palace. The central section, including a music room and chapel, was built, but after Pedro's marriage in 1760 to the future Maria I, the palace was again extended. The French architect, Jean-Baptiste Robillion, added the sumptuous Robillion Pavilion and gardens, cleared space for the Throne Room and redesigned the Music Room. During Maria's reign, the royal family kept a menagerie and went boating on the *azulejo*-lined canal.

Corridor of the Sleeves
Painted azulejo *panels (1784) representing the continents and the seasons, as well as hunting scenes, line the walls of the bright* Corredor das Mangas *(sleeves).*

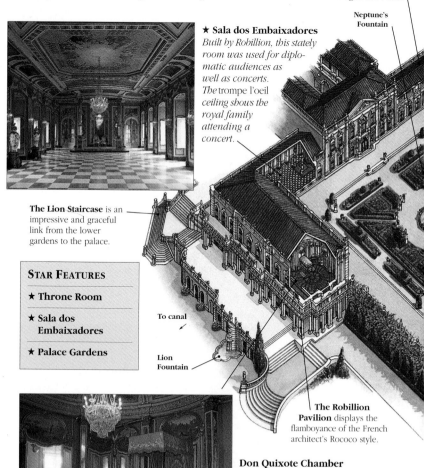

★ Sala dos Embaixadores
Built by Robillion, this stately room was used for diplomatic audiences as well as concerts. The trompe l'oeil *ceiling shows the royal family attending a concert.*

Neptune's Fountain

The Lion Staircase is an impressive and graceful link from the lower gardens to the palace.

STAR FEATURES

★ **Throne Room**

★ **Sala dos Embaixadores**

★ **Palace Gardens**

To canal

Lion Fountain

The Robillion Pavilion displays the flamboyance of the French architect's Rococo style.

Don Quixote Chamber
The royal bedroom, where Pedro IV (see p17) was born and died, has a domed ceiling and magnificent floor decoration in exotic woods, giving the square room a circular appearance. Painted scenes by Manuel de Costa (1784) tell the story of Don Quixote.

Music Room
Operas and concerts were performed here by Maria I's orchestra, "the best in Europe" according to English traveller, William Beckford. A portrait of the queen hangs above the grand piano.

VISITORS' CHECKLIST

Road map B5. Largo do Palácio, Queluz. 01-435 00 39. Queluz then 20-min walk. from Lisbon, Colégio Militar. 10am–1pm, 2–5pm Wed–Mon. 1 Jan, Easter, 1 May, 29 Jun, 25 Dec. Cozinha Velha (see p133).

Chapel

The royal family's living rooms and bedrooms opened out onto the Malta Gardens.

★ Throne Room
The elegant state room (1770) was the scene of splendid balls and banquets. The gilded statues of Atlas are by Silvestre Faria Lobo.

Entrance

Malta Gardens

The Hanging Gardens, designed by Robillion, were built over arches, raising the ground in front of the palace above the surrounding gardens.

MARIA I (1734–1816)

Maria, the eldest daughter of José I, lived at the palace in Queluz after her marriage to her uncle, Pedro, in 1760. Serious and devout, she conscientiously filled her role as queen, but suffered increasingly from bouts of melancholia. When her son José died from smallpox in 1788, she went hopelessly mad. Visitors to Queluz were dismayed by her agonizing shrieks as she suffered visions and hallucinations. After the French invasion of 1807, her younger son João (declared regent in 1792) took his mad mother to Brazil.

★ Palace Gardens
The formal gardens, adorned with statues, fountains and topiary, were often used for entertaining. Concerts performed in the Music Room would spill out into the Malta Gardens.

Sesimbra

Road map C5. 🏠 27,000. 🚌
ℹ️ *Largo da Marinha 26–7 (01-223
57 43).* 🛒 *1st & 3rd Fri of month.*

A STEEP NARROW ROAD leads
down to this busy fishing
village in a sheltered south-
facing bay. Protected from
north winds by the slopes
of the Serra da Arrábida, the
town has become a popular
holiday resort with Lisboetas.
It was occupied by the Romans
and later the Moors until King
Sancho II *(see p16)* conquered
its heavily defended forts in
1236. The old town is a maze
of steep narrow streets, with
the **Santiago Fort** (now a
customs post) in the centre
overlooking the sea. From the
terrace, which is open to the
public during the day, there
are views over the town, the
Atlantic and the wide sandy
beach that stretches out on
either side. Sesimbra is fast
developing as a resort, with
holiday flats mushrooming on
the surrounding hillsides and
plentiful pavement cafés and
bars that are always busy on
sunny days, even in winter.

The fishing fleet of brightly
painted boats is moored in
Porto do Abrigo to the west
of the main town. The harbour
is reached by taking Avenida
dos Náufragos, a sweeping

Colourful fishing boats in the harbour at Sesimbra

promenade that follows the
beach out of town. On the
large trawlers *(traineiras)*, the
catch is mainly sardines, sea
bream, whiting and swordfish;
on the smaller boats, octopus
and squid. In the late afternoon, when the fishing boats
return from a day at sea, a
colourful, noisy fish auction
takes place on the quayside.
The day's catch can be tasted
in the town's excellent fish
restaurants along the shore.

High above the town is the
Moorish castle, greatly
restored in the 18th century
when a church and small
flower-filled cemetery were
added inside the walls. There
are wonderful views from the
ramparts, especially at sunset.

Palmela

Road map C5. 🏠 14,000. 🚌 📖
ℹ️ *Castelo de Palmela (01-233 21 22).*
🛒 *every other Tue.*

THE FORMIDABLE castle at
Palmela stands over the
small hilltown, high on a north-
eastern spur of the wooded
Serra da Arrábida. Its strategic
position dominates the plain
for miles around, especially
when floodlit at night. Heavily
defended by the Moors, it was
finally conquered in the 12th
century and given by Sancho
I *(see p16)* to the Knights of
the Order of Santiago. In
1423, João I transformed the
castle into a monastery for the
Order, which has now been
restored and converted into a
splendid *pousada (see p119),*
with a restaurant in the monks'
refectory and a swimming
pool for residents, hidden
inside the castle walls. From
the castle terraces, and especially from the top of the
14th-century keep, there are
fantastic views all around,
over the Serra da Arrábida to
the south and on a clear day
across the Tagus to Lisbon. In
the town square below, the
church of **São Pedro** contains
18th-century tiles of scenes
from the life of St Peter.

The annual wine festival, the
Festa das Vindimas, is held in
September in front of the 17th-
century Paço do Concelho
(town hall). The villagers,
dressed in traditional costume,
press the wine barefoot and on
the final day of celebrations
there is a spectacular firework
display from the castle walls.

The castle at Palmela with views over the wooded Serra da Arrábida

Serra da Arrábida ⑮

Road map C5. 🚌 Setúbal.
🅸 Parque Natural da Arrábida, Praça
da República, Setúbal (065-52 40 32).

Portinho da Arrábida on the dramatic coastline of the Serra da Arrábida

THE PARQUE NATURAL da Arrábida covers the small range of limestone mountains which stretches east-west along the coast between Sesimbra and Setúbal. It was established to protect the wild, beautiful landscape and rich variety of birds and wildlife, including eagles, wildcats and badgers.

The name Arrábida is from Arabic meaning a place of prayer, and the wooded hill-sides are indeed a peaceful, secluded retreat. The sheltered, south-facing slopes are thickly covered with aromatic and evergreen shrubs and trees such as pine and cypress, more typical of the Mediterranean. Vineyards also thrive on the sheltered slopes and the town of **Vila Nogueira de Azeitão** is known for its wine, especially the Moscatel de Setúbal.

The **Estrada de Escarpa** (the N379-1) snakes across the top of the ridge and affords astounding views. A narrow road winds down to **Portinho da Arrábida**, a sheltered cove with a beach of fine white sand and crystal clear sea, popular with underwater fishermen. The sandy beaches of **Galapos** and **Figueirinha** are a little further east along the coast road towards Setúbal. Just east of Sesimbra, the Serra da Arrábida drops to the sea in the sheer 380-m (1,250-ft) cliffs of Risco, the highest in mainland Portugal.

🏠 Convento da Arrábida

Serra da Arrábida. 📞 01-352 70 02.
🅾 by appt only. 🗟
Half-hidden among the trees on the southern slopes of the Serra, overlooking the sea, this large 16th-century building was once a Franciscan monastery. The five round towers, perched along the slope of the hillside, were probably used for solitary medi-tation.

🏛 Museu Oceanográfico

Fortaleza de Santa Maria, Portinho da Arrábida. 📞 065-52 40 32.
🅾 Tue–Fri. 🗟
The small fort, just above Portinho da Arrábida, was built by Pedro, the Prince Regent, in 1676 to protect local commun-ities from attacks by Moorish pirates. It now houses a Sea Museum and Marine Biology Centre where visitors can see aquaria containing many local sea creatures, including sea urchins, octopus and starfish.

🌳 Quinta da Bacalhoa

Vila Fresca de Azeitão. 📞 01-218 00 11. **Gardens** 🅾 11am–1pm Mon–Sat. 🌑 public hols. 🗟
📷 compulsory. 🚻
Hidden by a thick hedge, this beautiful manor was built in 1480, in the early Renaissance style. In 1528 it was enlarged with a graceful loggia, over-looking a formal garden of low topiary hedges around a foun-tain. The sunken garden, with orange and lemon trees, leads to an ornamental pool and arched pavilion with a tile panel of Susannah and the Elders, dated 1565. In 1937 the estate was bought by an American, Mrs Scoville, whose family still owns it.

KEY

━━ Major road

▭▭▭ Minor road

══ Other road

0 kilometres 5

0 miles 3

Manueline interior of Igreja de Jesus, Setúbal

Setúbal 🔟

Road map C5. 🏙 *120,000.* 🚉 🚌
🚢 🅸 *Casa do Corpo Santo, Praça do Quebedo (065-53 42 22).*

Although this is an important industrial town, and the third largest port in Portugal (after Lisbon and Oporto), Setúbal is a good place to stay for a few days to explore the area. To the south of the central gardens and fountains are the fishing harbour, marina and ferry port, and a lively covered market. North of the gardens is the old town, with attractive pedestrian streets and squares full of shops and cafés.

The 16th-century **cathedral**, dedicated to Santa Maria da Graça, has glorious tiled panels dating from the 18th century, and gilded altar decoration. Street names commemorate two famous Setúbal residents: Manuel Barbosa du Bocage (1765–1805), whose satirical poetry landed him in prison, and Luísa Todi (1753–1833), a celebrated opera singer.

In Roman times, fish-salting was the most important industry here. Rectangular tanks, carved from stone, can be seen under the glass floor of the Regional Tourist Office at No. 10 Travessa Frei Gaspar.

⛪ Igreja de Jesus
Praça Miguel Bombarda. 🕻 *065-52 41 50.* 🕐 *Tue–Sun.* 🅱 **Museum** 🕐 *Tue–Sat.* 🔴 *public hols.*
To the north of the old town, this striking Gothic church is one of Setúbal's architectural treasures. Designed by the architect Diogo Boitac in 1494,

Fisherman's boat on the shallow mud flats of the Reserva Natural do Estuário do Sado

the lofty interior is adorned with twisted columns, carved in three strands from pinkish Arrábida limestone, and rope-like stone ribs decorating the roof, recognized as the earliest examples of the distinctive and ornate Manueline style.

On Rua do Balneário, in the now abandoned monastic quarters adjacent to the church, a **museum** houses 14 remarkable paintings of the life of Christ. Painted in glowing colours, the works are attributed to the followers of Jorge Afonso (1520–30), influenced by the Flemish school.

🏛 Museu de Arqueologia e Etnografia
Avenida Luísa Todi 162. 🕻 *065-393 65.* 🕐 *Tue–Sat.* 🔴 *public hols.*
The archaeological museum displays a wealth of finds from digs around Setúbal, including Bronze Age pots, Roman coins and amphorae made to carry wine and *garum*, a sauce made from fish marinated in salt and herbs considered a great delicacy in Rome. The ethnography display shows local arts, crafts and industries, including the processing of salt and cork over the centuries.

⚓ Castelo de São Filipe
Estrada de São Filipe. 🕻 *065-52 38 44.* 🕐 *daily.*
The star-shaped fort was built in 1595 by Philip II of Spain during Portugal's period under Spanish rule to keep a wary eye on pirates, English invaders and the local population. A massive gateway and stone tunnel lead to the sheltered interior, which now houses a *pousada (see p119)* and an exquisite small chapel, tiled with scenes from the life of São Filipe by Policarpo de Oliveira Bernardes (1695–1778). A broad terrace offers marvellous views over the city and the Sado estuary.

Environs: Setúbal is an excellent starting point for a tour by car of the unspoilt **Reserva Natural do Estuário do Sado**, a vast stretch of mud flats, shallow lagoons and salt marshes with patches of pine forest, which has been explored and inhabited since 3500 BC. Otters, water birds (including storks and herons), oysters and a great variety of fish are found in the reserve. The old tidal water mill at Mouriscas, 5 km (3 miles) to the east of Setúbal, uses the different levels of the tide to turn the grinding stones. Rice-growing and fishing are the main occupations today, and pine trees around the lagoon are tapped for resin.

☣ Reserva Natural do Estuário do Sado
ℹ Praça da República, Setúbal (065-52 40 32).

Península de Tróia ⑰

Road map C5. 🚌 ⛴ Tróia. ℹ Complexo Turístico de Tróia (065-441 51).

Thatched fisherman's cottage in the village of Carrasqueira

HIGH-RISE HOLIDAY apartments dominate the tip of the Tróia peninsula, easily accessible from Setúbal by ferry. The Atlantic coast, stretching south for 18 km (11 miles) of untouched sandy beach, lined with dunes and pine woods, is now the haunt of sunseekers in the summer.

Near Tróia, in the sheltered lagoon, the Roman town of **Cetóbriga** was the site of a thriving fish-salting business; the stone tanks and ruined buildings are open to visit. To the south, smart new holiday villas and golf clubs are springing up along the lagoon.

Further on, **Carrasqueira** is an old fishing community where you can still see traditional reed houses, with walls and roofs made from thatch. The narrow fishing boats

View over Alcácer do Sal and the River Sado from the castle

moored along the mud flats are reached by walkways raised on stilts. From here to Alcácer do Sal, great stretches of pine forest line the road, and there are the first glimpses of the cork oak countryside typical of the Alentejo region.

⋔ Cetóbriga
N253-1. 🄲 065-443 18. ◯ daily.

Alcácer do Sal ⑱

Road map C5. 🏘 15,000. 🚉 🚌 ℹ Praça Pedro Nunes (065-62 25 65). 🛒 1st Sat of month.

BYPASSED by the main road, the ancient town of Alcácer do Sal (al-kasr from the Arabic for castle, and do sal from its trade in salt) sits peacefully on the north bank of the River Sado. The imposing castle was a hillfort as early as the 6th century BC.

The Phoenicians established an inland trading port here, and the castle later became a stronghold for the Romans. Rebuilt by the Moors, it was finally conquered by Afonso II in 1217. The restored buildings have now taken on a new life as a pousada (see p118), with sweeping views over the rooftops and untidy storks' nests on top of trees and buildings.

There are pleasant cafés along the riverside promenade and several historic churches. The small church of Espírito Santo now houses a **Museu Arqueológico** exhibiting local finds and the 18th-century **Santo António** holds a marble Chapel of the 11,000 Virgins. The bullring is a focus for summer events and hosts the agricultural fair in October.

🏛 Museu Arqueológico
Igreja do Espírito Santo, Praça Pedro Nunes. 🄲 065-62 25 65. ◯ daily.

BIRDS OF THE TAGUS AND SADO ESTUARIES

Many waterbirds, including black-winged stilts, avocets, Kentish plovers and pratincoles are found close to areas of open water and mud flats as well as the dried out lagoons of the Tagus and Sado estuaries. Reed-beds also provide shelter for nesting and support good numbers of little bitterns, purple herons and marsh harriers. From September to March, the area around the Tagus estuary is extremely important for wildfowl and wintering waders.

Black-winged stilt, a wader that feeds in the estuaries

TRAVELLERS' NEEDS

WHERE TO STAY

LISBON AND ITS ENVIRONS offer a variety of accommodation, from restored palaces to family-run hostels. The hotels in Lisbon range from modern and luxurious or elegant and old-fashioned to cosy *pensões* and comfortable chain hotels. There are many hotels in and around the main sightseeing areas of the city.

The hotels in Estoril and Cascais along the Lisbon coast are mostly purpose-built and get busy in the summer. In the countryside

Porter services are available in Lisbon's top hotels

around Lisbon, hotels are fairly scarce, although Sintra offers a selection of places to stay and is a good base for exploring the area west of Lisbon. *Pousadas*, often historic buildings converted into hotels, are an alternative in the Lisbon Coast area. If you prefer self-catering, farmhouses, villas and apartments usually offer flexibility and good value. The hotels listed on pages 114–19 have been selected from every price category as offering the best value for money in each area.

Bedroom at the York House Hotel in Lisbon, a converted 16th-century convent *(see p116)*

CHOOSING A HOTEL

THE MAJORITY of the modern, luxury hotels in Lisbon are situated around Parque Eduardo VII, at the north end of Avenida de Liberdade.

Centrally located, the Baixa is an ideal district in which to stay, and has plenty of small *pensões* to offer. However, there is no shortage of hotels in other areas, although one problem which visitors may come across is a lack of midrange hotels.

Lapa and Rato, to the west of the city centre, offer a selection of older, more exclusive hotels. They are pleasant areas in which to stay and an alternative from the popular area around the Parque Eduardo VII.

TYPES OF HOTEL

HOTELS IN LISBON vary in quality, price and facilities. In addition to the conventional hotel there are other types of lodging, such as

albergarias (inns) that offer a pleasant stay at a lower price than a hotel of similar quality. *Pensões* or guesthouses are another alternative. They generally fall into the lowest price range and can be excellent value. At its simplest, accommodation in a *pensão* consists of a clean room with a shared bathroom. At the top end of the market, four-star *pensões* can rival the most luxurious hotels in terms of comfort. A *residencial* is like a *pensão* but only serves breakfast.

If you wish to stay outside Lisbon, then a *pousada*, a staterun country inn, is an ideal choice. These offer accommodation in scenic locations, and are often in converted country houses and palaces.

HOTEL CHAINS

AT THE TOP END of the market, two small hotel chains offer the most luxurious surroundings and facilities. The **Hotéis Alexandre de Almeida**, founded in 1917, is the older chain, and includes the gracious and appealing Metropole hotel *(see p115)*, which is located in the Baixa. The **Hotéis Tivoli** group has seven hotels in converted palaces, some of which are located in Lisbon and Sintra.

Lower down the scale, **Choice Hotels Portugal** operate two categories of modern hotel: Comfort Hotels and Quality Suites. The latter are usually rated at a higher level, but Comfort Hotels have better facilities for disabled travellers. The hotel group **Best Western** offers quality service and comfort in properties that each have their own style.

The impressive façade of the luxurious Hotel da Lapa *(see p116)*

◁ **Breakfasting beneath the wisteria at the Pousada da Palmela**

View from the Seteais Palace, Sintra, now a luxury hotel *(see p119)*

GRADINGS

MOST CATEGORIES of tourist accommodation are graded by the Portuguese Tourist Board with a star rating from one to five (five being the most luxurious). The stars indicate the size, degree of comfort and facilities offered, and bear no relation to the hotel's appeal or location. The establishment has to adhere to a set of criteria to achieve and maintain its star rating. However, the quality can vary from one type of lodging to another; for example, a three-star *pensão* can surpass a one- or two-star hotel in comfort.

PRICES

IN PORTUGAL, establishments are free to set their own prices, but tariffs must be clearly displayed at reception and in the rooms. The cost of the room usually includes all taxes and a continental breakfast. Other meals are charged as extras. It is sometimes possible to bargain for a better rate, especially in low season. As a rule, the cost of a single room is around 60 to 75 per cent of the cost of a double room. The coastal resort of Estoril can be expensive, but prices drop substantially out of season. *Pousadas* charge three rates for low (Nov–Mar), mid- (Apr–Jun, Oct) and high (Jul–Sep) season.

BOOKING

YOU WILL NEED to book in advance for locations in Estoril and Cascais in high season, when much accommodation is taken by tour operators. Hotels in central Lisbon are fairly easy to book all year round. Most hoteliers speak English so it should not be a problem to book by fax or phone. Deposits are not usually required and major credit cards are accepted.

If you wish to stay in a *pousada*, these can be booked through the **Portuguese National Tourist Office** *(see p146)* or **Enatur**, who will also supply information. The **Direcção-Geral do Turismo** (State Tourist Office) publishes two guides which are revised annually: *Guia do Alojamento Turístico*, (Guide to Tourist Accommodation) and *Turismo no Espaço Rural* (Guide to Tourism in the Country), both of which contain up-to-date listings of accommodation available in the area. However, these guides do not provide recommendations.

TRAVELLING WITH CHILDREN

THE PORTUGUESE adore children and will welcome them warmly into hotels and restaurants. Travellers who have children with them will find an immediate point of contact with their hosts.

DISABLED TRAVELLERS

THE PORTUGUESE National Tourist Office lists hotels with facilities for the disabled, and produces a general information leaflet. Some youth hostels and campsites provide special facilities and these are listed by the relevant organizations, and in a guide that is published by the **Secretariado Nacional de Reabilitação**.

DIRECTORY

HOTEL CHAINS

Best Western
UK: 0800-39 31 30.
Portugal: 0505-397 93 81.
(Both toll free.)

Choice Hotels Portugal
UK: 0800-44 44 44.
Portugal: 0500-11 66.
(Both toll free.)

Hotéis Alexandre de Almeida
Rua Dr Álvaro de Castro 73,
1600 Lisbon.
01-793 10 24.
FAX 01-793 04 45.

Hotéis Tivoli
Avenida da Liberdade 185,
1250 Lisbon.
01-353 01 81.
FAX 01-357 94 61.

BOOKING

Direcção-Geral do Turismo
Avenida António Augusto de Aguiar 86, 1050 Lisbon.
01-357 50 15.
FAX 01-357 52 20.

Enatur
Lisbon: 01-848 90 70.
FAX 01-848 92 57.
UK: 0171-402 8182.

DISABLED TRAVELLERS

Secretariado Nacional de Reabilitação
Avenida Conde de Valbom 63,
1050 Lisbon.
01-793 65 17.
FAX 01-796 51 82.

Choosing a Hotel

The hotels in this guide have been selected across a wide price range for their excellent facilities and locations. Many also have a recommended restaurant. The chart lists the hotels by areas within Lisbon. Hotels in the Lisbon Coast area are listed separately on pages 118–9. For restaurant listings see pp128–133.

Lisbon

Hotel	Price	Credit Cards	Restaurant	Garden	Swimming Pool	Number of Rooms
Bairro Alto: *Camões* Travessa do Poço da Cidade 38, 1° E, 1200. **Map** 7 A3. ☎ & [FAX] *01-346 40 48.* Conveniently located in the heart of the Bairro Alto, this light and airy hotel offers comfortable rooms and a friendly atmosphere. 🛁	Ⓢ					18
Bairro Alto: *Borges* Rua Garrett 108, 1200. **Map** 7 A4. ☎ *01-346 19 51.* [FAX] *01-342 66 17.* The Borges, one of the few places to stay in the smart Chiado area, successfully combines elegant furnishings with pleasant surroundings. 🛁 ♿	ⓈⓈ	AE DC MC V				100
Bairro Alto: *Suíço Atlântico* Rua da Glória 3–19, 1250. **Map** 7 A2. ☎ *01-346 17 13.* [FAX] *01-346 90 13.* Tucked away in a small side street, this hotel has large old-fashioned rooms and public areas with stone arches and wooden beams. 🛁	ⓈⓈ	AE DC MC V				90
Baixa: *Alegria* Praça da Alegria 12, 1250. **Map** 4 F1. ☎ *01-347 55 22.* [FAX] *01-347 80 70.* This small, good-value *pensão* offers clean and homely rooms and is set in a pleasant park-like square with a central fountain. 🛁	Ⓢ					25
Baixa: *Beira Minho* Praça da Figueira 6, 2° E, 1100. **Map** 7 B3. ☎ *01-346 18 46.* [FAX] *01-886 78 11.* The spectacular views up towards the Bairro Alto from this simple *pensão* make up for the lack of facilities. 🛁	Ⓢ					24
Baixa: *Norte* Rua dos Douradores 159, 1100. **Map** 7 B3. ☎ *01-887 89 41.* Centrally located just off Praça da Figueira, this *pensão* has few facilities but the rooms are neat and comfortable. Good value. 🛁 [TV]	Ⓢ					36
Baixa: *Restauradores* Praça dos Restauradores 13, 4°, 1250. **Map** 7 A2. ☎ *01-347 56 60.* A very small and fairly basic *pensão* on the fourth floor of a building that has a great location in the busy centre of the city. 🛁 ♿	Ⓢ					30
Baixa: *Coimbra e Madrid* Praça da Figueira 3, 3°, 1100. **Map** 7 B3. ☎ *01-342 17 16.* [FAX] *01-342 32 64.* A plain and simple *pensão* with rather sparse decoration. Some of the rooms, however, have magnificent views of the Castelo de São Jorge. 🛁	ⓈⓈ					36
Baixa: *Duas Nações* Rua da Vitória 41, 1100. **Map** 7 B4. ☎ *01-346 07 10.* [FAX] *01-347 02 06.* The "Two Nations" is a friendly place to stay, right in the heart of the Baixa, but the rooms overlooking Rua Augusta can be noisy. 🛁 [TV] ▤	ⓈⓈ	AE DC MC V				66
Baixa: *Florescente* Rua das Portas de S. Antão 99, 1150. **Map** 7 A2. ☎ *01-342 66 09.* [FAX] *01-342 77 33.* For a *pensão* the rooms of the Florescente are extremely well equipped. This street is renowned for its many excellent restaurants. 🛁 [TV] ▤	ⓈⓈ	AE MC V				70
Baixa: *Internacional* Rua da Betesga 3, 1100. **Map** 7 B3. ☎ *01-346 64 01.* [FAX] *01-347 86 35.* Centrally located between Praça da Figueira and Rossio, this hotel features modern and spacious rooms. Residents can relax in the hotel's large, comfortable TV lounge and small bar. 🛁 [TV] ▤	ⓈⓈ	AE DC MC V				53
Baixa: *Nova Goa* Rua do Arco do Marquês de Alegrete 13, 1100. **Map** 7 C3. ☎ *01-888 11 37.* [FAX] *01-886 78 11.* Just around the corner from Praça da Figueira, this *pensão* is like many in the vicinity: clean, comfortable and fairly basic. 🛁 [TV] ♿	ⓈⓈ					42

<table>
<tr><td colspan="2">

Price categories for a standard double room per night, including breakfast:

$ under 7,000$00
$$ 7–12,000$00
$$$ 12–20,000$00
$$$$ 20–30,000$00
$$$$$ over 30,000$00.
</td><td colspan="2">

RESTAURANT
The hotel has one or more restaurants open for lunch and supper, sometimes reserved for residents.
GARDEN
A garden, courtyard or large terrace for the use of hotel guests.
SWIMMING POOL
The hotel has its own indoor or outdoor pool.
CREDIT CARDS
Major credit cards accepted: *AE* American Express, *DC* Diners Club, *MC* MasterCard and *V* Visa.
</td></tr>
</table>

	CREDIT CARDS	RESTAURANT	GARDEN	SWIMMING POOL	NUMBER OF ROOMS
BAIXA: *Portugal* $$ Rua João das Regras 4, 1100. **Map** 7 C3. [C] *01-887 75 81.* [FAX] *01-886 73 43.* Though plain on the outside, this hotel situated off Rua Martim Moniz is surprisingly elegant with stylish old-fashioned decor. ⊟ TV ▤	AE DC MC V				58
BAIXA: *Roma* $$ Travessa da Glória 22a, 1°, 1250. **Map** 7 A2. [C] *01-346 05 57.* [FAX] *01-346 05 57.* This simple *pensão* has a fine location just off Avenida da Liberdade, convenient for shops and sightseeing. There is a 24-hour bar service. ⊟ TV [&]	AE MC V				24
BAIXA: *Metrópole* $$$ Praça Dom Pedro IV 30, 1100. **Map** 7 B3. [C] *01-346 91 64.* [FAX] *01-346 91 66.* This turn-of-the-century building has been renovated in a style reminiscent of the 1920s. The result is a charming and elegant hotel. The famous Buçaco wines *(see p210)* can also be bought here. ⊟ TV ▤ [&]	AE DC MC V				36
BAIXA: *Avenida Palace* $$$$$ Rua 1° de Dezembro 123, 1200. **Map** 7 B3. [C] *01-346 01 51.* [FAX] *01-342 28 84.* The Avenida Palace hotel, with its Neo-Classical façade and enviable central location, offers both elegance and convenience. The luxurious interior decoration retains many charming original details. ⊟ TV ▤ P	AE DC MC V				100
BAIXA: *Orion Eden* $$$$ Praça dos Restauradores 24, 1250. **Map** 7 A2. [C] *01-321 66 00.* [FAX] *01-321 66 66.* The modern Orion Eden has apartments and studios, all with private kitchen. Three studios have been adapted for the disabled. ⊟ TV ▤ P [&]	AE DC MC V			●	137
BAIXA: *Tivoli Jardim* $$$$ Rua J. César Machado, 1250. **Map** 4 F1. [C] *01-353 99 71.* [FAX] *01-355 65 66.* The rooms of this smart hotel are well appointed with spacious bathrooms and a mini-bar. An unusual round pool graces the garden behind the hotel and there is use of extensive sports facilities. ⊟ TV ▤ P	AE DC MC V	●	■	●	119
BAIXA: *Sofitel Lisboa* $$$$$ Av. da Liberdade 123–5, 1250. **Map** 4 F1. [C] *01-342 92 02.* [FAX] *01-342 92 22.* The comfortable, modern Sofitel features an attractive piano bar called the "Molière", situated just off the lobby. ⊟ TV ▤ P [&]	AE DC MC V	●			170
BAIXA: *Tivoli Lisboa* $$$$$ Av. da Liberdade 185, 1250. **Map** 4 F1. [C] *01-353 01 81.* [FAX] *01-357 94 61.* This large and elegant hotel has modern rooms and a huge two-level central lobby. The suites are particularly spacious. ⊟ TV ▤ P	AE DC MC V	●	■	●	300
CAMPO PEQUENO: *Lar do Areeiro* $ Praça Francisco Sá Carneiro 4, r/c, 1000. **Map** 6 E1. [C] *01-849 31 50.* Conveniently located close to many shops, this *pensão* offers good-value accommodation that is clean and comfortable. ⊟	MC V				43
CASTELO: *Ninho das Águias* $ Costa do Castelo 74, 1100. **Map** 7 C3. [C] *01-886 70 08.* The simple "Eagle's Nest" *pensão* sits beneath the castle walls. A stuffed eagle welcomes visitors onto the terrace, which has spectacular views.			■		16
ENTRECAMPOS: *Quality Hotel Lisboa* $$$$ Campo Grande 7, 1700. [C] *01-795 75 55.* [FAX] *01-795 75 00.* A pleasant hotel that caters for the business traveller. Features include a health club, gymnasium and jacuzzi. ⊟ TV ▤ P [&]	AE DC MC V	●			83
ESTEFÂNIA: *Caravela* $ Rua Ferreira Lapa 38, 1150. **Map** 6 D4. [C] *01-353 90 11.* The rooms in this *pensão* have a slightly old-fashioned ambience. Each room has a direct outside line and there is a bar and TV room. ⊟ TV	AE DC MC V				45

For key to symbols see back flap

Price categories for a standard double room per night, including breakfast:
$ under 7,000$00
$$ 7–12,000$00
$$$ 12–20,000$00
$$$$ 20–30,000$00
$$$$$ over 30,000$00.

RESTAURANT
The hotel has one or more restaurants open for lunch and supper, sometimes reserved for residents.
GARDEN
A garden, courtyard or large terrace for the use of hotel guests.
SWIMMING POOL
The hotel has its own indoor or outdoor pool.
CREDIT CARDS
Major credit cards accepted: *AE* American Express, *DC* Diners Club, *MC* MasterCard and *V* Visa.

ESTEFÂNIA: *Sol Lisboa* $$$$
Av. Duque de Loulé 45, 1050. **Map** 5 C4. ☎ *01-353 21 08.* [FAX] *01-353 18 65.*
The modern Sol hotel has 84 well-equipped suites with kitchens, as well as a small shopping arcade and a rooftop pool and sauna. 🛁 [TV] ❄ [P] ♿

GRAÇA: *Mundial* $$$
Rua Dom Duarte 4, 1100. **Map** 7 B3. ☎ *01-886 31 01.* [FAX] *01-887 91 29.*
This hotel, located centrally off Praça da Figueira, has plain but comfortable rooms. The restaurant offers marvellous views. 🛁 [TV] ❄ [P] ♿

GRAÇA: *Senhora do Monte* $$$
Calçada do Monte 39, 1100. **Map** 7 D1. ☎ *01-886 60 02.* [FAX] *01-887 77 83.*
This *albergaria* is somewhat off the beaten track, but it is well worth the effort to find it. The rooms are fairly plain but the views, especially from the rooftop bar and garden, are simply the best in town. 🛁 [TV] ❄

LAPA: *As Janelas Verdes* $$$$
R. das Janelas Verdes 47, 1200. **Map** 4 D3. ☎ *01-396 81 43.* [FAX] *01-396 81 44.*
A delightful *pensão* housed in an 18th-century ivy-covered mansion, once owned by the Portuguese novelist Eça de Queirós *(see p55).* It has Neo-Classical decor and a peaceful, charming patio. 🛁 [TV] ❄ [P]

LAPA: *Hotel da Lapa* $$$$
R. do Pau da Bandeira 4, 1200. **Map** 3 C3. ☎ *01-395 00 05.* [FAX] *01-395 06 65.*
A gracious and charming hotel located in the city's diplomatic area. Each room in the Palace Wing is uniquely decorated in its own Portuguese style – from 18th-century Neo-Classical to Art Deco. 🛁 [TV] ❄ [P] ♿

LAPA: *York House* $$$$
Rua das Janelas Verdes 32, 1200. **Map** 4 D4. ☎ *01-396 24 35.* [FAX] *01-397 27 93.*
This enchanting *pensão* is housed in the 17th-century Convento dos Marianos. Set around a shady, plant-filled patio, the elegant rooms have wooden or terracotta floors and elegant antique furniture. 🛁 [TV]

RATO: *13 da Sorte* $
Rua do Salitre 13, 1100. **Map** 4 F1. ☎ *01-353 18 51.* [FAX] *01-353 18 51.*
This excellently located *pensão* offers some individual suites. The terrace bar "Gaivota" (meaning seagull) offers splendid views. 🛁 [TV] ♿

RATO: *Amazónia* $$$
T. da Fábrica dos Pentes 12–20, 1250. **Map** 5 B5. ☎ *01-387 70 06.* [FAX] *01-387 90 90.*
Conveniently close to the city centre, this stylish hotel has elegant public rooms, large bedrooms and a piano bar. 🛁 [TV] ❄ ♿

RATO: *Altis* $$$$
Rua Castilho 11, 1250. **Map** 4 F1. ☎ *01-314 24 96.* [FAX] *01-354 86 96.*
This huge hotel has every expected facility, including a rooftop grill and well-equipped health club with an indoor pool. 🛁 [TV] ❄ [P] ♿

RATO: *Lisboa Plaza* $$$$
Travessa do Salitre 7, 1250. **Map** 4 F1. ☎ *01-346 39 22.* [FAX] *01-347 16 30.*
Built in 1953, and situated off Praça da Alegria, the traditional decor of this hotel is by the Portuguese interior designer, Graça Viterbo. 🛁 [TV] ❄

RATO: *Ritz Intercontinental* $$$$$
Rua R. da Fonseca 88, 1093. **Map** 5 B5. ☎ *01-383 20 20.* [FAX] *01-383 17 83.*
The legendary Ritz is an elegant, comfortable hotel. Many of the rooms have balconies that overlook the Parque Eduardo VII. 🛁 [TV] ❄ [P] ♿

ROTUNDA: *Castilho* $
Rua Castilho 57, 1250. **Map** 4 F1. ☎ *01-386 08 22.* [FAX] *01-386 29 10.*
An excellent-value *pensão* with good facilities and clean and comfortable rooms, some of which have three or four beds. 🛁 [TV] ♿

Hotel	Credit Cards	Restaurant	Garden	Swimming Pool	Number of Rooms
Sol Lisboa	AE DC MC V	●	■	●	84
Mundial	AE DC MC V	●	■		147
Senhora do Monte	AE DC MC V		■		28
As Janelas Verdes	AE DC MC V		■		17
Hotel da Lapa	AE DC MC V	●	■	●	94
York House	AE DC MC V	●	■		34
13 da Sorte	DC MC V				24
Amazónia	AE DC MC V		■	●	192
Altis	AE DC MC V	●	■	●	303
Lisboa Plaza	AE DC MC V	●			112
Ritz Intercontinental	AE DC MC V	●	■		284
Castilho	MC V				25

ROTUNDA: *Jorge V* $$
Rua Mouzinho da Silveira 3, 1250. **Map** 5 C5. (*01-356 25 25.* FAX *01-315 03 19.*
This pleasant, comfortable hotel offers good value for the area. Roughly
half the rooms have balconies, so request one when checking in. 🔒 TV 📋
AE DC MC V — 49

ROTUNDA: *Britânia* $$$
Rua R. Sampaio 17, 1100. **Map** 5 C5. (*01-315 50 16.* FAX *01-315 50 21.*
Housed in a building designed by the architect Cassiano Branco in 1944,
this delightful hotel has a beautiful marble lobby. 🔒 TV 📋 P
AE DC MC V — 30

ROTUNDA: *Capitol* $$$
Rua Eça de Queirós 24, 1050. **Map** 5 C4. (*01-353 68 11.* FAX *01-352 61 65.*
A comfortable hotel just off Avenida de Duque de Loulé. The rooms
overlooking the market can be noisy early in the morning. 🔒 TV 📋 P 🔗
AE DC MC V — 57

ROTUNDA: *Diplomático* $$$
Rua Castilho 74, 1250. **Map** 5 B5. (*01-386 20 41.* FAX *01-386 21 55.*
The Diplomático has spacious rooms with modern facilities and offers
complimentary tea, coffee and chocolate in the rooms. 🔒 TV 📋 P 🔗
AE DC MC V — 90

ROTUNDA: *Le Méridien Lisboa* $$$$$
Rua Castilho 149, 1070. **Map** 5 B4. (*01-383 09 00.* FAX *01-383 32 31.*
Overlooking the Parque Eduardo VII from one of the city's seven hills, this
hotel has comfortable rooms and spectacular views. 🔒 TV 📋 P 🔗
AE DC MC V — 330

ROTUNDA: *Nacional* $$$
Rua Castilho 34, 1250. **Map** 5 B5. (*01-355 44 33.* FAX *01-356 11 22.*
This interesting glass-fronted hotel has comfortable rooms and extensive
facilities. There are also two suites available. 🔒 TV 📋 P 🔗
AE DC MC V — 61

ROTUNDA: *Rex* $$$
Rua Castilho 169, 1070. **Map** 5 B4. (*01-388 21 61.* FAX *01-388 75 81.*
The Rex is located close to the Parque Eduardo VII. The rooftop
restaurant has good views and offers a buffet breakfast. 🔒 TV 📋 P 🔗
AE DC MC V — 36

ROTUNDA: *Veneza* $$$
Avenida da Liberdade 189, 1250. **Map** 5 C5. (*01-352 67 00.* FAX *01-352 66 78.*
The ornate staircase decorated with modern murals by Pedro Luiz-Gomes
is the highlight of this spacious and comfortable hotel. 🔒 TV 📋 P 🔗
AE DC MC V — 36

SALDANHA: *Marisela* $
Rua Filipe Folque 19, r/c, 1050. **Map** 5 C3. (*01-353 32 05.* FAX *01-316 04 23.*
Located in a quiet street very close to the gardens of Parque Eduardo VII,
this good-value *pensão* has rather basic, but adequate, rooms. 🔒 🔗 TV
AE MC V — 34

SALDANHA: *Horizonte* $$
Av. António A. de Aguiar 42, 1050. **Map** 5 B4. (*01-353 95 26.* FAX *01-353 84 74.*
This large *pensão* offers good value for money for this area. The rooms at
the front look out over Avenida da Liberdade and can be noisy. 🔒 TV 📋 🔗
AE DC MC V — 53

SALDANHA: *VIP* $$
Rua Fernão Lopes 25, 1000. **Map** 5 C3. (*01-352 19 23.* FAX *01-315 87 73.*
A simple hotel built over shops in a busy part of the city, the VIP is neat
and tidy, although the decor is somewhat old-fashioned. 🔒 TV 📋
AE DC MC V — 54

SALDANHA: *Impala* $$$
Rua Filipe Folque 49, 1050. **Map** 5 C3. (*01-314 89 14.* FAX *01-357 53 62.*
All the rooms in the quiet Impala hotel are suites, each with its
own living room, kitchen, bar and refrigerator. 🔒 TV 🔗
AE DC MC V — 26

SALDANHA: *Príncipe* $$$
Avenida Duque de Ávila 201, 1050. **Map** 5 B3. (*01-353 61 51.* FAX *01-353 43 14.*
Most of the rooms in this modern hotel have their own balcony.
There is a small bar and lounge just off the lobby. 🔒 TV 📋 P 🔗
AE DC MC V — 67

SALDANHA: *Real Parque* $$$$$
Avenida L. Bivar 67, 1050. **Map** 5 C3. (*01-357 01 01.* FAX *01-357 07 50.*
This impressive modern hotel, located on a quiet side street, has seven
rooms specially designed for the disabled. 🔒 TV 📋 P 🔗
AE DC MC V — 153

SALDANHA: *Sheraton Lisboa* $$$$$
Rua L. Coelho 1, 1069. **Map** 5 C3. (*01-357 57 57.* FAX *01-354 71 64.*
On one of the city's vantage points, Lisbon's Sheraton offers spacious
rooms, a communications centre and a health club. 🔒 TV 📋 P 🔗
AE DC MC V — 384

Price categories for a standard double room per night, including breakfast:

$ under 7,000$00
$$ 7–12,000$00
$$$ 12–20,000$00
$$$$ 20–30,000$00
$$$$$ over 30,000$00.

RESTAURANT
The hotel has one or more restaurants open for lunch and supper, sometimes reserved for residents.

GARDEN
A garden, courtyard or large terrace for the use of hotel guests.

SWIMMING POOL
The hotel has its own indoor or outdoor pool.

CREDIT CARDS
Major credit cards accepted: *AE* American Express, *DC* Diners Club, *MC* MasterCard and *V* Visa.

THE LISBON COAST

	CREDIT CARDS	RESTAURANT	GARDEN	SWIMMING POOL	NUMBER OF ROOMS
ALCÁCER DO SAL: *Pousada de Vale do Gaio* $$ Torrão, 7595. **Road map** C5. ☎ 065-66 96 10. **FAX** 065-66 45 45. This peaceful and intimate *pousada* on the lakeside, converted from the dam engineer's residence, offers excellent country walks.	AE DC MC V	●			14
CARCAVELOS: *Praia Mar* $$$ Rua Gurué 16, 2775. **Road map** B5. ☎ 01-457 31 31. **FAX** 01-457 31 30. This delightful hotel overlooks the Estoril coast's largest sandy beach. Modern and elegant throughout, the rooms are spacious and comfortable. The famed wines from Buçaco *(see p210)* are also available.	AE DC MC V	●	●	●	148
CASCAIS: *Palma* $$ Avenida Valbom 15, 2750. **Road map** B5. ☎ 01-483 77 97. **FAX** 01-483 79 22. Conveniently located close to the centre of Cascais as well as the beach, this small *pensão* has simple yet comfortable rooms.	AE DC MC V		●	●	9
CASCAIS: *Casa da Pérgola* $$$ Avenida Valbom 13, 2750. **Road map** B5. ☎ 01-484 00 40. **FAX** 01-483 47 91. This Mediterranean-style mansion has rooms with stucco ceilings and marble floors. It closes from November until a week before Easter.			●		11
CASCAIS: *Cidadela* $$$ Avenida 25 de Abril, 2750. **Road map** B5. ☎ 01-482 76 00. **FAX** 01-486 72 26. A short walk from the town centre, the Cidadela is surrounded by gardens. Most of the rooms have spectacular views over the bay.	AE DC MC V	●	●	●	128
CASCAIS: *Albatroz* $$$$$ Rua F. Arouca 100, 2750. **Road map** B5. ☎ 01-483 28 21. **FAX** 01-484 48 27. Built in the 19th century as a retreat for the Portuguese royal family, the Albatroz sits perched on the rocks directly overlooking the ocean. Inside, the luxurious decoration is matched by excellent service.	AE DC MC V	●	●	●	40
CASCAIS: *Estoril Sol* $$$$$ Parque de Palmela, 2750. **Road map** B5. ☎ 01-483 28 31. **FAX** 01-483 22 80. As well as marvellous views over the bay of Cascais, the Estoril Sol has a sea-water pool and a health club with Turkish baths.	AE DC MC V	●		●	310
COSTA DA CAPARICA: *Praia do Sol* $$ Rua dos Pescadores 12a, 2825. **Road map** B5. ☎ 01-290 00 12. **FAX** 01-290 25 41. A small hotel, the Praia do Sol offers well-appointed rooms conveniently located close to the beach in this popular resort town.	AE DC MC V				53
COSTA DA CAPARICA: *Costa da Caparica* $$$ Av. Gen. Delgado 47, 2825. **Road map** B5. ☎ 01-291 03 10. **FAX** 01-291 06 87. This hotel, with an unusual semi-circular entrance, overlooks the beach. It has seven rooms adapted for the disabled.	AE DC MC V	●		●	353
ERICEIRA: *Vilazul* $$ Calçada da Baleia 10, 2655. **Road map** B5. ☎ 061-868 00 00. **FAX** 061-629 27. Only 500 m (550 yds) from the sea, this bright and airy *pensão* has panoramic views from the terrace and some of the bedrooms.	AE DC MC V	●	●		21
ESTORIL: *São Cristóvão* $$ Av. Marginal 7079, 2765. **Road map** B5. ☎ 01-468 09 13. **FAX** 01-468 09 13. This charming *pensão* is housed in an interesting old villa. Located on the ocean side of the Avenida Marginal, it offers spectacular views.			●		14
ESTORIL: *Hotel Alvorada* $$$ Rua de Lisboa 3, 2675. **Road map** B5. ☎ 01-468 00 70. **FAX** 01-468 72 50. Only a few minutes' walk from the beach, this newly decorated hotel offers friendly service and bright, well-appointed rooms.	AE DC MC V				54

ESTORIL: *Hotel de Inglaterra* $\$\$\$$
Rua do Porto 1, 2765. **Road map** B5. 01-468 44 61. FAX 01-468 21 08.
Many rooms in this impressive early 20th-century mansion have private
balconies with views over the Bay of Cascais or the Sintra Hills.

AE DC MC V — 52

ESTORIL: *Palácio* $\$\$\$\$\$$
Rua do Parque, 2765. **Road map** B5. 01-468 04 00. FAX 01-468 48 67.
An elegant hotel with a prime location between the sea and the casino.
It has an 18-hole golf course and tennis courts.

AE DC MC V — 162

GUINCHO: *Hotel do Guincho* $\$\$\$\$$
Praia do Guincho, 2751. **Road map** B5. 01-487 04 91. FAX 01-487 04 31.
Perched on a clifftop overlooking the ocean, this atmospheric hotel with
arched ceilings and medieval decor was once a fortress.

AE DC MC V — 31

GUINCHO: *Senhora da Guia* $\$\$\$\$$
Estrada do Guincho, 2750. **Road map** B5. 01-486 92 39. FAX 01-486 92 27.
Set in its own grounds with a sea-water pool, this charming *estalagem*
is housed in a comfortable and relaxing manor house.

AE DC MC V — 42

MAFRA: *Castelão* $\$\$$
Avenida 25 de Abril, 2640. **Road map** B5. 061-81 20 50. FAX 061-516 98.
Convenient as a base when visiting the fabulous monastery in Mafra,
this fairly small hotel is comfortable and clean.

AE DC MC V — 35

PALMELA: *Pousada de Palmela* $\$\$\$\$$
Castelo de Palmela, 2950. **Road map** C5. 01-235 12 26. FAX 01-233 04 40.
The fortified walls of this 12th-century castle now enclose a tranquil
pousada with whitewashed rooms and many plants.

AE DC MC V — 28

QUELUZ: *Pousada da Dona Maria I* $\$\$\$\$$
L. do Palácio Nacional, 2745. **Road map** B5. 01-435 61 58. FAX 01-435 61 89.
Once used by staff of the marvellous 18th-century Palácio de Queluz,
today the "Clock Tower" is an impressive *pousada*.

AE DC MC V — 26

SESIMBRA: *Hotel do Mar* $\$\$\$\$$
R. Gen. Delgado 10, 2970. **Road map** C5. 01-223 33 26. FAX 01-223 38 88.
This hotel, built on different levels on the cliffside, is surrounded by lush
gardens. The presidential suite has a private pool.

AE DC MC V — 169

SETÚBAL: *IBIS Setúbal* $\$\$$
N10, Vale de Rosa, 2910. **Road map** C5. 065-77 22 00. FAX 065-77 24 47.
Featuring the usual combination of IBIS comforts and economy, this
hotel is surrounded by its own peaceful gardens.

AE DC MC V — 102

SETÚBAL: *Pousada de São Filipe* $\$\$\$\$$
Castelo de Setúbal, 2900. **Road map** C5. 065-52 38 44. FAX 065-53 25 38.
This historic castle, built by Philip II of Spain *(see p50)* in 1590, is an
friendly pousada with fine views over the estuary.

AE DC MC V — 14

SINTRA: *Residencial Sintra* $\$\$$
T. dos Avelares 12, 2710. **Road map** B5. 01-923 07 38. FAX 01-923 07 38.
Located just east of Sintra town centre, in the residential area of São
Pedro, this rambling old *pensão* is friendly and full of character.

MC V — 10

SINTRA: *Central* $\$\$$
Praça da República 35, 2710. **Road map** B5. 01-923 09 63.
Heavy furniture and peeling paint give this hotel an old-fashioned atmos-
phere. It has an excellent position opposite the Palácio Nacional.

AE MC V — 10

SINTRA: *Tivoli Sintra* $\$\$\$$
Praça da República, 2710. **Road map** B5. 01-923 35 05. FAX 01-923 15 72.
The modern Tivoli Sintra, tucked away in a corner of Sintra's main square,
has wonderful views across the valley, a bar and a boutique.

AE DC MC V — 75

SINTRA: *Caesar Park* $\$\$\$\$\$$
Estr. da Lagoa Azul, Linhó 2710. **Road map** B5. 01-924 90 11. FAX 01-924 90 07.
This huge, luxurious complex in the Sintra hills has an 18-hole golf course,
designed by Robert Trent Jones Jr, and a health club.

AE DC MC V — 174

SINTRA: *Palácio de Seteais* $\$\$\$\$\$$
R. B. du Bocage 8, 2710. **Road map** B5. 01-923 32 00. FAX 01-923 42 77.
Just outside town, this elegant hotel occupies a delightful 18th-century
palace with tastefully decorated interiors and a topiary garden.

AE DC MC V — 30

RESTAURANTS, CAFÉS AND BARS

ARTICULARLY IN Lisbon and along the coast, there are many restaurants dedicated to cooking all manner of freshly caught fish and seafood. It may be grilled, pan-fried or turned into soup or a stew. However, meat dishes are also plentiful, some of the most popular being made of pork and lamb. Lisbon has an abundance of cheap restaurants and cafés, as well as more expensive ones. There are not

Drinks waiter at the Palácio de Seteais (see p133)

only typically Portuguese restaurants in Lisbon, but also Chinese, Indian, Indonesian, Brazilian and African, all of which reflect Portugal's colonial past. This section gives tips on the different types of restaurants and cafés, as well as advice on menus, drinks and ordering your meal. The listings found on pages 128–33 are a selection of the best restaurants in all price ranges to be found throughout the capital and in the Lisbon Coast area.

TYPES OF RESTAURANT

EATING VENUES in Lisbon come in all shapes and sizes and at all price levels. Among the most reasonable is the local *tasca* or tavern, often just a room with half-a-dozen tables presided over by a husband-and-wife team. *Tascas* are often frequented by locals and professionals at lunchtime, which is a good indication of quality food. The *casa de pasto* offers a budget three-course meal in a large dining room, while a *restaurante* is more formal and offers a wider choice of dishes. At a typical *marisqueira*, the emphasis is on seafood and fresh fish. A *churrasqueira*, originally Brazilian, specializes in spit-roasted foods. A *cervejaria* is the ideal place to go for a beer and snack, maybe of delicious seafood. The restaurants in better hotels are generally of good quality. *Pousadas (see p112)*, found mainly in country areas, offer a network of traditional restaurants, with the focus on local gastronomic specialities.

The pleasant courtyard of Lautasco (p128) along Beco do Azinhal in the Alfama

EATING HOURS

LUNCH is usually served between noon and 2pm, when many restaurants get very crowded. Dinner is served from 7pm until at least 10pm in most places, and can often be later. An alternative for a late dinner would be a *fado* house *(see pp142–3)*, usually open from about 9:30pm to 3 or 4am. However, a meal here will be somewhat more expensive as the price includes a show.

RESERVATIONS

IT IS A GOOD IDEA to book ahead for expensive restaurants, and for those in popular locations in high season. Disabled people should certainly check in advance on facilities and access. Special facilities are generally lacking but most places will try to be helpful.

THE MENU

MANY restaurants, in tourist areas particularly, offer an *ementa turística*, a cheap, daily-changing menu (hotels with several restaurants have to offer an *ementa turística* in just one). This is served with coffee and a drink (a glass of wine or beer, a soft drink or

The impressive interior of Cozinha Velha (see p133) at Queluz

Eating outside in Cascais along the Lisbon coast

water) and provides a full meal at a good price with no hidden costs. Lunch *(almoço)* generally consists of a soup or starter and a fish or meat dish with potatoes or rice. To sample a local speciality, you should ask for the *prato do dia* – dish of the day. The choice of sweets can be limited, but there is usually a good selection of fresh fruits in season or you can try a pastry such as a *pastel de nata*.

Dinner *(jantar)* may be two or more courses, perhaps rounded off with ice cream, fruit, a simple dessert or cheese. Casserole-style dishes, such as *cataplana* (a kind of tightly sealed wok in which the food steams in its own juice, often used for fish) or *porco à alentejana* (pork with clams), are brought to the table in a pot for diners to share. This is similarly done with large fish, such as sea bass, which are sold by weight. One serving is large and can easily be shared by two people, and it is perfectly acceptable to ask for a *meia dose* or half-portion. The Portuguese will be more than happy to supply these half-portions for adults if required, as well as for any children present.

Peculiar to Portugal is the plate of assorted appetizers – perhaps olives, cheese and sardine pâté – brought with bread at the start of a meal. However, these are not always included in the price of the meal and may be charged per item consumed.

Pasteís de nata (custard pastries)

VEGETARIANS

VEGETARIANS WILL not eat as well as fish lovers, although local cheeses and breads can be excellent. Chefs are usually happy to provide something meatless, although this will probably mean just a salad or omelette. A greater variety of vegetarian dishes can be found in ethnic restaurants.

WHAT TO DRINK

IT WOULD BE a pity to visit Portugal without sampling port *(see pp124–5)* and Madeira, the country's two most famous drinks. Some restaurants may suggest a glass of white port as an aperitif while you wait for your meal. As far as house wine is concerned, it is usually of an acceptable quality to wash down your meal whatever the standard of the restaurant. Otherwise, ask for the wine list *(carta de vinhos)* and choose one of the native Portuguese wines *(see pp124–5)*. As an alternative to wine, the mineral water is recommended. This is either *com gás* (sparkling) or *sem gás* (still). If you prefer to drink beer, Sagres and Super Bock are both good lagers. *Cervejarias*, such as the lively Cervejaria Trindade in the Bairro Alto *(see pp48–59)*, are ideal places to get a snack late at night and enjoy an excellent range of beers, from lagers to dark beers, many of which are draught.

PAYING

IT IS COMMON PRACTICE to add a ten per cent tip to bills where service is not included. The cover charge is extra, and you may need to check that the restaurant takes credit cards if this is how you want to pay.

CHILDREN

THE PORTUGUESE view children as a blessing rather than a nuisance, so Lisbon is an ideal city for families to eat out together. Children's portions at reduced prices are advertised in restaurants or will be provided on request.

SMOKING

SMOKING IS COMMON and permitted in all public places in Portugal, unless there is a sign saying *proibido fumar*. No-smoking areas in restaurants are very rare.

DRINKING COFFEE IN LISBON

Coffee is widely drunk in Lisbon and served in many forms. The most popular, *uma bica*, is a small cup of strong black coffee like an espresso. For a weaker version, ask for *uma carioca de café*. A strong *bica* is called *uma italiana*. *Uma meia de leite* is half coffee, half milk. Strong coffee with a dash of milk is known as *um garoto escuro* (*um garoto claro* is quite milky). If you like coffee with plenty of milk, ask for *um galão* (a gallon). It is served in a glass, and again you can order *um galão claro* (very milky) or *escuro* (strong).

Uma bica   **Um galão**

What to Eat in Lisbon

Serra cheese

GASTRONOMICALLY, the Lisbon region is immensely varied, incorporating many different foods from all over Portugal. Situated near the Atlantic, Lisbon and its coast enjoy a proliferation of excellent seafood, in particular shellfish, dried cod *(bacalhau)* and grilled sardines. A popular dish is *porco à alentejana*, a mixture of pork and clams, originating from southern Portugal. Milk from sheep and goats is turned into a variety of cheeses, one of the most popular being the buttery Serra, which becomes harder as it ages. Sweet dishes include a vanilla flavoured rice pudding and a rich, dark chocolate mousse.

Fresh fruit is plentiful in Lisbon and grapes and oranges from the Algarve are delicious when in season.

Pastéis de bacalhau *are a national addiction. These little salt-cod cakes are eaten cold as a snack or hot as a main dish.*

Caldo verde, *Portugal's most famous soup, gets its vibrant colour from its main ingredient, couve galega, a type of kale.*

Paio, sausage made from pork loin

Spiced chouriço (sausage)

Cured ham

Cured meats *play an important role in Portuguese cuisine. The chouriços are flavoured with paprika and often wine.*

Leitão à Bairrada, *roasted sucking pig with crisp crackling, is relished hot or cold, and can be bought in good delicatessens.*

Frango à piri-piri, *a great favourite from Portugal's former colonies in Africa, is barbecued chicken with chilli.*

Bife à café, *café-style steak, is tender steak with a creamy sauce, served with chips and topped with a fried egg.*

Bacalhau à Gomes de Sá *is a creation from Oporto, in northern Portugal, made of layers of salt cod, potato and onion, and garnished with egg and olives.*

Porco à alentejana, *a curious marriage of pork and clams, is usually cooked in a* cataplana, *a kind of tightly sealed wok which retains the flavours.*

Pãezinhos

Papo seco

Queijo de ovelha (ewe's milk cheese)

Requeijão

Fresh cheeses *made from ewe's or goat's milk are enjoyed with a variety of fresh rolls. Especially prized is* Requeijão.

Shellfish *is plentiful and much enjoyed in Portugal. Lisbon is full of specialist seafood restaurants artfully displaying lobsters, crayfish, oysters, prawns of all sizes, crabs and other lesser known delicacies. Cockles and clams find their way into many dishes, such as the rich seafood rice,* arroz de marisco.

Oysters

Crab

Lobster

Shrimps

Mussels

Prawns

Açorda de marisco *is a special and unusual dish: shellfish are added to a thick soup of mashed bread, oil, garlic and coriander.*

Sardinhas assadas, *charcoal-grilled sardines, are a seaside tradition – a feast in summer when they are at their best.*

DRINKS

Portugal produces many fine wines *(see pp124–5)*, from which houses such as Fonseca distil *aguardente* (brandy). Mineral waters, such as Luso, from the spa in central Portugal, are widely available. The tradition of beer-making in the Lisbon area is less well-known and there are many *cervejarias* (beer houses) in the city. *Medronheira* is a liqueur made from the fruit of the strawberry tree *(arbutus).*

Mousse de chocolate *can be spectacular when made with really good dark chocolate.*

Arroz doce, *creamy rice pudding rich with egg, is flavoured with lemon rind and vanilla.*

Aguardente Velha Reserva

Mineral water from Luso

Queijadas de Sintra (cheese tarts spiced with cinnamon)

Pastéis de nata (custard-cream tartlets)

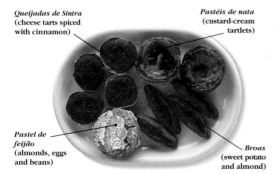

Pastel de feijão (almonds, eggs and beans)

Broas (sweet potato and almond)

Tartlets *such as* pastéis de nata *epitomize the region's infinite variety of cakes, many based on egg yolks, almonds and spices.*

Honey-sweetened Medronheira

Sagres beer

The Wines of Portugal

Since joining the EU in 1986, Portugal has been improving its range of wines. Long-established port *(see pp126–7)*, Madeira and *vinhos verdes* or "green wines", so called because they are drunk when young and fresh, are unique to the country. The classic fruity reds of Bairrada and Dão regions are now gaining much wider recognition, while the Alentejo and Ribatejo regions are starting to produce high-quality reds that are rapidly growing in popularity.

Rosés such as *Mateus are Portugal's great export success. To obtain the pink colour, the skins of the red grapes remain in contact with the must (juice) for a short time after crushing.*

WINE REGIONS

Each *região demarcada* (demarcated wine region) is designated by law and guarantees wine of high quality. The first region to be demarcated was the Douro, in the reign of King José (1750–77).

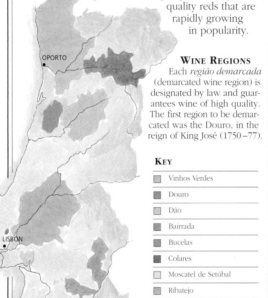

OPORTO

LISBON

KEY

▢	Vinhos Verdes
▨	Douro
▢	Dão
▩	Bairrada
▩	Bucelas
▨	Colares
▢	Moscatel de Setúbal
▩	Ribatejo
▢	Alentejo
▨	Lagoa

0 kilometres　50

0 miles　25

Vinho verde vineyards in the village of Lapela, near Monção in the Minho

Cellar of the Buçaco Palace Hotel, in Coimbra, famous for its red wine

HOW TO READ A WINE LABEL

Apart from *branco, tinto* and *rosado* (white, red and rosé), terms to note on a wine label are *adamado* or *doce* (sweet), *seco* (dry), *bruto* (dry, sparkling), *licoroso* (fortified), and *maduro* (aged in a vat). *Generoso* indicates an apéritif or dessert wine, *clarete* a Bordeaux-style wine, and *claro* is used for a new or *nouveau* wine. *Reserva* is used for wines from an outstanding vintage year. The phrase *engarrafado na origem* indicates that the wine is estate-bottled, while the words *adega* (cellar) and *quinta* (estate) often appear on wine labels as part of the producer's name.

Vinhos Sogrape is the name of the producer responsible for bottling and distributing this wine.

This wine is a *vinho verde,* a light and slightly sparkling white. *Vinho verde* may also be red.

Denominação de origem controlada is the Portuguese equivalent of the French *appellation contrôlée.*

The alcohol content at 9.5 per cent is fairly high for *vinho verde.*

The style of wine shows it to be a "dry white".

VINHOS V SOGRAPE

Chello
VINHO VERDE
DENOMINAÇÃO DE ORIGEM CONTROLADA
BRANCO SECO

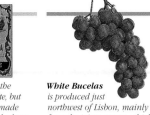

Vinhos verdes *from the Minho are usually white, but can be red. They are made from grapes grown high above the soil on fences or trees. The grapes are picked before fully ripe and the wine is fermented in the bottle, which ensures its delicacy and slight sparkle.*

White Bucelas *is produced just northwest of Lisbon, mainly from the* Arinto *grape, which grows especially well in the soil of this small district. Dry and exquisite, the wine has often been compared with Chablis, and goes well with fish dishes.*

Moscatel de Setúbal *is a world-famous dessert wine produced in the Arrábida hills around Palmela, mainly by the long-established firm of José Maria da Fonseca. Their cellars, where the wine is kept in oak casks for up to 50 years before bottling, are open to the public.*

The Douro *has about 80,000 vineyards along its valley, and although the region is more widely known for its port, just as many grapes are grown for making table wines. Portugal's most expensive table wine, the long-matured Barca Velha, comes from this region.*

Picking grapes for *vinho verde* in northern Portugal

The Ribatejo *is becoming a successful region for wine production, with red and white grapes growing abundantly on the sandy flood plain of the Tagus. The region of Coruche is becoming highly regarded for its soft and fruity reds.*

Full-bodied red Dão *is the most abundant of Portugal's vinhos maduros. Containing at least 20 per cent of the* Touriga Nacional *grape, it is aged in wood for several years to ensure quality. Crisp white Dão, which accounts for ten per cent of the region's production, should be drunk relatively young.*

The Alentejo region *is now making many of Portugal's best new wines. Single estates produce limited quantities of superlative reds, and labels such as Borba, Redondo, Moura and Reguengos are all worth looking out for. Both reds and whites are high in alcohol content.*

Bairrada *wines from the Beiras have been famous for over 1,000 years. The predominant red grape variety is the* Baga, *yielding the fruity and intense red which rivals Dão and also requires years of ageing. White wines are fewer and not so successful, with the exception of a sparkling version.*

Colares *is a small, historic wine region near Sintra. Vines are planted in trenches dug in sand dunes in order to protect the grapes from the Atlantic winds. The resulting reds are full-bodied and high in tannin, but soften with age; the rarer whites are dry* maduro *wines.*

Lagoa *produces the best wine from the recently demarcated region of the Algarve. It is a straightforward wine that does not travel well, but, especially when bought by the garrafão (flagon), it is very cheap and makes a suitable accompaniment for the local fish dishes.*

The Story of Port

THE "DISCOVERY" OF PORT dates from the 17th century. British merchants, keen to build up trade with Portugal, doctored the wine of the Douro region in northern Portugal with brandy to stop it from turning sour in transit. It was found that the stronger and sweeter the wine, the better flavour it acquired. Over the years, methods of maturing and blending were refined, and are continued today by the main port producers. Croft was one of the first big shippers, followed by other English and Scots firms, and much of the port trade is still in British control.

Barco rabelo ferrying port down the Douro river

THE PORT REGION

Port comes only from a demarcated region of the upper Douro valley, stretching 100 km (62 miles) to the Spanish border. Régua and Pinhão are the main centres of production, but most top-quality vineyards lie on estates or *quintas* in the harsh eastern terrain.

Map labels: OPORTO · Vila Real · Peso da Régua · Pinhão · Tua · Lamego · Corgo · Pinhão · Tua · Sabor · Douro · Douro

STYLES OF PORT

A classic after-dinner drink, port is rich, full-bodied and high in alcohol. The tawnies are lighter in taste and colour than ruby or vintage, but all are blended from several wines, selected from scores of samples.

Vintage

The star of any shipper's range is made from wines of a single vintage year, from the best vineyards. Blended and bottled after two years in oak casks, vintage port is then matured in tall black bottles.

LBV

LBV (Late Bottled Vintage) is wine of a single year that has been matured in wood for four to six years, before being bottled ready for drinking. The label gives the year of vintage and when it was bottled.

Aged Tawny

This light port, so-called because it pales to an amber colour as it ages, is less full-bodied than vintage or ruby ports. It may be labelled as 10, 20 or 30 years old, referring to the average age of its blend of old and young wines.

Tawny

Less sweet and lighter than ruby or vintage ports, tawny often appeals for those very reasons. It is blended from wines of different years after ageing in wood, or may even be a clever mixture of red and white.

Ruby

The full-bodied, fruity port named after its deep red colour is matured in wood until ready to drink. The younger ones take no more than three years. All are blended from wines of various ages.

White

The two styles of white port – dry and sweet – differ from the others as they are drunk as an aperitif, and are at their best chilled. White port is made only from white Malvasia grapes, hence the colour.

Collecting grapes in tall wicker baskets for transport to the wineries

HOW PORT IS MADE

The climax of the Douro farmers' year comes in late September. Bands of pickers from the outlying provinces congregate in the Douro valley to harvest the grapes. More than 40 varieties are used in the making of port.

Treading the grapes *in stone tanks or* lagares *to extract the juice is a feature of very traditional* quintas. *Some shippers believe it adds a special quality.*

Fermentation *in cement or steel tanks is a more common method. Carbon dioxide builds up within the tank, forcing the fermenting must (juice from the grapes) up a tube into an open trough at the top. The gas is released and the must sprays back over the pips and skins, in a process similar to treading.*

In the fortification *process, the semi-fermented must is run into a second vat where brandy – actually grape spirit – is added. This arrests the fermentation, leaving the wine sweet from natural grape sugar.*

Thousands of bottles *of Graham's vintage port from 1977, one of the best years, await full maturation at the lodge in Vila Nova de Gaia.*

All ports *apart from vintage are matured in oak casks in the port lodges. Once bottled, they are ready for drinking and do not require decanting.*

VINTAGE PORT

In years of outstanding quality, shippers may "declare" their best wine as "vintage" 18 months after the harvest. It is bottled six months later and begins its long, slow maturation. Shippers usually declare a "Vintage Year" about three times per decade. The minimum period for a good vintage to mature is about 15 years, but the best ones continue to improve indefinitely. Always decant vintage port before drinking it.

The following vintages are now ready to drink:

1960 Hard to find these days, but soft, mellow and mature if you do.

1963 A classic, full-bodied, rich vintage.

1966 A high-quality, low-yielding vintage; in short supply, but perhaps currently at its peak.

1970 All-time great vintage; magnificent now and will go on improving.

1975 Comparatively thin, unlikely to improve.

Vintages not ready for drinking yet:

1977 A superb vintage, possibly a second great from the 1970s.

1980 Initially viewed as mediocre by the experts, some of whom are now changing their minds.

1983 Full and powerful; may turn out to be excellent.

1985 Maturing quite rapidly; could be drinking within a few years.

1991 Declared by most shippers, though a few maintain the quality was not high enough.

1994 The most recent declaration, confidently expected to prove the best vintage year for a decade.

Graham's 1980 vintage

Choosing a Restaurant

THE RESTAURANTS in this guide have been selected for their good value, exceptional food or interesting location. This chart highlights some of the factors which may influence your choice. This chart lists the restaurants by areas within Lisbon. Restaurants in the Lisbon Coast area are listed separately on pages 132–33.

	CREDIT CARDS	LATE OPENING	OUTDOOR TABLES	GOOD WINE LIST

LISBON				

ALCÂNTARA: *Espalba Brasas* $$$
Doca de Santo Amaro, Armazém 12. **Map 3 A5.** (01-396 20 59.
A restaurant with architectural style and a light-hearted menu that includes daily specials and cocktails. Enjoy the live music in the summer. ● *lunch (Aug); Sun.* 🍴
— AE DC MC V · ■ ● ■

ALFAMA: *Hua-Ta-Li* $$
Rua dos Bacalhoeiros 109–115a. **Map 7 C4.** (01-887 91 70.
This is a large Chinese restaurant close to the docks that serves all the regular rice and noodle favourites. Fast and efficient service. 🍴
— · ■ · ·

ALFAMA: *Lautasco* $$
Beco do Azinhal 7 (off Rua de São Pedro). **Map 8 E4.** (01-886 01 73.
Rustically decorated with wooden panelling and wagon-wheel chandeliers, Lautasco specializes in typical Portuguese cuisine. ● *Sun; 20 Dec–15 Jan.*
— AE DC MC V · ■ ● ·

ALFAMA: *Sol Nascente* $$
Rua de São Tomé 86. **Map 8 D3.** (01-886 16 33.
On the main road up to the castle from Alfama, this restaurant has fine views over the Tagus. Try the seafood rice or the pork with clams. ● *Mon.* 🍴 ⅼ
— AE DC MC V · ■ ● ·

ALFAMA: *Senbor Leitão do Arco da Conceição* $$
Rua dos Bacalhoeiros 4. **Map 7 C4.** (01-886 98 60.
As its name suggests, this attractive restaurant with antiques around the walls specializes in *leitão* (roast sucking pig). ● *Sun.* 🎵 *Tue, Thu & Fri.*
— AE MC V · ■ · ·

ALFAMA: *Gargalbada Geral* $$$
Costa do Castelo 7. **Map 7 C3.** (01-886 14 10.
Part of the Chapitô artistic complex *(see p64)*, this cheerful restaurant with a bar and fine views over the harbour serves innovative cuisine. ● *Sun.* 🎵 ⅼ
— AE DC MC V · ■ ● ■

ALFAMA: *Casa do Leão* $$$$
Castelo de São Jorge. **Map 8 D3.** (01-888 01 54.
Beneath arched brick ceilings, inside part of Castelo de São Jorge *(see pp78–9)*, this restaurant offers superb service and excellent traditional Portuguese cuisine. Sit outside to enjoy the magnificent views. 🍴 🎵 *Wed–Fri.*
— AE DC MC V · · ● ■

ALFAMA: *Faz Figura* $$$$
Rua do Paraíso 15b. **Map 8 F2.** (01-886 89 81.
A smart restaurant, where panoramic views of the river and city can be enjoyed from the covered terrace. Specialities include *cataplana* dishes *(see p288)* and *picanha* (steak grilled over an open fire). ● *Sat lunch; Sun.* 🍴
— AE DC MC V · · ● ■

ALMADA: *Atira-te ao Rio* $$$
Cais do Jinjal 69–70. (01-275 13 80.
View Lisbon from the other bank of the Tagus and enjoy the restaurant's Brazilian specialities. Live samba music on Fridays and Saturdays. ● *Mon.* 🎵
— · ■ ● ·

BAIRRO ALTO: *Ali-A-Papa* $$$
Rua da Atalaia 95. **Map 4 F2.** (01-347 21 16.
This North African restaurant serves couscous and kebabs, and has a good selection of dishes for vegetarians. 🍴
— MC V · ■ · ·

BAIRRO ALTO: *Bota Alta* $$$
Travessa da Queimada 37. **Map 7 A3.** (01-342 79 59.
The "High Boot" is an attractive restaurant with original paintings on the walls. The menu consists of traditional Portuguese dishes. ● *Sat lunch; Sun.*
— AE DC MC V · · · ·

BAIRRO ALTO: *Casanostra* $$$
Travessa do Poço da Cidade 60. **Map 7 A3.** (01-342 59 31.
Within the green, white and black interior of this Italian restaurant you can choose from a six-page menu full of Italian delicacies. ● *Mon.* 🍴
— AE DC MC V · ■ · ·

Price categories are for a three-course meal for one with half a bottle of wine, including cover charge, service and VAT:

$ under 2,000$00
$$ 2,000–3,000$00
$$$ 3,000–4,500$00
$$$$ 4,500–6,000$00
$$$$$ over 6,000$00.

LATE OPENING
The kitchen stays open after 10pm, and you can usually have a meal up until at least 11pm.

OUTDOOR TABLES
Tables for eating outdoors, in a garden or on a balcony, often with a pleasant view.

GOOD WINE LIST
The restaurant will have a good selection of quality wines.

CREDIT CARDS
This indicates which of the major credit cards are accepted: *AE* American Express, *DC* Diners Club, *MC* MasterCard and *V* Visa.

	Credit Cards	Late Opening	Outdoor Tables	Good Wine List
BAIRRO ALTO: *El Último Tango* $$$ Rua Diário de Notícias 62. **Map** 7 A4. 01-342 03 41. In this Argentinian restaurant the most popular choice is meat grilled over an open fire. It also has interesting cocktails. ● *Sun; 2 weeks in Jun; 2 weeks in Oct.* ▤	MC V	■		■
BAIRRO ALTO: *Canto do Camões* $$$$ Travessa da Espera 38. **Map** 7 A4. 01-346 54 64. This small, tiled *fado (see pp66–7)* restaurant has traditional Portuguese food and international dishes with a Scandinavian influence. ● *Sun (Nov–Mar).* ▤ ♫ ♿	AE DC MC V	■		
BAIRRO ALTO: *Massima Culpa* $$$$ Rua da Atalaia 35–7. **Map** 4 F2. 01-342 01 21. This restaurant has a simple, uncomplicated decor with a very Italian atmosphere, and offers numerous antipasti and pasta dishes. ● *lunch; Wed.* ▤ ♿	AE DC MC V	■		■
BAIRRO ALTO: *Pap'Açorda* $$$$$ Rua da Atalaia 57. **Map** 4 F2. 01-346 48 11. Both Lisboetas and tourists come here for the *açorda de mariscos* (bread and seafood), served in a light dining room. The menu is traditional Portuguese with some novel touches. ● *Mon lunch; Sun; 2 weeks in Jul; 2 weeks in Oct.* ▤ ♿	AE DC MC V	■		■
BAIRRO ALTO: *Tavares* $$$$$ Rua da Misericórdia 37. **Map** 7 A4. 01-342 11 12. Lisbon's oldest restaurant, Tavares, dates from 1784. Its reputation is maintained with dishes such as breast of partridge on toast with *foie gras* and fillets of sea bass *au gratin* with prawn sauce. ● *Sat; Sun lunch.* ▤ ♿	AE DC MC V	■		■
BAIXA: *Casa do Alentejo* $$ Rua das Portas de Santo Antão 58. **Map** 7 A2. 01-346 92 31. Set in a fine 17th-century house, this restaurant specializes entirely in Alentejan food such as *açorda alentejana* (coriander and bread soup). ● *1–19 Aug.*				
BAIXA: *Paris* $$ Rua dos Sapateiros 126. **Map** 7 B4. 01-346 97 97. Open for nearly half a century, Paris offers a delicious mixture of Portuguese and Galician cuisine. Try the swordfish steak or the Alentejan pork. ▤ ♿	AE DC MC V			
BAIXA: *Lagosta Real* $$$ Rua das Portas de Santo Antão 37. **Map** 7 A2. 01-342 39 95. Fish, and particularly shellfish, is the order of the day here. Shellfish casserole, lobster stew and a grilled seafood platter are house specialities. ▤ ♿	AE DC MC V	■	●	■
BAIXA: *Ribadouro* $$$$ Rua do Salitre 2–12. **Map** 4 F1. 01-354 94 11. Popular with the locals who flood in for a drink after work, this restaurant is part café and part bar, and offers a tremendous shellfish menu. ▤	AE DC MC V	■		■
BAIXA: *Solar dos Presuntos* $$$$ Rua das Portas de Santo Antão 150. **Map** 7 A2. 01-342 43 53. An enticing window display of fish and shellfish draws diners inside. Caricatures of famous footballers adorn the walls. ● *Sun; 1 week in Jun; 1 week in Oct.* ▤	AE DC MC V	■		■
BAIXA: *Gambrinus* $$$$$ Rua das Portas de Santo Antão 23–5. **Map** 7 A2. 01-342 14 66. Renowned throughout Portugal, this is an exceptional and expensive restaurant. The service is impeccable, the cuisine delectable and the extensive wine list includes an array of vintage ports. ● *1 May.* ▤ ♿	AE DC MC V	■		■
BELÉM: *São Jerónimo* $$$$ Rua dos Jerónimos 12. **Map** 1 C4. 01-364 87 97. São Jerónimo is an elegant, spacious restaurant with 1930s decor. The excellent mixed menu of Portuguese and French cuisine includes skate in peach sauce and duck with nuts in wine sauce. ● *Sat lunch; Sun.* ▤	AE DC MC V			

Price categories are for a three-course meal for one with half a bottle of wine, including cover charge, service and VAT:

- $ under 2,000$00
- $$ 2,000–3,000$00
- $$$ 3,000–4,500$00
- $$$$ 4,500–6,000$00
- $$$$$ over 6,000$00.

Late Opening
The kitchen stays open after 10pm, and you can usually have a meal up until at least 11pm.

Outdoor Tables
Tables for eating outdoors, in a garden or on a balcony, often with a pleasant view.

Good Wine List
The restaurant will have a good selection of quality wines.

Credit Cards
This indicates which of the major credit cards are accepted: *AE* American Express, *DC* Diners Club, *MC* MasterCard and *V* Visa.

	Credit Cards	Late Opening	Outdoor Tables	Good Wine List
Belém: *Vela Latina* $$$$ Doca do Bom Sucesso. **Map 1 B5.** ☎ *01-301 71 18.* On the waterfront, this restaurant has a bar and terrace overlooking the Torre de Belém. The speciality is *cataplana rica do mar* (seafood). ● *Sun.* ▤ ♿	*AE DC MC V*	■	●	■
Belém: *O Nobre* $$$$$ Rua das Mercês 71a–b. **Map 2 D3.** ☎ *01-362 21 06.* Worth searching out on a day trip to Belém, O Nobre serves crab soup, game stew, partridge, fish with olives and roast pork with grapes. ● *Sat; Sun lunch.*	*AE MC V*	■		■
Campo Pequeno: *Chimarrão* $$$$ Campo Pequeno 79. **Map 5 C1.** ☎ *01-793 97 60.* This Brazilian restaurant specializes in dishes grilled on an open fire. Try *rodízio* (unlimited amount of grilled meat) with salad, rice and black beans. ▤ ♫	*AE DC MC V*	■		■
Campo Pequeno: *António Clara – Clube dos Empresários* $$$$$ Avenida da República 38. **Map 5 C1.** ☎ *01-796 63 80.* This wonderful old mansion offers a French-influenced menu in dining areas that were once individual rooms in the house. ● *Sun.* ▤	*AE DC MC V*			■
Chiado: *Tágide* $$$$$ Largo da Academia Nacional de Belas Artes 18–20. **Map 7 B5.** ☎ *01-342 07 20.* An elegant restaurant with 18th-century tiles, a 17th-century fountain and a superb view over the Tagus. Luxurious dishes include marinated salmon, baby octopus in red wine sauce and partridge in port sauce. ● *Sat lunch; Sun.* ▤	*AE DC MC V*			■
Entrecampos: *A Gondôla* $$$ Avenida de Berna 64. **Map 5 B2.** ☎ *01-797 04 26.* A Gondôla is a charming restaurant offering a wide choice of dishes ranging from stuffed trout to roast pork and Italian specialities. In the summer enjoy your meal in the pleasant surrounding gardens. ● *Sat eve; Sun.* ▤	*MC V*		●	■
Estefânia: *Espiral* $ Praça da Ilha do Faial 14a–b. **Map 6 D3.** ☎ *01-357 35 85.* This vegetarian restaurant, set in a pleasant square, has a plain interior but a large menu, with fresh juice drinks and organic wine. ● *1 Jan; 1 May.* ▤ ♫ *Fri & Sat.*	*AE DC MC V*			
Estefânia: *Clara Restaurante* $$$$$ Campo dos Mártires da Pátria 49. **Map 6 D5.** ☎ *01-885 30 53.* This is a spacious and luxurious restaurant in a green-tiled mansion, complete with garden terrace and a fountain. The excellent menu is predominantly French. ● *Sat lunch; Sun; 1–15 Aug.* ▤ ♫ ♿	*AE DC MC V*	■	●	■
Estrela: *Xêlê Bananas* $$$ Praça das Flores 29. **Map 4 E2.** ☎ *01-395 25 15.* This restaurant, near the parliament building, is decorated with artificial palms and bananas. It offers innovative combinations such as cod with bananas, *cherne* (stone bass) with apple, and roast pork with nectarine. ● *Sat lunch; Sun.* ▤	*AE DE MC V*	■		■
Estrela: *Conventual* $$$$ Praça das Flores 45. **Map 4 E2.** ☎ *01-60 91 96.* Decorated with religious antiques, this restaurant has an interesting menu that includes fried baby eels and ox tongue in egg sauce. ● *Sat lunch; Sun.* ▤ ♿	*AE DC MC V*	■		■
Graça: *Via Graça* $$$ Rua Damasceno Monteiro 9b. **Map 8 D1.** ☎ *01-887 08 30.* Via Graça offers some fine views of the castle and the Baixa, and well-presented traditional Portuguese cuisine. ● *Sat lunch; Sun.* ▤ ♿	*AE DC MC V?*	■		■
Lapa: *Café d'Arte* $ Rua das Janelas Verdes, Museu de Arte Antiga. **Map 4 D4.** ☎ *01-396 41 51.* An excellent opportunity to combine lunch with a museum trip in this fantastic riverside setting. ● *lunch (Jun–Aug); Mon; Tue.* ▤ ♿	*MC V*		●	

LAPA: *Picanha* $$$
Rua das Janelas Verdes 96. **Map 4** D4. 01-397 54 01.
Picanha sells one dish: *picanha*, which is rump steak grilled on an open fire, served with potatoes, rice, salad and beans. ● *Sat; Sun lunch.* 目 ᕯ

LAPA: *Restaurante Virtual* $$$ | AE / MC / DC / V
Rua da Esperança 100. **Map 4** E3. 01-397 64 51.
Located in a quiet street, this restaurant has great style. A relatively inexpensive menu includes duck supreme, monkfish and garlic prawns. ● *Sat; Sun.* 目 ᕯ

LAPA: *Sua Excelência o Conde* $$$$ | AE / MC / V
Rua do Conde 34. **Map 4** D3. 01-60 36 14.
The owner here can recite the menu in five languages. Classical Portuguese dishes served in a relaxed atmosphere. ● *Sat & Sun lunch; Wed; Sep.* 目 ᕯ

LAPA: *York House* $$$$ | AE / DC / MC / V
Rua das Janelas Verdes 32. **Map 4** D4. 01-396 24 35.
This delightful hotel restaurant has a varied menu. Sit inside and admire the tiled walls, or outside below a towering palm on the flower-laden terrace.

LAPA: *Embaixada Restaurant* $$$$$ | AE / DC / MC / V
Hotel da Lapa, Rua do Pau da Bandeira 4. **Map 3** C3. 01-395 00 05.
This restaurant is as refined and classical as the hotel. It offers a lunch buffet and Sunday brunch with a typical *cozido* (hearty meat casserole). 目 ᕯ

RATO: *Os Tibetanos* $$ | AE / MC / V
Rua do Salitre 117. **Map 4** F1. 01-314 20 38.
This vegetarian restaurant, in a Tibetan Buddhist centre, has much character and offers a tasty and inexpensive Tibetan menu. ● *Sun.* 目

RATO: *Casa da Comida* $$$$$ | AE / DC / MC / V
Travessa das Amoreiras 1. **Map 5** B5. 01-388 53 76.
A refined Lisbon restaurant with a charming patio, and an exquisite menu offering caviar, frogs' legs, goat, duck and pheasant. ● *Sat lunch; Sun.* 目 ᕯ

ROTUNDA: *Restaurante 33A* $$$$ | AE / DC / MC / V
Rua Alexandre Herculano 33. **Map 5** C5. 01-354 60 79.
Offering traditional Portuguese cuisine, this restaurant also has a small lounge with a country ambience and decor to match. ● *Sat lunch; Sun.* 目 🎵 ᕯ

ROTUNDA: *Pabe* $$$$$ | AE / DC / MC / V
Rua do Duque de Palmela 27a. **Map 5** C5. 01-353 74 84.
Pabe looks like a Tudor house and specializes in grilled dishes. A medieval atmosphere is accentuated by wooden-beamed ceilings and copper tables. 目 ᕯ

ROTUNDA: *O Terraço* $$$$$ | AE / DC / MC / V
Hotel Tivoli Lisboa, Avenida da Liberdade 185. **Map 4** F1. 01-353 01 81.
This delightful restaurant serves an innovative lunchtime special each day of the week. The dinner menu offers international dishes. 目 🎵 ᕯ

SALDANHA: *António* $$ | MC / V
Rua Tomás Ribeiro 63. **Map 5** C3. 01-353 87 80.
This restaurant is a good stop for lunch. The cooking is straightforward, and includes steak and fries and roast chicken. ● *eve; Sun.* 目

OLAIAS: *Navegadores* $$$ | AE / DC / MC / V
Altis Park Hotel, Avenida Engenheiro Arantes e Oliveira. 01-846 08 66.
Northeast of the city centre, Navegadores offers a terrific, reasonably priced buffet. Choose from salads, smoked fish and Portuguese specialities. 目 🎵 ᕯ

SALDANHA: *O Polícia* $$$ | MC / V
Rua Marquês Sá da Bandeira 112a. **Map 5** B3. 01-796 35 05.
A pleasant restaurant with an attractive bar, so named because the owner's father was a policeman. The menu changes daily. ● *Sat eve; Sun.* 目 🎵 ᕯ

SALDANHA: *Café Creme* $$$$ | AE / DC / MC / V
Avenida Conde de Valbom 52a. **Map 5** B2. 01-796 43 60.
An attractive, open and airy restaurant, Café Creme offers a wide choice of pastas, salads, cod, beef and grilled dishes. ● *Sat lunch; Sun.* 目 🎵 ᕯ

XABREGAS: *D'Avis* $$$ | DC / MC / V
Rua do Grilo 98. 01-868 13 54.
Specialities at this restaurant, located east of the city centre, include cod with coriander and *migas* (bread dish with spare ribs). ● *Sun; 2 weeks in Aug.* 目 ᕯ

	CREDIT CARDS	LATE OPENING	OUTDOOR TABLES	GOOD WINE LIST

Price categories are for a three-course meal for one with half a bottle of wine, including cover charge, service and VAT:

Ⓢ under 2,000$00
ⓈⓈ 2,000 – 3,000$00
ⓈⓈⓈ 3,000 – 4,500$00
ⓈⓈⓈⓈ 4,500 – 6,000$00
ⓈⓈⓈⓈⓈ over 6,000$00.

LATE OPENING
The kitchen stays open after 10pm, and you can usually have a meal up until at least 11pm.

OUTDOOR TABLES
Tables for eating outdoors, in a garden or on a balcony, often with a pleasant view.

GOOD WINE LIST
The restaurant will have a good selection of quality wines.

CREDIT CARDS
This indicates which of the major credit cards are accepted: *AE* American Express, *DC* Diners Club, *MC* MasterCard and *V* Visa.

THE LISBON COAST

		CREDIT CARDS	LATE OPENING	OUTDOOR TABLES	GOOD WINE LIST
CASCAIS: *Dom Manolo* Avenida Marginal 11. **Road map** B5. 【 01-483 11 26. A good-value mixed menu; the house speciality is *frango no churrasco* (spit-roast chicken). *Pastéis de bacalhau* (cod croquettes) are also good. ● *Jan.* 🍴	Ⓢ		■	●	
CASCAIS: *O Dragão* Rua Frederico Arouca 72. **Road map** B5. 【 01-486 86 31. This Chinese restaurant offers chicken with almonds, beef chop suey and sweet-and-sour pork. Glass doors overlook the beach. ● *Mon; 2 weeks in Nov.* 🍴	ⓈⓈ	AE DC MC V			
CASCAIS: *Estrela da India* Rua Freitas Reis 15b. **Road map** B5. 【 01-484 65 40. Some distance from the waterfront, this unpretentious Indian restaurant has a good choice of vegetarian dishes and a takeaway service. ● *Mon.* 🍴	ⓈⓈ	MC V		●	
CASCAIS: *Casa Velha* Avenida Valbom 1. **Road map** B5. 【 01-483 25 86. With a regional menu and decor that includes a boat in the dining room, Casa Velha also boasts a table always reserved for the president. ● *Wed.* 🍴 ♿	ⓈⓈⓈ	AE DC MC V	■	●	■
CASCAIS: *Novomar* Beco Torto 1. **Road map** B5. 【 01-484 42 96. A wide range of fish and shellfish dishes. Lookout for the house specialities, both for two people: *cataplana à moda de Cascais* (fish and shellfish steamed in their own juice) and *caldeirada à Novomar* (fresh fish stew). ● *Wed (Oct–Mar).* 🍴	ⓈⓈⓈ	AE DC MC V	■	●	■
CASCAIS: *Reijos* Rua Frederico Arouca 35. **Road map** B5. 【 01-483 03 11. Located in a busy shopping street, Reijos offers a good selection of grilled fish and shellfish. Also worth trying are the baked Virginia ham, the roast beef and the spare ribs with mushrooms and cream. ● *Sun; Dec.* 🍴	ⓈⓈⓈ	AE DC MC V	■	●	■
CASCAIS: *Eduardo's* Largo das Grutas 3. **Road map** B5. 【 01-483 19 01. Tucked away in a quiet corner, Eduardo's serves a mix of Belgian cuisine and Portuguese dishes, many of which are flambéed at the table. ● *Wed.*	ⓈⓈⓈⓈ	AE MC V	■	●	■
CASCAIS: *O Pescador* Rua das Flores 10b. **Road map** B5. 【 01-484 60 37. A well-known seaside restaurant, decorated with old boats, nets and pictures of famous people who have eaten here. Specializes in seafood. ● *Sun.* 🍴	ⓈⓈⓈⓈⓈ	AE MC V	■	●	■
ERICEIRA: *O Barco* Rua Capitão João Lopes 14. **Road map** B5. 【 061-627 59. O Barco has excellent sea views. The fish specialities include *feijoada de marisco* (seafood and bean stew) and seafood curry. ● *Thu; Dec.* 🍴	ⓈⓈⓈ	AE MC V			
ESTORIL: *Pinto's* Arcadas do Parque 18b. **Road map** B5. 【 01-468 72 47. Close to the Palácio Hotel, Pinto's is a mix of bar, cafeteria and restaurant. It serves pizzas and pastas, as well as a large selection of shellfish. 🍴	ⓈⓈ	AE DC MC V	■	●	
ESTORIL: *Four Seasons* Hotel Palácio Estoril, Rua do Parque. **Road map** B5. 【 01-468 04 00. Exposed beams and leather seats furnish this luxurious restaurant. Try the flambéed prawns with Pernod, cream and hollandaise sauce. 🍴 🎵 ♿	ⓈⓈⓈⓈⓈ	AE DC MC V			■
GUINCHO: *Estalagem Muchaxo* Praia do Guincho. **Road map** B5. 【 01-487 02 21. Overlooking Cabo da Roca, Muchaxo offers an extensive seafood menu. A popular dish is lobster in a tomato, cream and port sauce. 🍴 🎵 *Sat & Sun.* ♿	ⓈⓈⓈⓈ	AE DC MC V			■

GUINCHO: *Porto de Santa Maria* $$$$$
Estrada do Guincho. **Road map** B5. ☎ *01-487 02 40.*
This is one of the best seafood restaurants in the area. Choose your meal from the fish tanks and marble table where the best fish is displayed. ● *Mon.* ▤ ♿

AE MC DC V | | | ■

MONTE ESTORIL: *O Sinaleiro* $
Avenida de Sabóia 595. **Road map** B5. ☎ *01-468 54 39.*
O Sinaleiro serves excellent food and is popular with locals. Try *escalopes à Zíngara* (in Madeira wine sauce with cream). ● *Wed; 2 weeks in Apr & Oct.* ♿

AE MC V | | ● |

MONTE ESTORIL: *O Festival* $$$$
Avenida de Sabóia 515d. **Road map** B5. ☎ *01-468 85 63.*
This delightful restaurant serves traditional dishes with interesting touches. Try the duck à l'orange or the seafood casserole. ● *Mon; Tue lunch; Jan.* ▤ ♿

MC V | ■ | ● | ■

PAÇO D'ARCOS: *La Cocagne* $$$$
Avenida Marginal (Curva dos Pinheiros). **Road map** B5. ☎ *01-441 42 31.*
One of the best French restaurants in Portugal, La Cocagne has refined decor, impeccable service, exquisite dishes and magnificent views of the ocean. ▤ ♿

AE DC MC V | ■ | ● | ■

PALMELA: *Pousada de Palmela* $$$
Pousada de Palmela, Castelo de Palmela. **Road map** C5. ☎ *01-235 12 26.*
The converted refectory of the 15th-century monastery offers such delicacies as trout stuffed with smoked ham and pears in Muscatel wine. ▤ ♫ *Fri & Sat.* ♿

AE DC MC V | | ● | ■

PORTINHO DA ARRÁBIDA: *Beira-Mar* $$$
Portinho da Arrábida. **Road map** C5. ☎ *01-218 05 44.*
Enjoy specials such as *arroz de tamboril* (monkfish rice) and *arroz de marisco* (seafood rice) in this stunning seaside setting. ● *Wed (Oct–Mar); 15 Dec–15 Jan.* ♿

AE DC MC V | | ● | ■

QUELUZ: *Cozinha Velha* $$$$$
Largo Palácio Nacional de Queluz. **Road map** B5. ☎ *01-435 07 40.*
Set in the old kitchens of the Queluz Royal Palace, this spacious restaurant is famous for its typical Portuguese fare, such as pork with clams. ▤ ♫ ♿

AE DC MC V | | ● | ■

SESIMBRA: *Ribamar* $$
Avenida dos Náufragos 29. **Road map** C5. ☎ *01-223 48 53.*
Right next to the sea and offering fantastic views, Ribamar serves some unusual specialities; try fish with seaweed, or cream of sea-urchin soup. ▤ ♿

AE MC V | ■ | ● | ■

SETÚBAL: *Copa d'Ouro* $$
Rua João Soveral 12. **Road map** C5. ☎ *065-52 37 55.*
A superb fish menu here features *caldeirada à Setubalense* (seafood stew) and *cataplana de cherne* (stone bass steamed in its own juice). ● *Tue; Sep.* ▤

AE MC V | ■ | ● |

SETÚBAL: *Pousada de São Filipe* $$$
Pousada de São Filipe, Castelo de São Filipe. **Road map** C5. ☎ *01-848 46 02.*
This restaurant is part of a *pousada* that overlooks Setúbal and the Sado estuary. Its regional dishes include pumpkin cream soup and aromatic pork loin. ▤

AE DC MC V | | ● | ■

SINTRA: *Tulhas Bar* $$
Rua Gil Vicente 4–6. **Road map** B5. ☎ *01-923 23 78.*
This rustic restaurant, decorated with blue and yellow Sintra *azulejos*, serves superb traditional dishes such as veal steaks in Madeira sauce. ● *Wed.* ▤

AE DC MC V | | | ■

SINTRA: *Solar de São Pedro* $$$
Praça Dom Fernando II 12, São Pedro de Sintra. **Road map** B5. ☎ *01-923 18 60.*
French and Portuguese specialities, such as lobster crepes and *açorda de marisco* (a seafood bread dish), are served in this marketplace restaurant. ● *Wed.* ▤ ♿

AE MC V | | | ■

SINTRA: *Panorâmico* $$$$
Hotel Tivoli Sintra, Praça da República. **Road map** B5. ☎ *01-923 35 05.*
Overlooking the lush, verdant Sintra valley, this restaurant offers a different speciality as a main dish each evening, as well as a regular menu. ▤ ♿

AE DC MC V | | | ■

SINTRA: *Restaurante Palácio de Seteais* $$$$$
Avenida Barbosa du Bocage 8, Seteais. **Road map** B5. ☎ *01-923 32 00.*
Set in an 18th-century palace, which is now a hotel, this restaurant has a daily-changing menu of international and traditional Portuguese cuisine. ▤ ♫ ♿

AE DC MC V | | | ■

VILA FRESCA DE AZEITÃO: *Oh Manel!* $$
Largo Dr Teixeira 6a. **Road map** C5. ☎ *01-219 03 36.*
A family-run restaurant with a good-value menu. Specialities here are cod in cream sauce and *feijoada de gambas* (seafood and bean stew). ● *Sun; Oct.* ▤

MC V | | |

Cafés and Bars

T HE PORTUGUESE LOVE COFFEE, and an entire culture has developed around it *(see p121)*. Relaxing over a coffee and a pastry in a café is a way of life in Lisbon.

Some of the most famous and delicious pastries served include *travesseiros* (almond pastries) and *bolos de arroz* (rice cakes). Belém is famous for its *pastéis de nata*, custard pastries, while Sintra is renowned for its *queijadas*, cinnamon cheesecakes *(see p123)*. Most of the bars and restaurants are in Bairro Alto and along the riverfront, and most offer a pleasant view.

Evening drinking is equally popular, and Lisbon and its coast offer a range of night-time venues, from sophisticated bars serving wine and cocktails to brasher venues pumping out beer and live music.

On the Lisbon Coast, there are many bars in central Cascais and plenty of cafés along the seafront promenade. In the countryside, Sintra's cafés are famous for their fine selections of mouthwatering pastries.

LISBON

ALCÂNTARA: *Alcântara Café*
Rua Maria Luísa Holstein 15. **Map** 3 A4.
🄲 *01-363 71 76.*
Catering to a fashionable clientele, this bar/restaurant has sophisticated decor. Food is only served in the evenings. ▮

ALCÂNTARA: *Doca de Santo*
Doca de Santo Amaro. **Map** 3 A5.
🄲 *01-396 35 22.*
This is one of several warehouses along the marina which have been converted into a bar. It is a pleasant spot to enjoy an evening drink and has a wonderful view of the marina and river from the terrace. ▮ ▦

ALCÂNTARA: *Salsa Latina*
Gare Alcântara-Mar. **Map** 3 B4.
🄲 *01-395 05 55.*
This smart bar and restaurant with a terrace overlooking the river, caters to an affluent crowd. Salsa and Latin music are played most evenings. ▮ ▦ ♫

ALFAMA: *Bar Cerca Moura*
Largo das Portas do Sol 4. **Map** 8 D3.
🄲 *01-887 48 59.*
A pleasant place for a drink, the bar has a wonderful panoramic view of Alfama and the river below. Mainly serves snacks such as salads and finger food. ▦

ALFAMA: *Bar das Imagens*
Calçada Marquês de Tancos 1b.
Map 7 C3. 🄲 *01-888 46 36.*
This bar and restaurant serves delicious African dishes and has a superb view over Lisbon. The atmosphere is trendy but pleasantly relaxed. ▮ ▦ ♫

ALFAMA: *Chapitô*
Costa do Castelo 1–7. **Map** 7 C3.
🄲 *01-887 82 25.*
An arts centre with bar and restaurant, the Chapitô enjoys a view of the Alfama and the river. ▮ ▦

BAIRRO ALTO: *A Brasileira*
Rua Garrett 120. **Map** 7 A4.
🄲 *01-346 95 41.*
One of Lisbon's oldest and best-known cafés, A Brasileira was founded in 1895. It became a haunt for artists and poets. ▮ ▦

BAIRRO ALTO: *Bar Pintái*
Largo da Trindade 22. **Map** 7 A3.
🄲 *01-342 48 02.*
There is live Brazilian music daily in this large cavernous bar and plentiful *caipirinha*, a drink made of *cachaça* (sugar cane spirit), lemon, sugar and crushed ice. ♫

BAIRRO ALTO: *Café Pastelaria Benard*
Rua Garrett 104. **Map** 7 A4.
🄲 *01-347 31 33.*
This café serves an excellent selection of cakes and pastries. It also has a pleasant outdoor terrace. ▦

BAIRRO ALTO: *Café Rosso*
Galerias Garrett Rua Ivens 57.
Map 7 A4. 🄲 *01-343 26 71.*
This pleasant courtyard café serves a superb variety of sandwiches. The bar is open until 2am. ▦

BAIRRO ALTO: *Califórnia*
Rua Bernardino da Costa 39–41.
Map 7 A5. 🄲 *01-346 79 54.*
The Califórnia has a disco on the ground floor and a restaurant and café upstairs. Lively atmosphere. ▮ ♫

BAIRRO ALTO: *Casa da Loucos*
Rua da Barroca 30. **Map** 4 F2.
🄲 *01-342 71 49.*
A lively bar on two floors with wooden interiors, it serves some interesting cocktails.

BAIRRO ALTO: *Cervejaria Trindade*
Rua Nova da Trindade 20c.
Map 7 A4. 🄲 *01-342 35 06.*
A huge beer hall-style restaurant with beautiful *azulejo* panels, it specializes in seafood. ▮

BAIRRO ALTO: *Henry J. Beans*
Rua da Misericórdia 74. **Map** 7 A4.
🄲 *01-343 07 77.*
This international, trendy and fashionably decorated bar and restaurant serves cocktails and a wide variety of foreign beers. ▮

BAIRRO ALTO: *Mesón El Gordo Tapas Bar*
Rua São Boaventura 16–18.
Map 4 F2. 🄲 *01-342 42 66.*
This tastefully decorated bar and restaurant has a selection of 73 different *tapas*. Fine Portuguese wines are served by the glass. ▮

BAIRRO ALTO: *O'Gillins*
Rua dos Remolares 8–10.
Map 7 A5. 🄲 *01-342 18 99.*
This Irish-style pub has a wooden interior. The atmosphere is lively, especially on band nights. ▮ ♫ ♫

BAIRRO ALTO: *Pavilhão Chinês*
Rua Dom Pedro V 89. **Map** 4 F2.
🄲 *01-342 47 29.*
This eccentrically decorated bar is full of bizarre artefacts from all over the world and serves a long list of equally strange cocktails.

BAIRRO ALTO: *Rock City*
Rua Cintura do Porto de Lisboa 225.
🄲 *01-342 86 40.*
A huge atmospheric American bar, Rock City has live music and a restaurant. ▮ ▦ ♫

BAIRRO ALTO: *Solar do Vinho do Porto*
Rua de São Pedro de Alcântara 45.
Map 4 F2. 🄲 *01-347 57 07.*
Set in an old mansion *(see p54)*, this establishment serves over 300 different ports, including some fine vintages.

BAIXA: *Café Martinho da Arcada*
Praça do Comércio 3. **Map** 7 C5.
🄲 *01-886 62 13.*
A traditional Lisbon café under the arches of Praça do Comércio, it was once frequented by Fernando Pessoa *(see p53)*. ▦

BAIXA: *Café Nicola*
Praça Dom Pedro IV 26. **Map** 7 B3.
C 01-346 05 79.
One of Lisbon's oldest and most famous terraced cafés, this is a charming spot for breakfast, served by smart waiters. It is famous as the haunt of the satirical poet Manuel du Bocage (1765–1805). Wall paintings inside the café illustrate his life. **II** 🖼

BAIXA: *Chiadomel Restaurant Bar*
Alto do Elevador de Santa Justa.
Map 7 B3. **C** 01-346 95 98.
Situated at the top of the Santa Justa lift, the Chiadomel serves a variety of foreign beers, snacks and fine Portuguese cuisine. **II** 🖼

BAIXA: *Confeitaria Nacional*
Praça da Figueira 18b. **Map** 7 B3.
C 01-342 44 70.
This classic café has wonderful Art Nouveau decor. Pastries and cakes baked on the premises include good *pastéis de nata* and *bolo rei*.

BAIXA: *Ginginha*
Largo de São Domingos 8. **Map** 7 B3.
The smallest bar in Lisbon, off Rossio, is dedicated entirely to serving shots of *ginginha* (cherry liqueur) and nothing else.

BAIXA: *Pastelaria Suiça*
Praça Dom Pedro IV. **Map** 7 B3.
C 01-342 80 92.
A good place to have breakfast outdoors before a day of sightseeing, this café serves a wide variety of pastries. Overlooking the square, it is popular with Lisboetas stopping off on their way to work. **II** 🖼

BELÉM: *Antiga Casa dos Pastéis de Belém*
Rua de Belém 90. **Map** 1 C4.
C 01-363 74 23.
A trip to Belém is not complete without visiting this charming tiled café to sample its delicious *pastéis de nata* and excellent coffees.

CAMPO PEQUENO: *Galeto*
Avenida da República 14. **Map** 5 C1.
C 01-354 44 44.
A restaurant and snack bar on two floors, Galeto is a good place to visit for a late night snack as it serves food into the early hours.
II 🖼

CAMPO PEQUENO: *Versailles*
Avenida da República 15a. **Map** 5 C1.
C 01-354 63 40.
A well-known, turn-of-the-century restaurant café, the Versailles is ornately decorated in the Parisian style. Smartly attired waiters serve lunches, teas and dinners to a well-heeled clientele. **II**

GRAÇA: *Bar da Graça*
Travessa da Pereira 43. **Map** 8 E2.
C 01-886 37 44.
A trendy bar with live music, art exhibitions and theatre shows. Serves an excellent variety of foreign beers. 🎵

PENHA DA FRANÇA: *Portugália*
Avenida Almirante Reis 117.
Map 6 E5. **C** 01-314 00 02.
This is a classic beer-hall restaurant that is always popular. **II**

RATO: *Real Fábrica*
Rua da Escola Politécnica 275.
Map 4 E1. **C** 01-385 20 90.
A tastefully renovated old ceramic factory on two floors. The bar on the ground floor serves beers and snacks. There is a smart restaurant on the upper floor. **II** 🖼

THE LISBON COAST

CASCAIS: *Bar 24*
Rua Marquês Leal Pancada 24.
C 01-482 12 71.
One of the tiniest bars in town, with trendy decor, Bar 24 attracts a young crowd and can get quite packed. It offers a great range of alcoholic drinks.

CASCAIS: *Bar Trem Velho*
Alameda Duquesa de Palmela.
C 01-486 73 55.
This relaxed bar is in a converted train carriage next to Cascais train station. Serves snacks and litre mugs of beer called *girafas*. **II**

CASCAIS: *Beefeaters*
Rua Visconde da Luz 1a.
C 01-484 06 96.
This bar serves English ales, Dutch beer and Guinness among other beers. Also offers traditional British pub food. **II** 🖼

CASCAIS: *Casa do Largo*
Largo da Assunção 6.
C 01-486 70 14.
The Casa do Largo is a favourite haunt of the chic Cascais elite. Subdued atmosphere. **II**

CASCAIS: *John Bull*
Largo Luís de Camões 14.
C 01-483 33 19.
A British institution with wooden interiors on two floors, the John Bull serves a variety of local and foreign beers on tap. **II** 🖼

CASCAIS: *Le Tosca Bar*
Rua Marquês Leal Pancada 28a.
C 01-486 19 40.
Another small but lively bar on the same street as Bar 24, it tends to cater for a slightly older clientele. Small outside terrace. 🖼

ESTORIL: *Deck Bar*
Arcadas do Parque 21–22.
C 01-468 03 66.
One of Estoril's most popular terraced cafés, the Deck Bar is situated under arches opposite elegant gardens. Serves meals till 1am. Closed Mondays. **II** 🖼

ESTORIL: *Frolic*
Avenida Clotilde, Estoril.
C 01-468 12 19.
The Frolic is a pleasant bar, restaurant and café. It has a covered terrace and a relaxed atmosphere. Open until 2am on Friday and Saturday. **II** 🖼

ESTORIL: *Tamariz Caramba Bar*
Praia do Tamariz.
A lively, terraced bar overlooking Praia do Tamariz, the Tamariz Caramba Bar is a venue for live music every weekend. Serves salads, burgers and a variety of drinks including *caipirinhas* and jugs of *sangria*. Only open during summer months. 🖼 🎵

SINTRA: *Café da Natália*
Rua 1° de Dezembro 3–5, São Pedro de Sintra. **C** 01-923 56 79.
This old manor house, converted into an airy café, serves local food and wines. Dona Natália is known for her delicious quiches and crepes. Closed Thursdays and São Pedro market days. **II**

SINTRA: *Café Paris*
Largo Rainha Dona Amélia 32.
C 01-923 23 75.
An elegant, terraced café located on the main square opposite the Palácio Nacional, Café Paris is also open for lunches and dinners. **II** 🖼

SINTRA: *Casa da Sapa*
Volta do Duche 12. **C** 01-923 04 93.
A tiny cake shop, it has been baking its famous *queijadas* (cinnamon cheesecakes) since the mid-18th century. Lovely view of the Sintra valley. 🖼

SINTRA: *Pastelaria Piriquita*
Rua das Padarias 1–3.
C 01-923 06 26.
One of Sintra's oldest cafés, it is situated on a narrow street opposite the Palácio Nacional. Serves good *queijadas* and *travesseiros* (almond pastries).

SINTRA: *Restaurante Café Cintia*
Avenida Miguel Bombarda 49.
C 01-923 27 12.
A typical Portuguese café with a dark interior, it offers a glorious view of the Sintra valley and serves excellent *travesseiros*. **II** 🖼

Shops and Markets

Lisbon offers a wide variety of shops to the visitor, with its combination of elegant high street shops, flea markets and modern shopping centres. The cobbled streets of the Baixa, and the chic Chiado district have traditionally been Lisbon's main shopping areas, but now the new out-of-town shopping centres are becoming increasingly

Portuguese ceramic cockerel

popular. Numerous markets in Lisbon, Sintra and Cascais provide more adventurous shopping. If you are after something typically Portuguese, the handwoven tapestries and lacework are worth buying. Most of all, choose from a range of ceramics, such as *azulejos* or Vista Alegre porcelain. For wine lovers, Lisbon's wine merchants offer the best from all over the country.

A delicatessen in the Bairro Alto

Opening Hours

Traditional shopping hours are Monday to Friday 9am to 1pm and 3pm to 7pm, and Saturday 9am to 1pm.

However, in order to satisfy consumer demand, many shops, especially those in the Baixa, are now staying open during the lunch hour and on Saturday afternoons. Specialist shops such as hardware stores generally close for lunch at 12:30pm and reopen at 2:30pm. Shopping centres are open daily from 10am to midnight with most shops closing at 11pm. Convenience shops, such as the **Pão de Açucar Extra** chain, are open daily from 7am to 2am.

How to Pay

Most shops in Lisbon accept Visa and, to a lesser extent, American Express and MasterCard. Many smaller shops outside the main shopping areas will

not. An alternative is to obtain a cash advance with a credit card from one of the many Multibanco teller machines (ATMs). Note that these charge interest on the withdrawal from day one, in addition to a currency conversion fee.

Vat and Taxes

Non-European Union residents are exempt from IVA (Value Added Tax) in Portugal provided they remain in the country for no longer than 180 days. However, obtaining a rebate may be complicated in small shops or in areas less frequented by tourists. It is much simpler to buy in shops with a Tax Free sign outside.

To get your rebate, ask the shop assistant for an *Isençao na Exportaçao* form. This must then be presented to a customs

officer on your departure from Portugal. The original of the document will be returned to the vendor who is responsible for the reimbursement.

Shopping Centres

Modern shopping centres have become increasingly popular in Lisbon and most have been built recently. The **Amoreiras Shopping Centre** is a huge complex, with cinema, underground parking and a range of shops and restaurants.

Monumental Galerias is a smaller complex with four cinemas, a supermarket, restaurant and bar, clothes shops and underground parking. **Espaço Chiado**, a small centre, is in the Chiado district; its architecture features part of Lisbon's city wall.

Libersil is on two floors with parking, several restaurants and a variety of shops. **Cascaishopping** is the largest centre outside Lisbon, with 130 shops, seven cinemas, restaurants and parking; it is located between Sintra and Estoril. The largest of all, **Centro Colombo**, features not only shops and restaurants but also an amusement park.

The vast and modern Amoreiras Shopping Centre, home to international chain stores

Shoppers browsing among the bric-a-brac in the popular Feira da Ladra

MARKETS

THERE ARE numerous markets in Lisbon, of every variety. One of the most famous of the markets is **Feira da Ladra** (Thieves' Market), a flea market on the slopes of the Alfama district. Although some stalls just sell junk, some good bargains can be found among the wide array of second-hand clothes, bric-a-brac and general arts and crafts.

For more specialized markets, the **Feira Numismática** in Praça do Comércio has a fascinating selection of old Portuguese coins and notes. Just a little further down the river is **Mercado 24 de Julho**, an atmospheric fish and flower market close to Cais do Sodré.

Set in picturesque surroundings outside Lisbon, the **Feira de São Pedro**, in Sintra, is a wonderful market selling everything from new clothes and old bric-a-brac, to maturing cheeses and noisy livestock.

Along the coast, the **Feira de Cascais** has some good clothes bargains, as does the **Feira de Carcavelos**. Arrive early to beat the crowds.

Fresh fish for sale at the Mercado 24 de Julho

FOOD SHOPS

IT IS ALMOST IMPOSSIBLE to window shop in Lisbon's delicatessens *(charcutarias)* without buying. Lined with a vast array of mouth watering foods, from superb cheeses to tasty smoked meats and exquisite sweets, establishments such as **Charcutaria Brasil** are a must for all seasoned gourmets. Here you can buy almost all regional specialities, from cheeses such as *serra* and *ilhas* to wild game such as partidge. Smoked hams and spicy sausages are also popular. If you have a sweet tooth, try some delicious *ovos moles* (egg sweets) or an assortment of dried or crystallized fruits, including delicious Elvas plums.

Other good food shops include **Charcutaria Carvalho & Morais** and **Manteigaria Londrina**, which specializes in cheeses. **O Celeiro** is particularly good for sucking pig, smoked fish and the popular salted cod *(bacalhau).*

WINES AND SPIRITS

IN RECENT YEARS, the number of Portuguese wines has burgeoned and they have become popular internationally.

There is plenty of choice for the wine connoisseur, from lightly effervescent *vinhos verdes* and light rosés to more mature *tintos* (red wines) and fruity Muscatel dessert wines.

Fortified wines such as port and Madeira are widely available, and vary considerably in age and taste. Some of the most popular spirits and brandies on the market include Bagaceira Velha and Macieira, but these are very strong and not recommended for the faint-hearted. **Napoleão**, the best-known wine merchants in Lisbon, has outlets dotted all around the city, with its oldest shop in the Baixa. If you wish to buy port specifically, the best place to visit, though not the cheapest, is the **Solar do Vinho do Porto** (see p54), in the Bairro Alto, where you can sample some superb vintages before deciding what to buy. Alternatively, visit the cellars of **J.M. da Fonseca** in Azeitão, where you can taste and buy numerous different wines.

MUSIC AND MULTIMEDIA

THE MUSIC SCENE in Portugal has exploded recently and Portuguese rock music, which is influenced by African music from the former colonies has found international fame.

Virgin Megastore, the second largest of the chain in mainland Europe, is Lisbon's best equipped music store. Apart from CDs and cassettes, there are magazines, computer games, laser-discs, CD-ROMs, videos and T-shirts also on sale. **Valentim de Carvalho**, another music store, has outlets all over town with its main store in Rossio. Both stores stock a wide variety of Portuguese music, from the latest rock hits to more traditional *fado* and folk music.

Frontage of Livraria Bertrand, one of Lisbon's oldest bookshops

BOOKSHOPS

PORTUGAL ENJOYS a great literary tradition with a range of authors, past and present, such as Luís de Camões, Fernando Pessoa and José Saramago. Translated versions of their works are available in most large bookshops.

Three of Lisbon's oldest bookshops include **Livraria Bertrand** and **Livraria Portugal**, both in the Chiado, and **Livraria Bucholz** near Avenida da Liberdade. Here you can find a wide selection of both English and foreign-language books, from travel guides to dictionaries as well as paperback fiction novels and hardbacks on a range of subjects including art, history and literature.

For an interesting selection of second-hand books in both English and other languages, try visiting **Livraria Artes e Letras**, in Bairro Alto, which stocks a good range.

Terracotta ware for sale in Setúbal

CLOTHES

L ISBON has branches of many international chainstores, such as Marks and Spencer's and Benetton, most of which are in the city's purpose built shopping centres *(see p136)*. Amongst the Portuguese stores are a number of exclusive shops, including **Rosa & Teixeira**, a well-established tailors stocking classic menswear. **Loja das Meias** is a ladies' clothing store with several outlets in Lisbon. For something special, **Ana Salazar** is one of Portugal's most famous designers, but her prices are high.

CERAMICS

P ORTUGAL'S CERAMICS are famous for their quality and variety. In Lisbon you can find everything, from delicate porcelain to rustic terracotta, and from tiles to tableware.

The very fine **Vista Alegre** porcelain tableware is internationally known. Also famous are the hand-painted ceramics, including tiles from **Viúva Lamego**, **Sant'Anna** and **Cerâmica Artística de Carcavelos**. Known as *azulejos*, glazed tiles have long been used in Portugal to brighten up buildings. They are usually sold as complete paintings, 16 or 25 square in size. In Cascais, **Ceramicarte** is one of the largest ceramic centres. Perhaps the most ubiquitous pottery originates from Barcelos, famous for its decoratively painted cockerel which has become the unofficial national symbol.

REGIONAL CRAFTS

P ORTUGAL HAS a rich history of fine regional craftwork *(artesanato)*, in particular lace, wool, silver and gold items. There are plenty of handicraft and gift shops in the Restauradores and Rossio areas of Lisbon, though these can be a little touristy. **Arte Rustica**, in the Baixa, is excellent for genuine crafts.

Regionália, in Estoril, and **Sintra Bazar** in central Sintra, are also both good for arts. Visit the **Estoril Craft Fair** (July–August) for a wide variety of crafts, where artisans from all over Portugal come to exhibit their work. **Casa Quintão** specializes in fine hand-woven carpets and tapestries. Cork carvings and pottery can be found at **Santos Ofícios**. For more unusual souvenirs, try **Mercearia Liberdade**, which stocks sculptures carved from granite and toys made out of tin.

Mercearia Liberdade, one of Lisbon's best craft shops

ANTIQUES

A NTIQUES OFTEN TEND to be overpriced in Portugal, especially in Lisbon where the shops are mostly geared to a fairly up-market clientele. You will generally find better value in towns outside the city. Look for shops that are members of APA *(Associação Portuguesa de Antiquários)*, often indicated by a sign in the shop window.

The majority of Lisbon's antique shops, such as **Antiguidádes Moncada** and **Brique-à-Braque de São Bento**, are located in Rua Dom Pedro V, at the top of the Bairro Alto, in Rua de São Bento, by the Parliament building, and around the cathedral, in the Alfama. There are numerous religious artefacts at **Ricardo Hogan**, and **Solar** specializes in 16th–20th-century tiles *(azulejos)*.

Beautiful prints (known as *gravuras*), sold at various second-hand bookshops in the Bairro Alto, are usually good value for money. **Livraria Olisipo** stocks books and also old prints of landscapes, fauna and maps. For a good range of quality antiques, it is worth visiting the auctions held at **Cabral Moncada Leilões** (every Monday evening) and also the Antiques Fair, which is held in Lisbon annually during April.

SIZE CHART

Australia uses both British and American systems.

Women's dresses, coats and skirts

Portuguese	34	36	38	40	42	44	46
British	8	10	12	14	16	18	20
American	6	8	10	12	14	16	18

Women's shoes

Portuguese	36	37	38	39	40	41
British	3	4	5	6	7	8
American	5	6	7	8	9	10

Men's suits

Portuguese	44	46	48	50	52	54	56	58
British	34	36	38	40	42	44	46	48
American	34	36	38	40	42	44	46	48

Men's shirts

Portuguese	36	38	39	41	42	43	44	45
British	14	15	15½	16	16½	17	17½	18
American	14	15	15½	16	16½	17	17½	18

Men's shoes

Portuguese	39	40	41	42	43	44	45	46
British	6	7	7½	8	9	10	11	12
American	7	7½	8	8½	9½	10½	11	11½

DIRECTORY

SHOPPING CENTRES

Amoreiras
Avenida Eng. Duarte Pacheco, Amoreiras. **Map** 5 A5.
█ 01-381 02 00.

Cascaishopping
Estrada Nacional 9, Alcabideche - Estoril.
█ 01-460 06 46.

Centro Colombo
Avenida Lusiada Letras CC.
█ 01-716 02 50.

Espaçào Chiado
Rua da Misericórdia, 12–20 r/c, Chiado.
Map 7 A4.
█ 01-347 25 78.

Libersil
Avenida da Liberdade 38, Liberdade. **Map** 7 A2.
█ 01-346 77 46.

Monumental Galerias
Avenida Fontes Pereira de Melo 51e, Saldanha.
Map 5 C4.
█ 01-315 05 31.

MARKETS

Feira de Carcavelos
Carcavelos.

Feira de Cascais
Cascais.

Feira da Ladra
Alfama. **Map** 8 E3.

Feira Numismatica
Praça do Comércio.
Map 7 C5.

Feira de São Pedro
Sintra.

Mercado 24 de Julho
Avenida 24 de Julho, Cais do Sodré. **Map** 4 F4.

FOOD SHOPS

Charcutaria Brasil
Rua Alexandre Herculano 84–9, Rato. **Map** 5 C5.
█ 01-388 56 44.

Charcutaria Carvalho & Morais
Avenida João XXI 54, Arieiro. **Map** 6 E1.
█ 01-797 34 12.

Manteigaria Londrina
Rua das Portas de Santo Antão 53–5, Rossio. **Map** 7 A2.
█ 01-3 42 74 48.

O Celeiro
Rua 1º de Dezembro 67–83, Rossio. **Map** 7 B3.
█ 01-342 74 95.

WINES AND SPIRITS

J.M. da Fonseca
Vila Nogueira de Azeitão, Azeitão.
█ 01-218 02 27.

Napoleão
Rua dos Fanqueiros 70, Baixa. **Map** 7 C4.
█ 01-887 20 42.

Solar do Vinho do Porto
Rua São Pedro de Alcântara 45 r/c, Bairro Alto. **Map** 7 A3.
█ 01-347 57 07.

MUSIC AND MULTIMEDIA

Valentim de Carvalho
Praça Dom Pedro IV 59.
Map 4 F2.
█ 01-342 58 95.

Virgin Megastore
Praça dos Restauradores 18–22, Restauradores.
Map 7 A2.
█ 01-346 01 48.

BOOKSHOPS

Livraria Artes e Letras
Largo Trindade Coelho 3, Bairro Alto. **Map** 7 A3.
█ 01-347 16 75.

Livraria Bertrand
Rua Garrett 73, Chiado. **Map** 7 A4.
█ 01-342 19 41.

Livraria Bucholz
Rua Duque de Palmela 4, Rotunda. **Map** 5 C5.
█ 01-315 73 58.

Livraria Portugal
Rua do Carmo 70–74, Chiado. **Map** 7 B4.
█ 01-347 49 82.

CLOTHES

Ana Salazar
Avenida de Roma 16f, Alvalade. **Map** 6 D1.
█ 01-848 67 99.

Loja das Meias
Praça Dom Pedro IV 1, Rossio. **Map** 7 B3.
█ 01-347 41 81.

Rosa & Teixeira
Avenida da Liberdade 204, Liberdade. **Map** 5 C5.
█ 01-311 03 50.

CERAMICS

Ceramicarte
Largo da Assunção 3–4, Cascais.
█ 01-484 01 70.

Cerâmica Artistica de Carcavelos
Avenida Loureiro 47b, Carcavelos.
█ 01-456 32 67.

Sant'Anna
Rua do Alecrim 95, Chiado. **Map** 7 A5.
█ 01-347 67 46.

Vista Alegre
Largo do Chiado 18, Chiado. **Map** 7 A4.
█ 01-346 14 01.

Viúva Lamego
Calçada do Sacramento 29, Chiado. **Map** 7 B4.
█ 01-346 96 42.

REGIONAL CRAFTS

Arte Rustica
Rua Áurea 246–8, Baixa. **Map** 7 B4.
█ 01-342 11 27.

Casa Quintão
Rua do Alecrim 113–15, Chiado. **Map** 7 A4.
█ 01-346 36 86.

Mercearia Liberdade
Avenida da Liberdade 207, Liberdade. **Map** 4 F1.
█ 01-354 70 46.

Regionália
Arcadas do Parque 27, Estoril.
█ 01-468 16 19.

Santos Ofícios
Rua da Madalena 87, Baixa. **Map** 7 C4
█ 01-887 20 31.

Sintra Bazar
Praça da República 37, Sintra.
█ 01-923 05 14.

ANTIQUES

Antiguidades Moncada
Rua Dom Pedro V 34, Bairro Alto. **Map** 4 F2.
█ 01-346 82 95.

Brique-à-Braque de São Bento
Rua São Bento 542, São Bento. **Map** 4 E1.
█ 01-60 70 01.

Cabral Moncada Leilões
Praça Principe Real 33, Principe Real. **Map** 4 F1.
█ 01-342 89 68.

Livraria Olisipo
Largo Trindade Coelho 7–8, Bairro Alto. **Map** 7 A3.
█ 01-346 27 71.

Ricardo Hogan
Rua São Bento 281, São Bento. **Map** 4 E1.
█ 01-395 41 02.

Solar
Rua Dom Pedro V 68–70, Bairro Alto. **Map** 4 F2.
█ 01-346 27 71.

ENTERTAINMENT IN LISBON

THOUGH QUITE SMALL compared to other European capitals, Lisbon boasts an outstanding cultural calendar. Chosen as Cultural Capital of Europe 1994, the city hosts both modern and traditional events from classical music, ballet and opera to street festivals, fairs and bullfights.

Pop and rock concerts are held all year round and traditional *fado (see pp142–3)* is widely performed. Football fans can spend an afternoon watching Benfica or Sporting. The city also offers excellent late-night entertainment, focused on lively, fashionable clubs and bars along the waterfront and in the Bairro Alto.

BOOKING TICKETS

TICKETS CAN BE reserved by phoning the Agência de Bilhetes para Espectáculos Públicos (**ABEP**). Pay in cash when you collect them from the kiosk. Cinemas and theatres will not take phone or credit card bookings – only the major cultural centres do.

ABEP kiosk selling tickets on Praça dos Restauradores

LISTINGS MAGAZINES

PREVIEWS of forthcoming events and listings of bars and clubs appear in several magazines in Lisbon. English-language publications on offer include the monthly *What's On* and *LISBOAem,* which are available free from tourist offices. Also available free, but in Portuguese, is the monthly *Agenda Cultural.*

CINEMA AND THEATRE

MOVIE-GOERS are extremely well served in Lisbon. Films are shown in their original language with subtitles in Portuguese, and tickets are inexpensive. There are plenty of cinemas to choose from, and the futuristic **Amoreiras Shopping Centre** *(see p74)* has a multiplex centre with ten screens showing all the latest Hollywood releases. Cult movies and international art-house films can be seen at the

Cinemateca Portuguesa, which has a comprehensive monthly film calendar. Copies are available at the box office or tourist office. Most cinemas offer reductions on Mondays.

Theatre lovers can enjoy Portuguese and foreign language plays at the **Teatro Nacional Dona Maria II** and the **Teatro da Trindade**. For a slightly less formal but entertaining show try **Chapitô** in the Alfama quarter, an arts centre with splendid river views which stages open-air performances.

CLASSICAL MUSIC, OPERA AND DANCE

LISBON'S TOP CULTURAL centres are the modern **Centro Cultural de Belém** *(see p68)* and the **Fundação Calouste Gulbenkian** *(see pp76–9).* They host a variety of national and international events including concerts, ballet and opera. A calendar of events for each venue is available from the box office or the tourist office. Operas and classical concerts also take place at the **Teatro Nacional de São Carlos** *(see p53)* and the Coliseu dos Recreios.

Clowns performing at Chapitô, Alfama's informal arts centre

WORLD MUSIC, JAZZ, FOLK AND ROCK

THOUGH LISBON'S musical soul is *fado*, the city also swings to a variety of sounds from the rhythms of Africa and South America through contemporary jazz to heavy rock. For Brazilian music, try **Pé Sujo**, while **B. Leza** and **Ritz Clube** are popular for African music.

Every summer the Fundação Calouste Gulbenkian puts on the International Jazz Festival. The **Hot Clube** is a favourite

The house orchestra playing at the Fundação Calouste Gulbenkian

Brazilian musician at Pé Sujo

jazz spot on a smaller scale, and it also plays host to a variety of popular folk singers and bands, such as Fausto and Sérgio Godinho.

Top pop and rock bands play at large venues such as the **Coliseu dos Recreios** as well as in stadiums. Live rock is also on offer at bars such as **Johnny Guitar** and **Anos Sessenta**.

NIGHTCLUBS

FOR NIGHT-TIME DRINKING the most fashionable clubs and bars are largely concentrated in two areas of the city: the traditional nightspot of Bairro Alto and the riverside Avenida 24 de Julho. There are also bars underneath Ponte 25 de Abril. Bairro Alto has a range of popular and fashionable clubs and discotheques, including **Portas Largas**, **Três Pastorinhos** and the hip boogie club **Frágil**.

Avenida 24 de Julho is Lisbon's fastest-growing after-hours destination, with larger bars and nightclubs in converted warehouses and other attractive riverside buildings. The young and chic frequent fashionable **Kapital**, a nightclub on three floors with a rooftop veranda. Next door,

Kremlin is a lively haunt for fans of techno music, while **Plateau** is geared towards those clubbers seeking a heavy rock venue.

Details of recommended bars in Lisbon, Estoril, Cascais and Sintra can be found on pages 134–5.

SPORTS

MOST SPORTING action takes place outside the city, but Lisbon has two football teams, Benfica and Sporting. One or other plays at home almost every Sunday, Benfica at **Estádio da Luz**, and Sporting at **Estádio José Alvalade**.

Bullfights are held from April to October in Lisbon's Campo Pequeno *(see p80)*. Ticket prices vary depending on whether you sit in *sol* or *sombra* (sun or shade).

DIRECTORY

BOOKING TICKETS

ABEP
Praça dos Restauradores.
Map 7 A2.
☎ 01-347 58 24.

CINEMA AND THEATRE

Amoreiras Shopping Centre
Avenida Engenheiro Duarte Pacheco.
Map 5 A5.
☎ 01-381 02 00.

Chapitô
Costa do Castelo 1–7.
Map 7 C3.
☎ 01-886 14 10.

Cinemateca Portuguesa
Rua Barata Salgueiro 39.
Map 5 C5.
☎ 01-354 62 79.

Teatro da Trindade
Rua Nova da Trindade 9
Map 7 A3.
☎ 01-342 32 00.

Teatro Nacional Dona Maria II
Praça Dom Pedro IV.
Map 7 B3.
☎ 01-342 84 49.

CLASSICAL MUSIC, OPERA AND DANCE

Centro Cultural de Belém
Praça do Império.
Map 1 C5.
☎ 01-361 24 44.

Fundação Calouste Gulbenkian
Avenida de Berna 45.
Map 5 B2.
☎ 01-793 51 31.

Teatro Nacional de São Carlos
Rua Serpa Pinto 9.
Map 7 A4.
☎ 01-346 59 14.

WORLD MUSIC, JAZZ, FOLK AND ROCK

Anos Sessenta
Largo do Terreirinho 21.
Map 7 C2.
☎ 01-887 34 44.

B. Leza
Largo do Conde Barão 50.
Map 4 E3.
☎ 01-396 37 35.

Coliseu dos Recreios
Rua das Portas de Santo Antão 96.
Map 7 A2.
☎ 01-343 16 77.

Hot Clube
Praça da Alegria 39.
Map 4 F1.
☎ 01-346 73 69.

Johnny Guitar
Calçada Marquês de Abrantes 72.
Map 4 E3.
☎ 01-396 04 15.

Pé Sujo
Largo de S. Martinho 6–7.
Map 8 D4.
☎ 01-886 56 29.

Ritz Clube
Rua da Glória 57.
Map 4 F1.
☎ 01-342 51 40.

NIGHTCLUBS

Frágil
Rua da Atalaia 128.
Map 4 F2.
☎ 01-346 95 78.

Kapital
Avenida 24 de Julho 68.
Map 4 E3.
☎ 01-395 59 63.

Kremlin
Escadinhas da Praia 5.
Map 4 D3.
☎ 01- 60 87 68.

Plateau
Escadinhas da Praia 3.
Map 4 D3.
☎ 01-39 51 16.

Portas Largas
Rua da Atalaia 105.
Map 4 F2.
☎ 01-346 63 79.

Três Pastorinhos
Rua da Barroca 111.
Map 4 F2.
☎ 01-346 43 01.

SPORTS

Estádio José Alvalade
Alameda das Linhas de Torres.
☎ 01-759 94 59.

Estádio da Luz
Avenida General Norton Matos.
☎ 01-726 61 29.

Fado: the Music of Lisbon

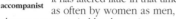

LIKE THE BLUES, *fado* is an expression of longing and sorrow. Literally meaning "fate", the term may be applied to an individual song as well as the genre itself. The music owes much to the concept known as *saudade*, meaning a longing both for what has been lost, and for what has never been attained, which perhaps accounts for its emotional power. The people of Lisbon have nurtured this poignant music in back-street cafés and restaurants for over 150 years, and it has altered little in that time. It is sung as often by women as men, always accompanied by the *guitarra* and *viola* (acoustic guitar). *Fado* from Coimbra has developed its own distinctive, light-hearted style.

A *guitarra* accompanist

A graphic depiction of the music's low-life associations from the 1920s

Argentina Santos is perhaps the leading traditional singer of today. All female *fadistas* wear a black shawl in memory of Maria Severa.

The *guitarrista* plays the melody and will occasionally perform a solo instrumental piece.

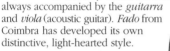

Maria Severa (1810–36) was the first great fadista *and the subject of the first Portuguese sound film in 1931. Her scandalous life and early death are pivotal to* fado *history, and her spiritual influence has been enormous, inspiring* fados, *poems, novels and plays.*

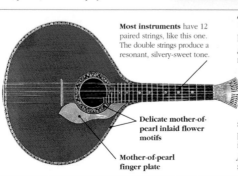

Most instruments have 12 paired strings, like this one. The double strings produce a resonant, silvery-sweet tone.

Delicate mother-of-pearl inlaid flower motifs

Mother-of-pearl finger plate

THE GUITARRA

Peculiar to Portuguese culture, the *guitarra* is a flat-backed instrument shaped like a mandolin, with eight, ten or twelve strings, arranged in pairs. It has evolved from a simple 19th-century design into a finely decorated piece, sometimes inlaid with mother-of-pearl. The sound of the *guitarra* is an essential ingredient of a good *fado*, echoing and enhancing the singer's melody line.

Alfredo Duarte (1891–1982) *was a renowned writer of* fado *lyrics dealing with love, death, longing, tragedy and triumph. Affectionately known as* O Marceneiro *(the master carpenter) because of his skill as a joiner, he is still revered and his work widely performed.*

All kinds of themes may occur in fado. *This song of 1910, for example, celebrates the dawning of the liberal republic. Such songsheets remained a favoured means of dissemination, even after the first records were made in 1904.*

A cultural icon for the Portuguese, Amália Rodrigues (born 1921) has been the leading exponent of fado for over 50 years. She crystallized the music's style in the postwar years, and made it known around the world.

The *viola* provides rhythm accompaniment, but the player will never take a solo.

The music has long inspired great writers and painters. O Fado (1910) by José Malhôa (1855–1933) shows it in an intimate setting with the fadista captivating his listener. The air of abandonment underlines the earthiness of many of the songs.

THE FADO HOUSE

Lisbon's best *fado* houses, such as the famous Parreirinha de Alfama, which belongs to Argentina Santos *(shown above)*, are run by the *fadistas* themselves for love of the music, not as a tourist attraction. They continue the tradition that began originally in the Alfama, whereby cafés and restaurants gave the music of the people a home. Such authentic venues still provide a good meal and a sense of history as well as entertainment. The oldest is Luso, which has been in existence since the 1930s.

WHERE TO ENJOY FADO IN LISBON

Any of these establishments will offer you the essential ingredients of Lisbon's nightlife: good food, wine and music to stir the emotions.

Adega Machado
Rua do Norte 91.
Map 7 A3. 01-392 87 13.

Lisboa à Noite
Rua das Gáveas 69.
Map 7 A3. 01-396 26 03.

Luso
Travessa da Queimada 10.
Map 7 A3. 01-342 22 81.

Parreirinha de Alfama
Beco do Espírito Santo 1.
Map 7 E4. 01-886 82 09.

Senhor Vinho
Rua do Meio à Lapa.
Map 4 D3. 01-397 26 81.

A Severa
Rua das Gáveas 51.
Map 7 A4. 01-342 83 14.

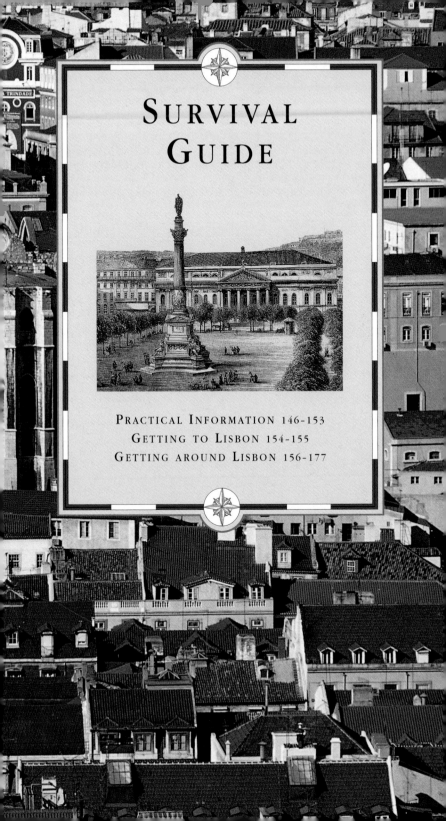

Survival
Guide

PRACTICAL INFORMATION

L ISBON IS becoming increasingly popular as a tourist destination. The best time to visit is in the spring or autumn when the weather is at its best. Lisbon and large towns in the area all have *Postos de Turismo* (tourist information offices) which will provide information about the immediate region,

Tourist information sign

town plans, maps and details on current events as well as accommodation. Check that sights are open before you visit, although most museums are open from Tuesday to Sunday. Banks are open from Monday to Friday and the ATM machines can be used 24 hours a day and accept many international credit and debit cards.

CUSTOMS

T HERE ARE no limits to the amount of goods visitors can import from one EU country to another, provided that tax has been paid in the country of purchase. Duty-free allowances for alcohol, perfumes and tobacco are the same as in other EU countries. Consulates will provide visitors with information on customs regulations. For more information on taxes see page 136.

VISAS

N ATIONALS of the European Union, Australia and New Zealand are permitted to stay up to 90 days without a visa as long as they hold a valid passport or identity card. American and Canadian nationals may stay up to 60 days in Lisbon with a visa.

TOURIST INFORMATION

T HE TOURIST OFFICES' opening hours are generally the same as those of local shops. Offices in the centre of Lisbon

have been marked on the Street Finder *(see pp170–77).* Offices may also be found at Portela airport and at Santa Apolónia station. Addresses of offices in the Lisbon Coast area are given in the information at the top of each sight entry. Portuguese tourist offices abroad can provide you with helpful information before you travel that will help you plan your holiday.

Museum tickets

ADMISSION CHARGES

M OST MUSEUMS and monuments, except churches, charge an entrance fee, which often increases in the summer. Entry is often free on Sunday mornings and public holidays. Pensioners and children under 14 are entitled to a 40 per cent discount. Visitors under 26 with a *Cartão Jóvem* (youth card) or an ISIC card (international student identity card) are entitled to half-price entrance. Visitors to Lisbon can buy a LISBOA card, which

permits free entry to Lisbon's state museums and also free travel on all the city's public transport *(see p158).*

OPENING TIMES

M OST MUSEUMS open from 10am–5pm daily with many closing for lunch from 12–2pm or from 12:30–2:30pm. Smaller museums, or privately-owned ones, may have different opening times. Note that state-run museums and some sights close on Mondays and public holidays. Major churches are open all day although some may close from 12–4pm. Smaller ones may only open for services.

FACILITIES FOR THE DISABLED

D ISABLED FACILITIES in Lisbon are slowly improving. Adapted toilets are available at airports and the main stations and reserved car-parking is now more evident. Ramps and lifts are gradually being installed in public places.

LANGUAGE

P ORTUGUESE is very similar to Spanish, so if you are familiar with Spanish you should have little difficulty reading Portuguese. However, the pronunciation of the language is very different. The Portuguese are proud of their language, and do not take kindly to being addressed in Spanish. A phrasebook containing useful words and phrases is on pages 191–2.

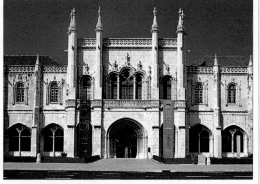

Façade of the Museu Nacional de Arqueologia in Lisbon

◁ **View across Lisbon's skyline, with the Elevador de Santa Justa in the foreground**

Respectably dressed Portuguese leaving church

ETIQUETTE

Tʜᴇ ᴘᴏʀᴛᴜɢᴜᴇsᴇ appreciate efforts by visitors, however small, to communicate in their language. A simple *bom-dia* (good day) will work wonders and earn a grateful smile. Generally open and friendly, the Portuguese are unerringly polite. It is considered courteous to address people as *senhor* or *senhora* and you are expected to shake hands when introduced to anyone, although a kiss on each cheek between females and among the young is more commonplace. Dress is relaxed but decorum should be observed especially when visiting churches; arms and legs should be covered.

PORTUGUESE TIME

Pᴏʀᴛᴜɢᴀʟ follows Britain in adopting Greenwich Mean Time (GMT) in winter and moving the clocks forward one hour in summer. The 24-hour clock is commonly used.

ELECTRICITY

Vᴏʟᴛᴀɢᴇ ɪɴ ᴘᴏʀᴛᴜɢᴀʟ is 220 volts. Plugs have two round pins and most hotel bathrooms offer built-in adaptors for shavers only.

NEWSPAPERS, RADIO AND TELEVISION

Portuguese newspapers

Eɴɢʟɪsʜ-ʟᴀɴɢᴜᴀɢᴇ newspapers printed in Europe are widely available on the day of publication. Various other European newspapers and periodicals are on sale the day after home publication. Portuguese daily newspapers include *Diário de Notícias* and *Público*. The *Anglo-Portuguese News* (APN) is Lisbon's main English-language publication. Published weekly, it provides information for the British expatriates in Lisbon. There are two state-owned television channels in Portugal, RTP1 and RTP2, and two privately-owned channels, SIC and TVI. Satellite television is also available, broadcasting in several languages. Listings of television programmes broadcast in English can be found in the *Anglo-Portuguese News*. Portuguese radio has programmes in English, French and German with information for tourists, but these only operate during the summer.

Newspaper stall in the Café Brasiliera (p53)

CONVERSION CHART

Imperial to Metric
1 inch = 2.54 centimetres
1 foot = 30 centimetres
1 mile = 1.6 kilometres
1 ounce = 28 grams
1 pound = 454 grams
1 pint = 0.6 litres
1 gallon = 4.6 litres

Metric to Imperial
1 millimetre = 0.04 inches
1 centimetre = 0.4 inches
1 metre = 3 feet 3 inches
1 kilometre = 0.6 miles
1 gram = 0.04 ounces
1 kilogram = 2.2 pounds
1 litre = 1.8 pints

DIRECTORY

EMBASSIES AND CONSULATES

Australia
Rua Marquês de Sá da Bandeira 8,
1ºD, 1300 Lisbon. **Map** 5 B3.
[*01-353 07 50.*

Canada
Avenida da Liberdade 144, 4º,
1250, Lisbon. **Map** 5 C5.
[*01-347 48 92.*

Republic of Ireland
Rua da Imprensa à Estrela 1, 4º,
1200 Lisbon. **Map** 4 E2.
[*01-396 15 69.*

United Kingdom
Rua de São Bernardo 33,
1200 Lisbon. **Map** 4 D2.
[*01-392 40 00 (embassy)*
[*01-392 41 60 (consulate).*

PORTUGUESE GOVERNMENT TOURIST OFFICES

In Lisbon:
Palácio Foz,
Praça dos Restauradores,
1200 Lisbon. **Map** 7 A2.
[*01-346 36 43.*

At Lisbon airport:
[*01-849 43 23.*

Canada
60 Bloor Street West,
Suite 1005, Toronto M4W 3B8.
[*1416-921 7376.*

United Kingdom
22/25a Sackville Street,
London W1X 1DE.
[*0171-494 14 41.*

Personal Health and Security

I N GENERAL, Lisbon is relatively free of crime, but simple precautions should always be taken. When parked, do not leave any valuable possessions in the car, and watch out for pickpockets in crowded areas and on public transport. Should you have serious medical problems, ring the emergency service number given in this section. For minor complaints, consult a pharmacist, who should be able to help.

Motorway SOS telephone

WHAT TO DO IN AN EMERGENCY

T HE NUMBER to contact in the event of an emergency is 112. Dial the number and then indicate which service you require – the police *(polícia)*, an ambulance *(ambulância)* or the fire brigade *(bombeiros)*. If you need medical treatment, the casualty department *(serviço de urgência)* of the closest main hospital will treat you. On motorways and main roads, use the orange SOS telephone to call for help should you have a car accident. The service is in Portuguese; press the button and then wait for an answer. The operator will put you through.

Pharmacy sign

HEALTH PRECAUTIONS

N O VACCINATIONS are needed for visitors, although it is a sensible precaution to have had a typhoid shot and a current polio booster. Tap water is safe to drink throughout the country. If you are visiting during the summer, it is advisable to bring insect repellent, as mosquitoes, while they do not present any serious health problems, can be a nuisance.

PHARMACIES

P HARMACIES *(farmácias)* in Lisbon can diagnose simple health problems and suggest appropriate treatment. Pharmacists can dispense a range of drugs that would normally only be available on prescription in many other countries. The sign for a *farmácia* is a green cross on a white background. They are open from 9am to 1pm and 3pm to 7pm. Each pharmacy displays a card in the window

showing the address of the nearest all-night pharmacy and a list of those that are open until late (10pm).

MEDICAL TREATMENT

S OCIAL SECURITY coverage is available for all EU nationals, although you may have to pay first and reclaim later. To reclaim, you must obtain an E111 form before you travel. This form is available at post offices throughout the UK or from the Department of Health. A booklet accompanies it, called *Health Advice for Travellers*, which explains what healthcare you are entitled to and how to claim for it. The E111 covers emergencies only, so visitors are advised to take out medical insurance for all other types of medical treatment. The **British Hospital** in Lisbon has English-speaking doctors, as do the international health centres in Estoril and Cascais along the Lisbon Coast. Details of these can be found in the local English newspapers.

PORTUGUESE POLICE

I N LISBON and other main towns, the police force is the *Polícia de Segurança Pública* (PSP). In rural areas, law and order is kept by the *Guarda Nacional Republicana* (GNR). The *Brigada de Trânsito* (traffic police) are a division of the GNR, and are recognizable by their red armbands. They are responsible for patrolling roads.

PERSONAL SECURITY

V IOLENT CRIME is extremely rare in Lisbon and in Portugal generally, and the vast majority of visitors to the country will experience no problems whatsoever, but sensible precautions should be taken. It is advisable to arrange travel insurance for your possessions before you

Traffic policeman

Male PSP officer

Female PSP officer

Fire engine

Ambulance

Police car

DIRECTORY

EMERGENCY NUMBERS

**General Emergency
(Fire, Police, Ambulance)**
 112.

**Associação Portuguesa
de Tradutores**
Rua de Ceuta 4b, Garagem 5,
2795 Linda-a-Velha, Lisbon.
 01-419 82 55.

British Hospital
Rua Saraiva de Carvalho 49,
1250 Lisbon.
 01-395 50 67.

Ordem dos Advogados
Largo de São Domingos 14, 1°,
1100 Lisbon.
 01-886 36 14.

LEGAL ASSISTANCE

An insurance policy that covers the costs of legal advice, issued by companies such as Europ Assistance or Mondial Assistance, will help with the legal aspects of your insurance claim should you have an accident. If you have not arranged this cover, call your nearest consulate or the **Ordem dos Advogados** (lawyers' association) who can give you names of English-speaking lawyers and help you with obtaining representation. Lists of interpreters, if you require one, are given in the local Yellow Pages (Páginas Amarelas) under *Tradutores e Intérpretes*, or can be contacted through the **Associação Portuguesa de Tradutores**, which is based in Lisbon.

PUBLIC CONVENIENCES

The portuguese for toilets is *retretes*. If the usual figures of a man or woman are not shown, look for *homens* (men) and *senhoras* (ladies). Toilet facilities are provided at service areas every 40 km (25 miles) and at drive-in rest areas on the motorways. In some cases you may have to pay to use ladies' toilets, but men's facilities are always free.

leave for Lisbon. Thieves do operate in certain areas in particular, and care should be taken after dark in the Alfama, Bairro Alto and Cais do Sodré districts of Lisbon, as well as in some areas of the coastal resorts. Personal belongings should be protected as much as possible and leaving anything inside a car, particularly a radio, is not recommended. When out walking, be sure to conceal wallets, and carry bags and cameras on your side away from the road so as not to tempt snatchers in cars or on motorbikes. If you are unfortunate enough to encounter thieves during your visit, you are advised not to attempt to resist and hand over your possessions immediately.

REPORTING A CRIME

If you have any property stolen, you should immediately contact the nearest police station. Theft of documents, such as a passport, should also be reported to your

consulate. Many insurance companies insist that policy holders report any theft within 24 hours. The police will file a report which you will need in order to claim from your insurance company on your return home. Contact the PSP in towns or cities, or the GNR in rural areas. In all situations, keep calm and be polite to the authorities to avoid delays. The same applies should you be involved in a car accident. In rural areas you may be asked to accompany the other driver to the nearest police station to complete the necessary paperwork. Ask for an interpreter if no one there speaks English.

Ladies' toilet sign

Men's toilet sign

Banking and Local Currency

BFB Bank Logo

Y OU CAN TAKE any amount of money into Portugal but if you import more than 2,500,000 escudos you must declare it at customs when entering the country. Eurocheques or traveller's cheques are the safest way to carry money in Lisbon, but credit cards are the most convenient. They can be used to withdraw Portuguese currency, for a fee, from ATMs (automatic teller machines) displaying the appropriate sign.

A 24-hour bank at Lisbon airport

BANKING HOURS

B ANK OPENING HOURS are from 8:30am to 3pm, Monday to Friday, although the major branches in Lisbon and those in the resorts close at 6pm. Banks are closed at weekends and on public holidays.

CHANGING MONEY

M ONEY CAN be changed at banks, at a bureau de change (câmbio) and in many hotels. The most convenient of these methods is to use banks as they are more common than bureaux de change and offer

a better rate of exchange than hotels. However, service in banks can sometimes be slow and usually involves filling in a number of forms. In addition, some banks restrict currency exchange to their customers.

The quickest and most practical way of changing money is to use the electronic currency exchange machines found outside the branches of most major banks, and at railway stations and the airport. They have the added advantage of allowing you to change money outside normal banking hours. The screen in the centre of the machine

displays the current exchange rates and gives instructions for use in several languages.

CHEQUES AND CARDS

T RAVELLER'S CHEQUES are available from most banks or from branches of Thomas Cook and American Express offices. They are a safe way of carrying money, but in Lisbon they are expensive to cash. Commission rates vary from bank to bank, so it is wise to shop around first.

A cheaper alternative is to buy Eurocheques from your bank together with a Eurocheque card. You can write out cheques in escudos for up to 30,000$00 per day, and many shops will accept them as payment. All banks showing the Eurocheque logo will also cash the cheques for you.

The credit cards that are most commonly accepted for payment are Visa, American Express and MasterCard. They can also be used to withdraw Portuguese currency at banks and bureaux de change.

CASH DISPENSERS

A PRACTICAL WAY of obtaining cash advances using your credit card with a PIN number is to use the MB (Multibanco) ATM (automatic teller machine) which is found outside most banks. Cards accepted are Visa, MasterCard, Amex, Eurocheque and Eurocard. A transaction tax is usually charged as well as a commission. It is worth looking around for the best rate first as tax and commission rates vary from bank to bank.

Indicator panel shows which denominations of each currency the machine accepts.

Foreign currency is inserted here.

Exchange rates and instructions are shown on this screen.

Portuguese notes and coins emerge from these slots.

Language and currency is selected using these buttons.

Currency Exchange Machine at Lisbon Airport
These machines provide a convenient way of changing foreign notes into Portuguese currency at any time of day or night.

CURRENCY

THE BASIC CURRENCY unit in Lisbon is the escudo ($), pronounced "ish-koo-doh", which is divided up into 100 centavos. Amounts are usually expressed with the escudo sign written before the centavos, so 1,000 escudos is shown as 1,000$00. The smallest coin still in circulation is the 1$00 (1 escudo) coin, and the largest bank note currently in circulation is the orange 10,000$00 (10,000 escudos) note.

1,000$00 are usually referred to as a *conto*, and this term can be used on cheques instead of escudos. For example, the Portuguese are more likely to refer to 12,000$00 as 12 *contos*.

It is advisable to carry smaller denomination notes and coins at all times when travelling in Lisbon. Buses, small shops and kiosks are often unable, or unwilling, to give you change if you use the larger notes to pay for small purchases.

10,000$00

5,000$00

2,000$00

1,000$00

Bank Notes
Denominations of notes are 10,000$00, 5,000$00, 2,000$00, 1,000$00 and 500$00. Older Portuguese bank notes are in the process of being phased out and replaced with newer designs, although at present both versions are in circulation. The smaller replacement designs are shown in the foreground, with the older notes behind. A replacement design for the 500$00 note is expected in 1997.

500$00

Coins
The following coins are currently in circulation in Portugal: 200$00, 100$00, 50$00, 20$00, 10$00, 5$00, 2$50 and 1$00. There are no centavo coins in circulation below 1$00; the only coin that incorporates centavos is the 2$50.

200$00   100$00   50$00   20$00

10$00   5$00   2$50   1$00

Using the Telephone

RECENT YEARS have seen a dramatic improvement in the Portuguese telecommunications system. Formerly, the antiquated equipment caused all manner of problems for visitors. Thankfully, it has been updated with the help of the latest technology, and visitors should now find that using the telephone in Lisbon is relatively free of complications. Public telephones may be used for phoning internally or abroad, either with coins or cards. It is generally much more convenient, especially when making international or long-distance calls, to use card phones instead of coin phones.

English-style phone box

Post office *cabine* phone

USING A COIN PHONE

1 Lift receiver and wait for the dialling tone.

2 Insert 10$00, 20$00 50$00, 100$00 or 200$00 coins.

3 The display shows amount of credit. If more money is required the message "*Inserir mais moedas por favor*" appears.

4 Key in telephone number and wait to be connected.

5 To make another call, press the follow-on call button.

6 Replace receiver after call. Unused coins will be refunded.

USING A TELECOM CARD PHONE

1 Lift receiver and wait for the dialling tone.

2 Insert phonecard arrow side up, or credit card magnetic strip down.

3 The screen will display number of units available, then tell you to key in telephone number.

4 Key in number and wait to be connected.

5 If phonecard runs out in the middle of a call, it will re-emerge. Remove it and insert another one.

6 Replace receiver after call. When card re-emerges, remove it.

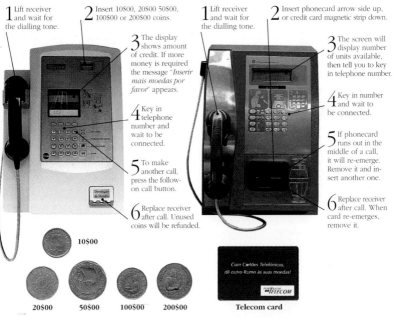

10$00

20$00   50$00   100$00   200$00

Telecom card

TELEPHONING IN LISBON

THERE ARE SIX different types of pay phone in the Lisbon area. Four use coins and two take cards, although one type of card is being phased out.

Telecom logo

There are two types of coin-operated phone in the street: the older green phones accept 10$00, 20$00 and 50$00 coins, and the newer beige phones accept these as well as the 100$00 and 200$00 coins. The red phones found in bars and newsagents accept only 10$00, 20$00 and 50$00 coins, whereas the new blue phones, in bars and shops, will also accept 100$00 and 200$00 coins.

Until recently, using a phonecard has been complicated because there were two types of card, the Telecom and the Credifone. The good news is that by the end of 1997, only the Telecom card will remain in use. Card phones are more convenient than coin phones, especially when making calls abroad, as they avoid the need to carry pockets full of change. Both cards are available in 50 and 120 units from post offices, Portugal Telecom outlets, tobacconists and newsagents.

You can also call from post offices. Queue at the cashier's window and you will be directed to a booth (*cabine*). Make your call first and then pay at the counter. The rate is much better than in hotels, which will add on a large surcharge. It is cheaper to phone in the evening or at weekends, when off-peak rates are charged.

REVERSE CHARGE CALLS

REVERSE CHARGE calls can be made from any telephone. First dial the *país directo* number for the country you wish to call. This number is listed in the opening pages of any telephone directory, after the list of city dialling codes for that country. This number will put you in direct contact with the local telephone operator. There are also separate numbers for calls to the USA using services such as ATT, MCI and Sprint.

A new-style beige coin telephone, covered by a shelter

DIALLING CODES

- If you are making a call from within Lisbon just dial the six- or seven-digit number.
- To phone Lisbon from outside the city dial 01.
- To phone Lisbon, and most places in the Lisbon Coast area, including Sintra, Cascais and Estoril, from abroad, first dial 00 35 11 and then the local number.
- To call abroad from Lisbon, dial 00 and then the country code. The code for Australia is 61; Ireland: 353; New Zealand: 64; UK: 44 and US and Canada 1.
- Lisbon's directory enquiries number is 118. For international directory enquiries dial 098.
- The Algarve is covered by Portimão (082), Faro (089), and Tavira (081). Madeira's code is 091.

Postal Services

Correios (postal service) logo

THE POSTAL SERVICE is known as the *Correios*. It is reasonably efficent: a letter sent to a country within the EU should take five to seven days, and a letter sent to the USA or further afield should take about seven to ten days. The *Correios* sign features a horse and rider in white on a red background.

SENDING A LETTER

FIRST-CLASS MAIL is known as *correio azul* and second-class mail is called *normal*. First-class letters are posted in blue postboxes and second-class post in red ones. At post offices there may be separate slots for national and international mail. There is also an express mail service called EMS, and for valuable letters, a recorded delivery service *(correio registado)* is available. Stamps *(selos)* can be bought from post offices or from any shop displaying the red and white *Correios* sign, and also from vending machines. These are found in airport terminals and in railway stations, as well as on the streets of large towns.

Portuguese stamps

POSTE RESTANTE

A MAIL-HOLDING service *(posta restante)* is also available at most major post offices. The envelope should carry the name of the recipient in block capitals, underlined, followed by *posta restante* together with the postcode and the name of the destination town. To collect the mail, take your passport and look for the counter that is marked *encomendas*. A small fee is charged for this service.

POST OFFICES

POST OFFICES are usually open from 8:30am until 6:30pm from Monday to Friday. Post offices in town or city centres have different opening times. These are 8am–10pm from Monday to Friday and 9am–6pm on Saturdays.

LISBON'S ADDRESSES

LISBON'S ADDRESSES often include both the storey of a building and the location within that floor. The ground floor is the *rés-do-chão* (r/c), first floor *primeiro andar* (1º), the second floor is expressed as 2º, and so on. Each floor is divided into left, *esquerdo* (E or Esq^{do}), right, *direito* (D or D^{to}).

Information on collection times **First-class postbox**

Lisbon's Postboxes
First-class letters should be posted in blue (Correio Azul) *boxes and second-class letters in red boxes.*

Second-class postbox

TRAVEL INFORMATION

L ISBON IS SERVED by an international airport as well as good road and rail links; it is also a popular port with cruise liners. Road networks into Lisbon have improved significantly in the last decade with the construction of new ring roads and motorways, whilst a second bridge across the Tagus will be completed in 1998, alleviating traffic congestion into the city. Trams provide fascinating trips through Lisbon's old neighbourhoods

TAP, the Air Portugal logo

which are also worth exploring on foot. However, travel in the city during peak hours can be frustrating. Despite modernisation of the city's public transport system, many still commute by car, creating endless traffic jams. Lisbon's surroundings offer an escape from the hubbub as well as some wonderful sightseeing opportunities – either by train to historic Cascais, across the Tagus by ferry to Caparica's beaches or by road to romantic Sintra.

AIR TRAVEL

L ISBON HAS regular scheduled flights from European capitals and major cities, including Paris, Frankfurt, Madrid, Milan and Zurich. Daily scheduled flights by TAP, the national airline of Portugal, and British Airways from London, and by TAP from Dublin, serve Lisbon. Travellers from North America can pick up a direct TWA, Delta or TAP flight to Lisbon from New York. TAP and its partner Varig also link major South American cities, such as Rio de Janeiro, São Paulo and Caracas, to the Portuguese capital. There are no direct flights to Lisbon from Canada, Australia or New Zealand, and the usual connecting point is London. Domestic flights also operate to destinations including Porto, Faro, Madeira and the Azores.

Airlines offer a host of options on flights to Lisbon. The cheapest scheduled flights from the UK, such as BA's periodic World Offer, usually have a fixed return date, requiring you to stay over one Saturday night. Midweek flights may also be discounted. These flights must usually be booked well in advance as seats are limited. Since refunds are not made, it is advisable to take out insurance

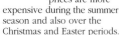

Signs at Lisbon's Portela airport

in case of last-minute alterations or cancellations. Few charter flights are available to Lisbon, and all have fixed outward and return dates.

Young people and students should consult agencies that specialize in student travel. If you are arranging a long-haul flight, it is worth enquiring whether you can take a budget flight to London, and continue to Lisbon from there. In general, ticket prices are more expensive during the summer season and also over the Christmas and Easter periods.

LISBON AIRPORT

P ORTELA AIRPORT is located only 7 km (4 miles) to the north of Lisbon city centre. Although airy and modern, it remains relatively small by international standards. All the facilities usually associated with an international airport are on offer, including shops,

cafés, bars, restaurants, duty free shops, bureaux de change and car hire agencies.

CONNECTIONS WITH THE AIRPORT

T HE AIRPORT'S proximity to the city centre means that it is reasonably cheap to get into to the heart of Lisbon. Taxis are readily available from the taxi rank just outside the International Terminal at Portela airport.

Express shuttle service aerobuses depart every 20 minutes (7am–9pm) from outside the International Terminal to Praça do Comércio, Praça Marquês de Pombal, Praça dos Restauradores, and Cais do Sodré station. The ticket is then valid for the rest of the day and can be used on local buses, trams and funiculars in the city. Cheaper local buses (No. 44 and No. 45) stop just outside the airport car park and also offer a service to Praça dos Restauradores and Cais do Sodré station. These buses operate from 6am–1am, but their timetable is less predictable than the aero-bus service.

Shuttle bus waiting to depart from the airport to the city centre

Entrance to the Ponte 25 de Abril, one of the main routes into Lisbon

ARRIVING BY TRAIN

To the east of the Alfama district, on Avenida Dom Henrique, is **Santa Apolónia**, the main station for long distance trains arriving from Coimbra, Porto and the north, as well as from Madrid and Paris. It is 15 minutes' walk east of Praça do Comércio.

For helpful advice about accommodation or to change money, there is a tourist information office (open 9am–7pm Mon–Sat) and a bureau de change inside the station. To get to your hotel, there is a taxi rank outside the station's main entrance.

Santa Apolónia train station

From 1998, a new station at the Expo site, the **Gare do Oriente**, will provide an alternative international terminus to Santa Apolónia. Although much further north, it will have excellent links by bus and metro into the city.

Trains from the south and east of the city arrive at **Barreiro** station on the south bank of the Tagus and connect with the ferry which docks at Terreiro do Paço. Nearby, **Cais do Sodré** station serves Cascais and Estoril. **Rossio** station, on Praça dos Restauradores, serves Queluz, some 20 minutes away, and Sintra, about 45 minutes from Lisbon. For more details on travelling by train, see page 161.

ARRIVING BY ROAD

There are at present four entry routes into Lisbon with a fifth via the new Vasco da Gama bridge to the north of the city due to open soon.

For those arriving from the Algarve and the south as well as Madrid and the east, the standard route is via the A2 motorway and the Ponte 25 de Abril.

From Oporto and the north the A1 motorway brings you to Lisbon's outskirts, where there is a motorway toll to be paid. In order to reach the centre of Lisbon, simply follow signs indicating *Centro*.

However, if you prefer not to go into Lisbon itself but wish to head straight to the coastal resorts of Cascais and Estoril, or to Sintra, then turn off the motorway at Alverca, 20 km (12 miles) north of Lisbon, where there are signs marked Cascais/C.R.E.L. (the outer ring road).

Those arriving from Cascais and the coast enter Lisbon via the A5 motorway, while the A8 is the main entry point for traffic from Torres Vedras and the coastal region.

The new bridge at Montijo will provide better access to the northern end of the city, including the Expo and the airport, via the C.R.I.L. (the inner ring road).

If you are arriving in Lisbon by bus, the main bus station is centrally located at Avenida Casal Ribeiro, and has good transport connections as well as a taxi rank. For further information on bus travel, see page 160.

LISBON'S BRIDGES

One of Lisbon's most famous landmarks, the Ponte 25 de Abril, provides the main link between Lisbon and the southern bank of the Tagus. Built in the 1960s, this bridge is usually overloaded with traffic. The best time to cross is outside the rush hours when it is least busy. To improve traffic flow, a toll is charged only on the way into Lisbon, and this covers the exit cost as well.

In order to ease traffic pressure, a second bridge, the Vasco da Gama, near the Expo site, is planned for completion by March 1998. This will provide a much needed link between the north of Lisbon and Montijo, on the south side of the Tagus, from where motorways lead south to the Alentejo and Algarve regions.

Getting Around Lisbon

A**N ATTRACTIVE CITY**, Lisbon is a pleasure to explore and walking can be one of the best ways to see it. However, it is also hilly and even the fittest of sight-seers will soon tire. The trams, lifts *(elevadores)* and buses come as a welcome rest for the foot-weary tourist and offer some excellent views (see pages 158–60 for information on public transport). Driving around the city can be a hair-raising experience, with its maze of one-way streets and impatient *Lisboeta* drivers, and it is not generally recommended. However, taxis offer the convenience of road travel without the troubles of parking and finding your way around in an unfamiliar city. They are also relatively cheap.

A typical alleyway in the Alfama district, Lisbon

WALKING AROUND LISBON

L**ISBON IS** a delightful city to wander around taking in the sights, especially in the old neighbourhoods such as the Alfama and Bairro Alto. Narrow cobbled streets, picturesque buildings and alleyways provide a charming setting to experience traditional Lisbon life.

However, it is important to remember that Lisbon is built on seven hills, and unless you are fairly fit, it is wise to take advantage of public transport as much as possible for the uphill climbs. Both old-fashioned and ultra-new trams, known as *eléctricos*, go almost as far as Castelo de São Jorge. You can then walk down through the Alfama, and enjoy the views.

The heart of Lisbon's commercial area is made up of Chiado and the Baixa, where pedestrianized streets are filled with bustling shoppers and street artists. A wide variety of shops, department stores, outdoor cafés and banks offer plenty of opportunity to buy souvenirs, change money or enjoy a coffee whilst soaking up the atmosphere.

When walking around the old neighbourhoods such as the Alfama, beware of pickpockets and thieves that may prey on unsuspecting tourists.

DRIVING AROUND LISBON

U**SING A CAR** to get around the busy city centre of Lisbon is not advisable. Portuguese drivers can be intimidating and parking can often be difficult since there are few car parks. The city centre is also full of partially hidden one-way traffic signs, which can be frustrating, if not somewhat expensive, should you come across an unsympathetic policeman who may issue an on-the-spot fine to visitors. Having said this, most policemen in Lisbon are generally

RETIRE AQUI O SEU BILHETE

Pay and display sign

understanding of, and tolerant towards confused drivers and puzzled tourists, and will be willing to guide you back in the right direction.

There are relatively few roundabouts in Lisbon; the larger ones, such as Marquês de Pombal and Rotunda do Relógio by the airport, have traffic lights, although many of the smaller ones do not. Cars on roundabouts travel anticlockwise and have priority over waiting traffic. However, unless there are signs to the contrary, traffic from the right has priority at squares, cross-roads, junctions and even minor side roads.

If it is absolutely necessary for you to drive in Lisbon, keep calm and try to avoid the worst of the rush hour traffic (8–10am and 5:30–7:30pm). You should also look out for pedestrian crossings as these are often badly marked.

PARKING

P**RESSURED BY** the chaotic state of parking on its streets, Lisbon City Council has embarked on a massive underground and outdoor car park construction programme. By 1998, a total of around 20,000 above- and underground parking spaces will be available in the city.

The main underground car parks are located at Avenida 5 de Outubro, Avenida de Roma, Praça de Londres, Praça dos Restauradores, Praça da Figueira and Alameda.

Car parks are signposted by a white P on a blue background and are relatively inexpensive. Most are located in the city centre. The largest, and newest, is situated in Praça Marquês de Pombal and has over 1,000 spaces.

Central Lisbon also has pay and display zones on weekdays between 8am and 8pm. They are identified by the car park sign plus a hand and a card or a coin. The tickets are bought from machines; unfortunately most do not give out change, so be sure to have coins to

The Marquês de Pombal roundabout in central Lisbon

hand if you intend to park in the city centre. Parking illegally will result in either a hefty fine or your car being towed away. If it is impounded, the car will then only be released upon payment of a large fine.

CAR HIRE

M OST OF THE major hire companies such as Hertz and Avis have offices at the airport inside the International Terminal. To rent a car in Portugal you must have an international driving licence (unless you hold a licence from an EU member state). Drivers must be over the age of 21 and have held their licence for at least one year.

It is usually more expensive to hire a car at an airport, as is renting in summer; most companies offer special off-peak and weekend deals. The price depends on whether unlimited mileage is included and if you want comprehensive insurance *(todos-os-riscos)*. Normally, the car is provided with a full tank of petrol; it is best to return it with the tank full, as the agency will charge to fill it themselves.

`79·40·ET`

A typical Lisbon taxi

PETROL

P ETROL, CALLED *gasolina*, is relatively expensive in Portugal and is the same price countrywide. Diesel *(gasoleo)* is the cheapest and high octane leaded petrol *(super)* is the most expensive. Unleaded *(gasolina sem chumbo)* is slightly cheaper than *super*.

In order to help differentiate between different fuels, a colour coding system exists: unleaded petrol is marked green, leaded is blue and diesel is yellow.

The majority of petrol stations are located on Lisbon's outskirts so try not to get caught in town with an empty tank. Those outside town are generally self-service and open 24 hours daily. The few that operate in the city centre are manned but usually close by 11pm. Filling up your tank is referred to as *atestar* and it is considered customary to give the attendant a small tip.

TAXIS

C OMPARED TO THE rest of Europe, taxis in Portugal remain relatively inexpensive, although it is not unknown for taxi drivers to take advantage of unsuspecting tourists, either by following a much longer route or by charging for extras such as luggage. Officially, taxi drivers are only allowed to charge a flat rate for any luggage. However, if you think you have been overcharged for any

reason, ask for a receipt *(recibo)* with the driver's name and number on it.

Most taxis are beige but some of the older black and green cabs still exist. All are metered. Costs depend on the time of day. There are two green lights on their roofs to indicate the rate: one light (6am–10pm) means normal rates apply, and two indicates the higher tariff (10pm–6am, weekends, public holidays).

You can either flag a taxi down in the street (but check that the "taxi" light on the roof is on) or call a radio taxi, which costs more.

DIRECTORY

CAR HIRE AGENCIES AT LISBON AIRPORT

Auto Jardim
01-846 29 16.

Avis Rent-a-Car
01-356 11 76.

Eurodollar
01-940 52 40.

Guérin
01-388 27 24.

Hertz
01-355 73 01.

24-HOUR TAXI SERVICES

Autocoope
01-793 27 56.

Centtures
01-483 60 30.

Retális
01-815 50 61.

24-HOUR PETROL PUMPS

Garagem Almeida Navarro
Rua da Palma 256, Almirante Reis. **Map** 7 B2.

Miranda & Ferrão
Avenida António Serpa 22, Campo Pequeno. **Map** 5 C1.

Mobil
Avenida Almirante Gago Coutinho, Areeiro. **Map** 6 E1.

Getting Around by Public Transport

Metro logo

As a result of the ever increasing traffic on its streets, Lisbon City Council has made huge efforts to improve the capital's public transport system. To date, the *Metropolitano* has seen the most significant improvement. New trams with much greater capacity have also been introduced to replace their much loved but ageing predecessors, built at the beginning of the 20th century. Lisbon's orange buses have a more extensive network than trams and are another good way to get around and see the sights at the same time. Buses, trams and funiculars are all run by Carris, a state-owned company.

TICKETS

Lisbon's transport system offers a wealth of choice regarding different ticket types. Value for money depends on how long you wish to stay and how many different types of transport you want to use.

If you wish to remain as flexible as possible it is best to buy tickets on boarding. Single tickets on all Carris transport (bus, tram and funicular) are bought from the driver or lift operator. However, if you buy Carris tickets beforehand at one of their kiosks (at Praça da Figueira, Elevador de Santa Justa or Sete Rios) you are entitled to two journeys for the price of one.

For visitors wishing to spend a whole day sightseeing and travelling around Lisbon, it is better to buy a one- or three-day ticket at a Carris kiosk. These allow travel on all Carris transport and are excellent value for money if you intend to make

numerous journeys in a short period. Both tickets must be validated at the beginning of the first journey.

Should you intend to stay longer and wish to use the metro as well, it is worth investing in a Tourist Pass, available for four or seven days, and also sold at Carris kiosks. You will need to show your passport or some relevant identification in order to get one. LISBOA cards, which entitle the holder to free public transport and entry to state museums, are also available for a charge.

If you just want to use the metro, tickets can be bought either from the ticket office or from an automatic vending machine at the station. It is cheaper to buy them from the vending machines, which accept coins from 5$00 to 200$00 and will give change. Metro tickets usually cover only one journey, but a one-

Metro *obliterador* machine

day *(bilhete de um dia)* or seven-day ticket *(bilhete de sete dias)* is available and worth buying, as well as a set of ten *(dez)*, known as a *caderneta*. Children between the ages of four and twelve, students and adults over 65 all pay half price on public transport. Children under the age of four are permitted to travel free of charge.

TRAVELLING BY METRO

The quickest and cheapest way by far to get around town is by the *Metropolitano*. Metro stations are signposted with a red M and the service operates from 6:30–1am each day. Although the metro becomes quite packed during the morning and evening rush hours, there are frequent trains. The system is safe to travel on, even at night, since the stations and trains are patrolled regularly 24 hours a day by the metro police. Tickets must be validated in the *obliterador*, usually located at the entrance to the station, before you board a train, or else you can face a hefty fine.

Only two unnamed metro lines are in operation at the moment, but two more are under construction. Despite this expansion programme, the service still does not reach many areas of Lisbon, the west of the city in particular. At present one line starts at Roma, in the north of Lisbon

---

BUYING TICKETS

Buses, trams and funiculars accept the same tickets. Discounted ones can be bought from the various Carris kiosks around the city centre. Metro tickets sold from self-service station machines are cheaper, and discounted ones are also available.

One-day metro ticket

One-day travel ticket

Half-price Carris ticket

The LISBOA card *permits travel on public transport for 1, 2 or 3 days and allows entry to the main museums. It is available from Carris kiosks.*

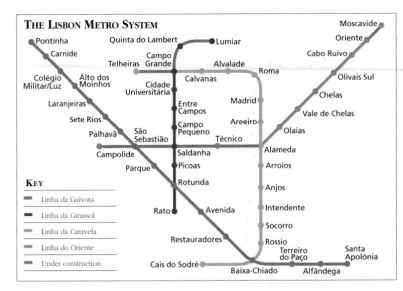

THE LISBON METRO SYSTEM

Pontinha
Carnide
Quinta do Lambert
Lumiar
Moscavide
Oriente
Campo
Grande
Telheiras
Alvalade
Cabo Ruivo
Colégio
Militar/Luz
Alto dos
Moinhos
Calvanas
Roma
Olivais Sul
Cidade
Universitária
Laranjeiras
Entre
Campos
Madrid
Chelas
Sete Rios
São
Sebastião
Campo
Pequeno
Areeiro
Vale de Chelas
Palhavã
Técnico
Olaias
Campolide
Saldanha
Alameda
Parque
Picoas
Arroios
Rotunda
Anjos
Rato
Avenida
Intendente
Socorro
Restauradores
Rossio
Santa
Apolónia
Cais do Sodré
Terreiro
do Paço
Baixa-Chiado
Alfândega

KEY

— Linha da Gaivota
— Linha da Girassol
— Linha da Caravela
— Linha do Oriente
— Under construction

and runs south down to the Rotunda before swinging back up towards the northwest of the city, to terminate at Colégio Militar, the home of the Benfica football ground. At Rotunda, the other line connects and goes directly north, terminating at Campo Grande, home to Benfica's rival, Sporting.

By 1998 there will be four lines operating: the Gaivota (Seagull line), the Girassol (Sunflower line), the Caravela (Caravel line) and the Oriente (Orient line). These lines will link the metro to major bus, train and ferry services, and will also provide transport from Lisbon's suburbs (including the Expo site which will be linked by the new station, Oriente) to the commercial heart of the city, along the north bank of the river.

TRAVELLING BY TRAM

TRAMS *(eléctricos)* are one of the most pleasant ways of sightseeing in Lisbon. However, they only operate in a very limited area of the city, along the river to Belém and around the hilly parts of Lisbon. There are presently two types of tram operating in Lisbon, the charming, old, pre-World War I models, and the much longer new trams with sleek interiors.

Single tickets for all rides are very cheap except for those on the red *Colinas* or *Tejo* trams, which provide special sightseeing rides for tourists and are much more expensive than the ordinary routes. These sightseeing services operate from March to October and take you through the hilly parts of Lisbon and along the Tagus. However, it is better value to catch one of the following trams:

No. 12 follows a route from Largo Martin Moniz (near Praça da Figueira) to São

Tomé, in the picturesque Alfama district *(see p30–9)*.

No. 15 goes from Praça do Comércio along the river to Belém where you can admire the beautiful architecture of the Torre de Belém and the Mosteiro dos Jerónimos, and also visit the new Cultural Centre of Belém (CCB).

No. 28 starts at São Vicente de Fora and provides a fascinating trip through some of the oldest parts of Lisbon, passing close to the Castelo de São Jorge and including Graça and Estrela.

New-style tram

Old-style tram

Lisbon's Elevador da Glória ascending to the Bairro Alto

FUNICULARS AND LIFTS

DUE TO LISBON'S hilly terrain, funiculars and lifts are a convenient and popular means of getting from river level to the upper parts of the city, namely Bairro Alto, Alfama and Graça. Although expensive in relation to the distance covered, this form of transport certainly helps take the effort out of negotiating Lisbon's hills, and in addition offers some superb views over the city.

Elevador da Bica climbs from the São Paulo area, close to Cais do Sodré station, up to the lower end of Bairro Alto. **Elevador da Glória** goes from Praça dos Restauradores to the upper end of Bairro Alto. The **Elevador de Santa Justa** lift takes passengers from the Rua do Ouro, the old shopping district, to the Largo do Carmo, beside the ruins of the old Igreja do Carmo *(see p52)*.

TRAVELLING BY BUS

BUS TRANSPORT in Lisbon is more expensive than travelling by metro and less reliable. Although buses are fairly frequent, they are often packed. However, the service is presently more extensive than either the metro or the tram system and offers better access to sights for visitors.

Lisbon buses *(autocarros)* are orange and easily recognizable. All services run approximately every 15 minutes from 6:30am to midnight. Some night buses operate until 1:30am.

Stops are indicated by a sign marked *paragem* where details of the specific route are shown. The final destination is always displayed on the front of the bus. Tickets bought at Carris kiosks need to be validated in an *obliterador* machine on the bus, although those purchased from the driver do not. A set of ten tickets can be bought for half price at news stands. They are valid on buses and trams.

Orange and white Lisbon bus heading for Praça do Comércio

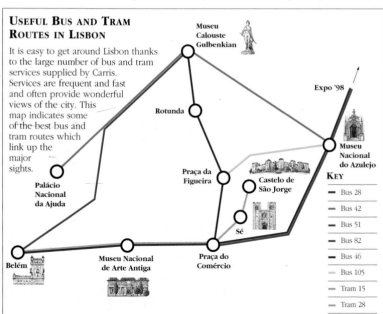

USEFUL BUS AND TRAM ROUTES IN LISBON

It is easy to get around Lisbon thanks to the large number of bus and tram services supplied by Carris. Services are frequent and fast and often provide wonderful views of the city. This map indicates some of the best bus and tram routes which link up the major sights.

Museu Calouste Gulbenkian

Expo '98

Rotunda

Museu Nacional do Azulejo

Praça da Figueira

Castelo de São Jorge

Palácio Nacional da Ajuda

Sé

Belém

Museu Nacional de Arte Antiga

Praça do Comércio

KEY

— Bus 28
— Bus 42
— Bus 51
— Bus 82
— Bus 46
— Bus 105
— Tram 15
— Tram 28

Travelling Around the Lisbon Coast

Logo for Caminhos de Ferro Portugueses

Lisbon and its surroundings offer numerous sightseeing opportunities and the good road network around the area means that most sights are only 30 minutes or so from the city centre. Buses and coaches are available for visiting Cascais and Estoril and there is also a good local train service. Although no public bus services go to Sintra, there are organized coach tours to the palaces and the glorious countryside around the town. A frequent rail service operates from Rossio station to Sintra. To visit Sesimbra and other areas to the south of the Tagus, ferries depart from Praça do Comércio, in Lisbon, and offer a more leisurely way to cross the river than the busy Ponte 25 de Abril. Trains and buses can then be picked up on the south bank of the river.

High-speed Alfa train at Santa Apolónia station in Lisbon

TRAVELLING BY TRAIN

The state-owned railway company, Caminhos de Ferro Portugueses (CP), operates all trains in Portugal.

There are four main rail lines out of Lisbon. Most popular with tourists is the line which runs from Cais do Sodré to Cascais on the coast, and the line linking Rossio station to the town of Sintra. Rossio station (metro Restauradores) is situated next to Praça dos Restauradores. There are regular trains from there to Sintra (departing every 15 minutes at peak hours) and the journey takes about 45 minutes.

Santa Apolónia is the main station for trains travelling north as well as for most international arrivals. For those travelling east or south of Lisbon, a ferry departs from Fluvial station, on the north bank of the Tagus, to Barreiro station on the south side, from where train services depart.

Façade of Rossio station

A new station, the Gare do Oriente near the Expo site, is due to open in 1998. It will be an alternative international terminus as well as an interchange for local destinations.

To reach Estoril and Cascais take the train from Cais do Sodré station. The journey follows the coastline and takes about 45 minutes. Check destinations on the screens at the station before you travel as some trains terminate at Oeiras. You can also catch the train to Alcântara from Cais do Sodré, only five minutes away, or to Belém, ten minutes away.

TICKETING SYSTEM

Discounts of 50 per cent are available on all CP tickets for children aged from four to twelve years, students (you will need to show your student ID), and adults over 65. Children under the age of four travel free. However, there are no special discounts available for groups travelling together.

Return tickets can be bought on the Cais do Sodré-Cascais and Rossio-Sintra lines; however this will only save time rather than money, as returns are simply double the cost of single tickets.

If you wish to take a bicycle on these trains you will only be permitted to do outside rush hours and an additional fee will be charged. Never get on a train without a ticket as you will be liable to a fine.

DIRECTORY

RAILWAY STATIONS

Barreiro
§ 01-207 30 28.
Cais do Sodré
(01-37 01 81. **Map** 4 F4.
Rossio
(01-346 31 81. **Map** 7 A3.
Santa Apolónia
(01-86 41 42. **Map** 8 F3.

Train information (CP)
(01-888 40 25.

Departures board in Santa Apolónia station giving times and destinations

TRAVELLING BY CAR

WHEN DRIVING, always carry your passport, licence, car insurance and rental contract. Failure to produce these *documentos* if the police stop you will incur a fine.

The road network in and around Lisbon has seen significant improvements in the last decade, with the construction of new ring roads as well as motorways. If you are heading west out of Lisbon towards the coast and Estoril and Cascais, the quickest route is to take the A5 motorway.

Local signs giving directions to Estoril, the south via the bridge and Sete Rios

However, try to avoid rush hour traffic (8–10am and 5:30–7pm). To get on to the A5, follow the road out from Praça de Espanha or from Rotunda past Amoreiras.

Alternatively, if you prefer to take the scenic coastal route (N6), follow the A5 out of Lisbon for 8 km (5 miles), and turn off at the sign to Avenida Marginal.

To get to Sintra, the best route to take is either the A5 motorway or to follow the IC19 past Queluz. Parts of the A5 motorway pass through picturesque countryside.

To reach Caparica, Tróia and Setúbal, south of the Tagus, you can either cross the Ponte 25 de Abril at Alcântara or catch the car ferry which departs regularly from Cais do Sodré port to Cacilhas. Once across the river, follow the A2 motorway south.

MOTORWAYS

MOTORWAYS AROUND Lisbon have toll charges since they are privately owned by a company called **Brisa**.

In general, they are the quickest way to travel around Portugal, as they have better surfaces than minor roads. There are also motorway rest areas where you can have something to eat and fill the car up with petrol.

There are two systems for paying tolls on motorways. Most drivers take a ticket *(título)* at the entrance and pay at the exit where the fee is displayed at the toll booth.

The other system, known as the Via Verde, is primarily for residents in the area and is not intended for general use. Drivers subscribing to the system pay an annual fee and are permitted to drive straight through the Via Verde channel without stopping. It is strictly forbidden for anyone who does not subscribe to drive through the *Via Verde*, so make sure that you are in the correct lane as you approach the toll booths.

BREAKING DOWN

THE LOCAL motoring association, **ACP** (Automóvel Club de Portugal), has a reciprocal breakdown service with most other international motoring organizations. To qualify, drivers should take out European cover with their own organization.

Should you suffer a road accident, the emergency services number is 112. If you have simply broken down, call the ACP. There are SOS phones at regular intervals along motorways. Unless you state that you are a member of an ACP-affiliated organization, a private tow truck will be sent to help you. Breakdown assistance will try to repair your car on the spot, but if it is a more serious problem they will **ACP logo** tow your car to a garage. Depending on your insurance, the ACP can make arrangements for you to have a hire car until yours is repaired.

In Portugal, international rules apply to breakdowns, including placing a red warning triangle behind the car to alert other drivers. Be sure to check that you have one in your car before you travel.

A sightseeing coach from one of the many tour operators

TRAVELLING BY COACH

FOLLOWING the privatization of the Rodoviária Nacional (RN), concessions have been made available to private enterprise, and hence competitive pricing has developed between rival coach companies. However, the absence of a central coach service sometimes makes it difficult to know which company serves the destination you wish to reach.

Each of the companies operates its own ticketing system. As a general rule, however, you buy your ticket from the driver when you board the coach, although it is possible to get cheaper tickets, known as *modulos*, beforehand from the relevant coach company's kiosk. As on the trains, there are no group discounts though children between the ages of four and twelve travel half price. At present, the only direct coach service operating between Lisbon and Cascais is the **Praiamar Expresso**. However, this service is limited to two buses in the afternoon to Cascais and two buses in the morning into Lisbon. Express buses leave from Campo Grande (metro Entre Campos), in Lisbon, to Cascais, via Oeiras, Carcavelos and Estoril. The trip takes about an hour.

For destinations south of the Tagus, the two main companies which run bus services are **Belos** and **TST** (Transportes Sul do Tejo). Buses leave from Praça de Espanha (metro Palhava) for destinations such as Costa da Caparica (1hr) and Sesimbra (1hr 45 mins).

For destinations northwest of Lisbon, contact **Empresa Barraqueiro**. This company operates regular services to places such as Ericeira (1hr 50 mins) and Mafra (1hr 30 mins), from Rua Fernandes da Fonseca, near Largo Martim Moniz (metro Socorro).

To date there is no coach link between Lisbon and Sintra. However, the Scottish company **Stagecoach** operates two routes to Sintra from Cascais and Estoril. The No. 403 departs from outside Cascais railway station every 90 minutes, via Guincho and Cabo da Roca. The No. 418 departs hourly from outside Estoril railway station. Both buses stop at Sintra station and in the town centre. In Sintra, Stagecoach also runs a service from the train station to Palácio da Pena and Castelo dos Mouros from Tuesday to Sunday.

COACH TOURS

THERE ARE MANY coach tours operating in the Lisbon area, offering a wide choice of destinations, from a short local trip around the city's sights to longer trips to other cities in Portugal such as Oporto. For those who just

wish to tour Lisbon itself, short half-day tours are available. Sintra, Cabo da Roca, Estoril and Cascais are all easily reached in a day trip. Alternatively, you can head southwards to Sesimbra and Arrábida, or north to Mafra. Prices depend on whether meals or special events, such as *fado* or bull-fighting, are included. Most tours offer reductions to children under the age of ten. Tours can be booked directly with the tour operator, through a travel agent or at some hotels. If you are staying at one of Lisbon's major hotels, some tours will provide a pick-up service.

FERRIES ACROSS THE TAGUS

MOST FERRY SERVICES are operated by **Transtejo**. There are several different points at which you can cross the Tagus by ferry. The trips are worth making purely for the fabulous views of Lisbon.

From Praça do Comércio (Estação Fluvial) there are crossings to Cacilhas (daily from 6am to 10:30pm) which take 15 minutes. Fast new ferries also cross from Praça do Comércio to Seixal and Montijo (daily from 6am to 10:30pm) and take 15 and 30 minutes respectively. Ferries owned by Soflusa operate a 15 minute service from Fluvial to Barreiro (daily from 5:45am to 2:45am). From Belém, ferries go to Trafaria (daily from 7am

to 9pm), where you can get a bus to the beaches at Caparica.

If you wish to take your car across the river, the ferry from Cais do Sodré makes regular crossings to Cacilhas and only takes about 15 minutes. This service operates daily from 5:30am to 2:30am.

Transportes Sul do Tejo

TST coach operator logo

Ferry docking at Praça do Comércio

LISBON STREET FINDER

AP REFERENCES given in this guide for sights and entertainment venues in Lisbon refer to the Street Finder maps on the following pages. Map references are also given for Lisbon's hotels *(see pp114–119)* and restaurants *(see pp128–33)*. The first figure in the map reference indicates which Street Finder map to turn to, and the letter and number which follow refer to the grid reference on that map. The map below shows the area of Lisbon covered by the eight Street Finder maps. Symbols used for sights and useful information are displayed in the key below. Lisbon's Metro network *(see pp158–9)* is being extended; and those stations marked on the map include those scheduled to open in 1998.

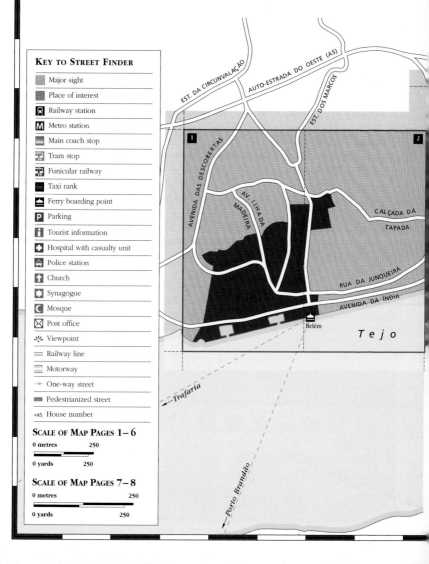

KEY TO STREET FINDER

- Major sight
- Place of interest
- **R** Railway station
- **M** Metro station
- Main coach stop
- Tram stop
- Funicular railway
- Taxi rank
- Ferry boarding point
- **P** Parking
- **i** Tourist information
- Hospital with casualty unit
- Police station
- Church
- Synagogue
- **C** Mosque
- Post office
- Viewpoint
- Railway line
- Motorway
- One-way street
- Pedestrianized street
- «45 House number

SCALE OF MAP PAGES 1–6

| 0 metres | 250 |
| 0 yards | 250 |

SCALE OF MAP PAGES 7–8

| 0 metres | 250 |
| 0 yards | 250 |

Street Finder Index

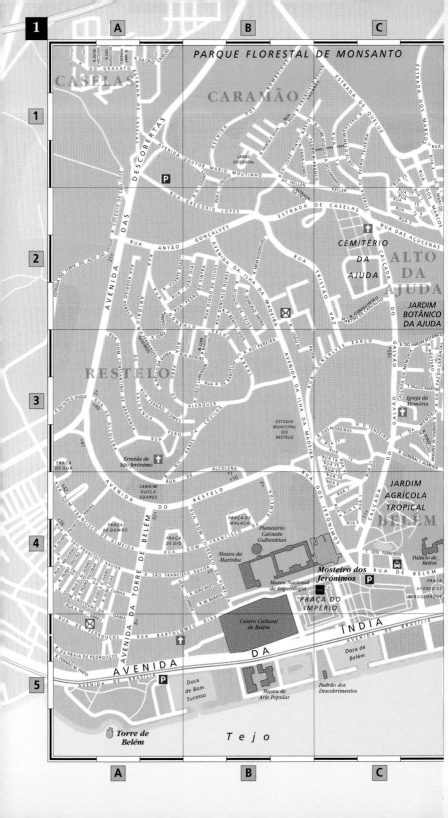

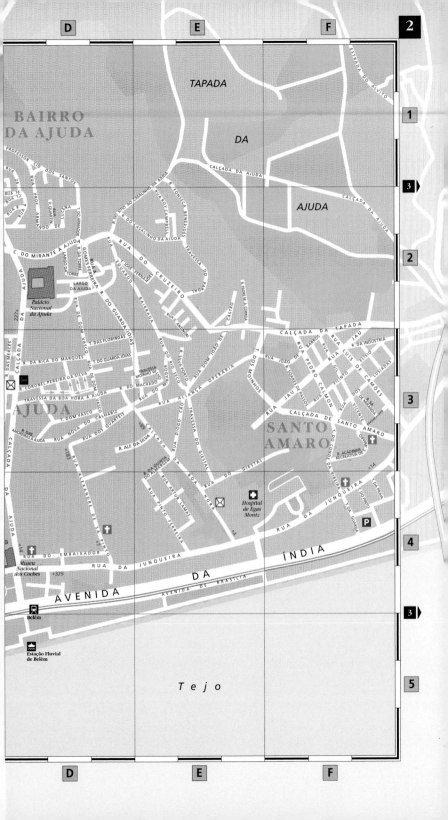

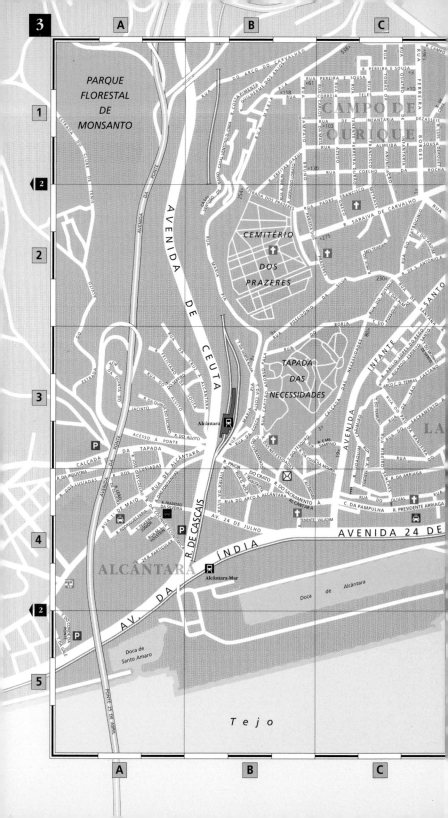

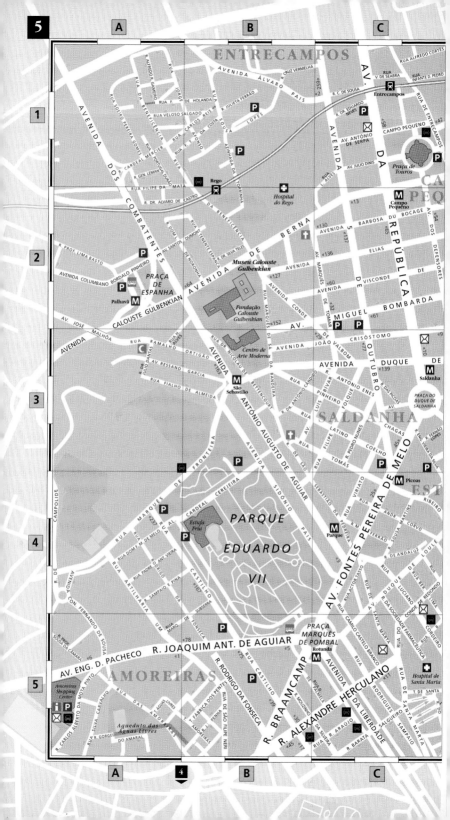

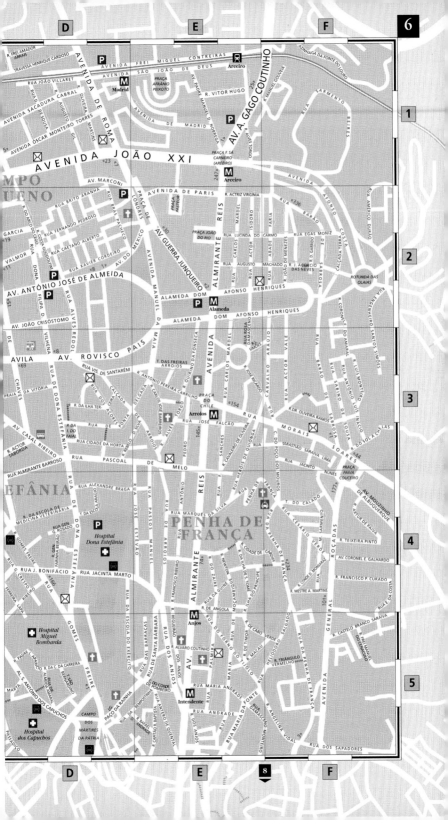

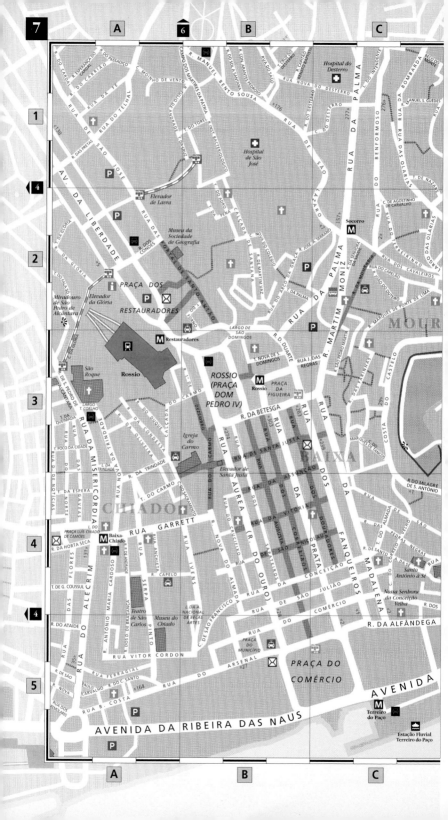

General Index

Acknowledgments

DORLING KINDERSLEY would like to thank the following people whose contributions and assistance have made the preparation of this book possible.

CONTRIBUTORS

SUSIE BOULTON studied History of Art at Cambridge University. A freelance travel writer, she is the author of *Eyewitness Venice and the Veneto.*

SARAH McALISTER is a freelance writer and editor for the *Time Out* guides. Her knowledge of Lisbon and the surrounding area is a result of extensive visits to the country.

CONSULTANT

MARTIN SYMINGTON was born in Portugal and is a freelance travel writer. He contributes to numerous British newspapers including the *Daily Telegraph* and the *Sunday Telegraph.* He is the author of guides to *The Loire Valley* (Hodder and Stoughton), *Portugal* (AA) and *Denmark* (AA/Thomas Cook). He has also contributed to *The Algarve and Southern Portugal* (AA/Thomas Cook), *Portugal* (Insight), *Eyewitness Great Britain* and *Eyewitness Seville and Andalusia.*

ADDITIONAL CONTRIBUTORS

Paul Vernon, Edite Vieira.

DESIGN AND EDITORIAL ASSISTANCE

Gillian Andrews, Angela Marie Graham, Felicity Laughton, Helen Markham, Robert Mitchell, Adam Moore, Naomi Peck, Jake Reimann, Amanda Tomeh, Ingrid Vienings, Fiona Wild.

INDEXER

Hilary Bird.

ADDITIONAL PHOTOGRAPHY

Steve Gorton, John Heseltine, Dave King, Martin Norris, Roger Philips, Clive Streeter.

PHOTOGRAPHIC AND ARTWORK REFERENCE

Joy FitzSimmons, Veronica Wood.

PHOTOGRAPHY PERMISSIONS

DORLING KINDERSLEY would like to thank the following for their assistance and kind permission to photograph at their establishments:

Instituto Português do Património Arquitectónico e Arqueológico (IPPAR), Lisboa; Instituto Português de Museus (IPM), Lisboa; Museu do Mar, Cascais; Museu da Marinha, Lisboa; Fundação da Casa de Alorna, Lisboa, and all other churches, museums, parks, hotels, restaurants and sights too numerous to thank individually.

SPECIAL ASSISTANCE

Emília Tavares, Arquivo Nacional de Fotografia, Lisboa; Luísa Cardia, Biblioteca Nacional e do Livro, Lisboa; Marina Gonçalves and Aida Pereira, Câmara Municipal de Lisboa; Caminhos de Ferro Portugueses; Carris; Enatur, Lisboa; Karen Ollier-Spry, John E. Fells and Sons Ltd; Maria Helena Soares da Costa, Fundação Calouste Gulbenkian, Lisboa; Pilar Serras and José Aragão, ICEP, London; Instituto do Vinho de Porto, Porto; Simoneta Afonso, IPM, Lisboa; Mário Abreu, Dulce Ferraz, IPPAR, Lisboa; Pedro Moura Bessa and Eduardo Corte-Real, Livraria Civilização Editora, Porto; Metropolitano de Lisboa; Raquel Florentino and Cristina Leite, Museu da Cidade, Lisboa; Joao Castel Branco G. Pereira, Museu Nacional do Azulejo; and the staff at all the other tourist offices and town halls in Portugal.

PICTURE CREDITS

t = top; tl = top left; tlc = top left centre; tc = top centre; tr = top right; cla = centre left above; ca = centre above; cra = centre right above; cl = centre left; c = centre; cr = centre right; clb = centre left below; cb = centre below; crb = centre right below; bl = bottom left; b = bottom; bc = bottom centre; bcl = bottom centre left; br = bottom right; d = detail.

Works of art have been reproduced with the permission of the following copyright holders: The work illustrated on page 80tl, *Reclining Figure*, 1982, is reproduced by kind permission of the Henry Moore Foundation; *Terreiro do Paço* by Dirk Stoop 81b is reproduced by kind permission of the Museu da Cidade, Lisboa.

DORLING KINDERSLEY would like to thank the following individuals, companies and picture libraries for permission to reproduce their photographs:
AISA: 16tr, 17tc/br, 66b; ARQUIVO NACIONAL DE FOTOGRAFIA-INSTITUTO PORTUGUÊS DE MUSEUS: Museu Conde de Castro Guimarães/Manuel Palma 12; Biblioteca da Ajuda/José Pessoa 14c; Museu Nacional dos Coches/José Pessoa 17bc, 63bl;

Henrique Ruas 64b; Igreja São Vicente de Fora/Carlos Monteiro 17bl; Museu Nacional de Arte Antiga/Luis Pavão 16tl, 28t, 56bl/br, 57t/c/b, 59c; Francisco Matias 19tl, José Pessoa 19tr, 56tl/tr, 58b, 59b; Pedro Ferreira 58t, 59t; Museu Nacional de Arqueologia/ José Pessoa 65c; Arnaldo Soares 142tr, 143tl; Museu Nacional do Teatro/Arnaldo Soares 142cl; Luisa Oliveira 143tr; José Pessoa 142b; TONY ARRUZA: 16c.

INSTITUTO DA BIBLIOTECA NACIONAL E DO LIVRO, Lisboa: 13b, 14b, 105bl; © TRUSTEES OF THE BRITISH MUSEUM, London: 18br; BOUTINOT PRINCE WINE SHIPPERS, Stockport: 126br.

CÂMARA MUNICIPAL DE OEIRAS: 15c; CÂMARA MUNICIPAL DE LISBOA: Antonio Rafael 20cl; CEPHAS: Peter Stowell 24b; Mick Rock 124cb, 125c, Peter Stowell 24b; CHAPITÔ: 140tr; COCKBURN SMITHES & CIA, S. A. – an Allied Domecq Company: 228crb.

D & F WINE SHIPPERS, London: 125bc.

MARY EVANS PICTURE LIBRARY: 21tr, 101b.

FOTOTECA INTERNACIONAL, Lisboa: César Soares 16bl; Luís Elvas 25b/t; FUNDAÇÃO RICARDO DO ESPÍRITO SANTO SILVA: Museu-Escola de Artes Decorativas Portuguesas 35c.

GIRAUDON: 18cl; CALOUSTE GULBENKIAN FOUNDATION, Lisboa: 141tl.

THE IMAGE BANK: José Manuel 4b, 23b; Moura Machado 24c.

LUSA: Luis Vasconcelos 52b; André Kosters 53t; António Cotrim 143c.

JOSÉ MANUEL: 21br; 125br; MUSEU CALOUSTE GULBENKIAN, Lisboa: Enamelled Silver Gilt Corsage Ornament, Rene Lalique, © ADAGP, Paris and DACS, London 1997, 76ca; 76t/ca/cb/b, 77t/ca/cb/b, 78c/b/t,79b/t/c; Museu da Cidade, Lisboa: Antonio Rafael 20tl/bl/br; 21c/bl; Museu da Marinha, Lisboa: 16br, 68b.

NATIONALMUSEET, Copenhagen: 18tr; NATURPRESS: Juan Hidalgo-Candy Lopesino 22t.

ORONOZ, Madrid: 16bc.

QUINTA DO BOMFIM LODGE: 125cl, 127t/cla/cra; Claudio Capone 127bc.

RCL, PAREDE: Rui Cunha 140b; REX FEATURES: Sipa Press, Michel Ginies 15b.

SCIENCE PHOTO LIBRARY/CNES 1993, DISTRIBUTION SPOT IMAGE: 10.

SYMINGTON PORT & MADEIRA SHIPPERS: 126cla/cra.

PETER WILSON: 136b, 137c, 138c, 155bl, 163t; WOODFALL WILD IMAGES: Mike Lane 109b; WORLD PICTURES: 23t.

Jacket: All special photography except ARCHIVO NACIONAL DE FOTOGRAFIA-INSTITUTO PORTUGUÊS DE MUSEUS, Lisboa: José Pessoa front cover bc.

Phrase Book

IN EMERGENCY

Help!	Socorro!	soo-**koh**-roo
Stop!	Páre!	pahr'
Call a doctor!	Chame um médico!	shahm' ooñ meh-dee-koo
Call an ambulance!	Chame uma ambulância!	shahm' oo-muh añ-boo-lañ-see-uh
Call the police!	Chame a polícia!	shahm' uh poo-lee-see-uh
Call the fire brigade!	Chame os bombeiros!	shahm' oosh bom-**bay**-roosh
Where is the nearest telephone?	Há um telefone aqui perto?	ah ooñ te-le-**fon**' uh-**kee pehr**-too
Where is the nearest hospital?	Onde é o hospital mais próximo?	ond' eh oo ohsh-pee-**tahl**' mysh **pro**-see-moo

COMMUNICATION ESSENTIALS

Yes	Sim	seeñ
No	Não	nowñ
Please	Por favor/ Faz favor	poor fuh-**vor** fash fuh-**vor**
Thank you	Obrigado/da	o-bree-**gah**-doo/duh
Excuse me	Desculpe	dish-**koolp**'
Hello	Olá	oh-**lah**
Goodbye	Adeus	a-**deh**-oosh
Good morning	Bom-dia	boñ dee-uh
Good afternoon	Boa-tarde	boh-uh tard'
Good night	Boa-noite	boh-uh noyt'
Yesterday	Ontem	oñ-**tayñ**
Today	Hoje	ohj'
Tomorrow	Amanhã	ah-mañ-**yañ**
Here	Aqui	uh-**kee**
There	Ali	uh-**lee**
What?	O quê?	oo keh
Which	Qual?	kwahl'
When?	Quando?	**kwañ**-doo
Why?	Porquê?	poor-keh
Where?	Onde?	oñd'

USEFUL PHRASES

How are you?	Como está?	**koh**-moo shtah
Very well, thank you.	Bem, obrigado/da.	bayñ o-bree-**gah**-doo/duh
Pleased to meet you.	Encantado/a.	eñ-kañ-**tah**-doo/duh
See you soon.	Até logo.	uh-**teh** lh-loo
That's fine.	Está bem.	shtah bayñ
Where is/are . . . ?	Onde está/estão . . . ?	ond' shtah/ shtowñ
How far is it to . . . ?	A que distância fica . . . ?	uh kee dish-**tañ**-see-uh **fee**-kuh
Which way to . . . ?	Como se vai para . . . ?	**koh**-moo seh vy puh-ruh
Do you speak English?	Fala inglês?	**fah**-luh eeñ-glehsh
I don't understand.	Não compreendo.	nowñ kom-pree-**eñ**-doo
Could you speak more slowly please?	Pode falar mais devagar por favor?	pohd' fuh-**lar** mysh d-va-**gar** poor fuh-**vor**
I'm sorry.	Desculpe.	dish-**koolp**'

USEFUL WORDS

big	grande	grañd'
small	pequeno	pe-**keh**-noo
hot	quente	keñt'
cold	frio	**free**-oo
good	bom	boñ
bad	mau	**mah**-oo
enough	bastante	bash-**tañt**'
well	bem	bayñ
open	aberto	a-**behr**-too
closed	fechado	fe-**shah**-doo
left	esquerda	**shkehr**-duh
right	direita	dee-**ray**-tuh
straight on	em frente	ayñ freñt'
near	perto	**pehr**-too
far	longe	loñj'
up	suba	**soo**-buh
down	desça	**deh**-shuh
early	cedo	**seh**-doo
late	tarde	tard'
entrance	entrada	eñ-**trah**-duh
exit	saída	sa-**ee**-duh
toilets	casa de banho	**kah**-zuh d' **bañ**-yoo
more	mais	mysh
less	menos	**meh**-noosh

MAKING A TELEPHONE CALL

I'd like to place an international call.	Queria fazer uma chamada internacional.	kree-uh fuh-**zehr** oo-muh sha-**mah**-duh in-ter-na-**see**-oo-**nahl**'
a local call.	uma chamada local.	oo-muh sha-**mah**-duh loo-**kahl**'
Can I leave a message?	Posso deixar uma mensagem?	poh-soo day-**shar** oo-muh meñ-**sah**--jayñ

SHOPPING

How much does this cost?	Quanto custa isto?	**kwañ**-too koosh-tuh **eesh**-too
I would like . . .	Queria . . .	kree-uh
I'm just looking.	Estou só a ver obrigado/a.	shtoh soh uh vehr o-bree-**gah**-doo/uh
Do you take credit cards?	Aceita cartões de crédito?	kar-**toinsh** de **kreh**-dee-too
What time do you open?	A que horas abre?	uh **kee** oh-rash **ah**-bre
What time do you close?	A que horas fecha?	uh **kee** oh-rash **fay**-shuh
This one	Este	ehst'
That one	Esse	ehss'
expensive	caro	**kah**-roo
cheap	barato	buh-**rah**-too
size (clothes/shoes)	número	**noom**'-roo
white	branco	**brañ**-koo
black	preto	**preh**-too
red	roxo	**roh**-shoo
yellow	amarelo	uh-muh-**reh**-loo
green	verde	vehrd'
blue	azul	uh-**zool**'

TYPES OF SHOP

antique shop	loja de antiguidades	**loh**-juh de añ-tee-gwee-**dahd'sh**
bakery	padaria	**pah**-duh-ree-uh
bank	banco	**bañ**-koo
bookshop	livraria	lee-vruh-**ree**-uh
butcher	talho	**tah**-lyoo
cake shop	pastelaria	pash-te-luh-**ree**-uh
chemist	farmácia	far-**mah**-see-uh
fishmonger	peixaria	pay-shuh-**ree**-uh
hairdresser	cabeleireiro	kab'-lay-**ray**-roo
market	mercado	mehr-**kah**-doo
newsagent	kiosque	kee-**yohsk**'
post office	correios	koo-ray-oosh
shoe shop	sapataria	suh-puh-tuh-**ree**-uh
supermarket	supermercado	soo-**pehr**-mer-**kah**-doo
tobacconist	tabacaria	tuh-buh-kuh-**ree**-uh
travel agency	agência de viagens	uh-jen-**see**-uh de vee-**ah**-jayñsh

SIGHTSEEING

cathedral	sé	seh
church	igreja	ee-**gray**-juh
garden	jardim	jar-**deeñ**
library	biblioteca	bee-blee-oo-**teh**-kuh
museum	museu	moo-zeh-oo
tourist information office	posto de turismo	posh-**too** d' too-**reesh**-moo
closed for holidays	fechado para férias	fe-**sha**-doo puh-ruh **feh**-ree-ash
bus station	estação de autocarros	shta-**sowñ** d' oh-too-kah-roosh
railway station	estação de comboios	shta-**sowñ** d' koñ-**boy**-oosh

STAYING IN A HOTEL

Do you have a vacant room?	Tem um quarto livre?	tayñ ooñ **kwar**-too leevr'
room with a bath	um quarto com casa de banho	ooñ **kwar**-too koñ **kah**-zuh d' bañ-yoo
shower	duche	doosh
single room	quarto individual	**kwar**-too een-dee-vee-doo-**ahl**'
double room	quarto de casal	**kwar**-too d' kuh-**zahl**'
twin room	quarto com duas camas	**kwar**-too koñ **doo**-ash **kah**-mash
porter	porteiro	poor-**tay**-roo
key	chave	shahv'
I have a reservation.	Tenho um quarto reservado.	**tayñ**-yoo ooñ **kwar**-too re-ser-**vah**-doo

EATING OUT

Have you got a table for . . . ?	**Tem uma mesa para . . . ?**	tayñ oo-muh **meh**-zuh puh-ruh
I want to reserve a table.	**Quero reservar uma mesa.**	keh-roo re-zehr-**var** oo-muh **meh**-zuh
The bill please.	**A conta por favor/ faz favor.**	uh **kohn**-tuh poor fuh-**vor**/ fash fuh-**vor**
I am a vegetarian.	**Sou vegetariano/a.**	Soh ve-je-tuh-ree-ah-noo/uh
Waiter!	**Por favor!/ Faz favor!**	poor fuh-**vor** fash fuh-**vor**
the menu	**a lista**	uh **leesh**-tuh
fixed-price menu	**a ementa turística**	uh ee-**mehñ**-tuh too-**reesh**-tee-kuh
wine list	**a lista de vinhos**	uh **leesh**-tuh de **veeñ**-yoosh
glass	**um copo**	ooñ **koh**-poo
bottle	**uma garrafa**	oo-muh guh-**rah**-fuh
half bottle	**meia-garrafa**	**may**-uh guh-**rah**-fuh
knife	**uma faca**	oo-muh **fah**-kuh
fork	**um garfo**	ooñ **gar**-foo
spoon	**uma colher**	oo-muh kool-**yair**
plate	**um prato**	ooñ **prah**-too
napkin	**um guardanapo**	ooñ goo-ar-duh-**nah**-poo
breakfast	**pequeno-almoço**	pe-**keh**-noo-ahl-**moh**-soo
lunch	**almoço**	ahl-**moh**-soo
dinner	**jantar**	jan-**tar**
cover	**couvert**	koo-**vehr**
starter	**entrada**	eñ-**trah**-duh
main course	**prato principal**	**prah**-too prin-see-**pahl**'
dish of the day	**prato do dia**	**prah**-too doo **dee**-uh
set dish	**combinado**	koñ-bee-**nah**-doo
half portion	**meia-dose**	may-uh **doh**-se
dessert	**sobremesa**	**soh**-bre-**meh**-zuh
rare	**mal passado**	**mahl**' puh-**sah**-doo
medium	**médio**	**meh**-dee-oo
well done	**bem passado**	**bayñ** puh-**sah**-doo

MENU DECODER

abacate	uh-buh-**kaht**'	avocado
açorda	uh-**sor**-duh	bread-based stew (often seafood)
açúcar	uh-soo-**kar**	sugar
água mineral	**ah**-gwuh mee-ne-**rahl**'	mineral water
(com gás)	koñ **gas**	sparkling
(sem gás)	sayñ **gas**	still
alho	**ay**-oo	garlic
alperce	ahl'-**pehrce**	apricot
amêijoas	uh-may-**joo**-ash	clams
ananás	uh-nuh-**nahsh**	pineapple
arroz	uh-**rohsh**	rice
assado	uh-**sah**-doo	baked
atum	uh-**tooñ**	tuna
aves	**ah**-vesh	poultry
azeite	uh-**zayt**'	olive oil
azeitonas	uh-zay-**toh**-nash	olives
bacalhau	buh-kuh-**lyow**	dried, salted cod
banana	buh-**nah**-nuh	banana
batatas	buh-**tah**-tash	potatoes
batatas fritas	buh-**tah**-tash **free**-tash	french fries
batido	buh-**tee**-doo	milk-shake
bica	**bee**-kuh	espresso
bife	beef	steak
bolacha	boo-**lah**-shuh	biscuit
bolo	**boh**-loo	cake
borrego	boo-**reh**-goo	lamb
caça	**kah**-ssuh	game
café	kuh-**feh**	coffee
camarões	kuh-muh-**roysh**	large prawns
caracóis	kuh-ruh-**koysh**	snails
caranguejo	kuh-rañ-**gay**-joo	crab
carne	**karn**'	meat
cataplana	kuh-tuh-**plah**-nuh	sealed wok used to steam dishes
cebola	se-**boh**-luh	onion
cerveja	sehr-**vay**-juh	beer
chá	**shah**	tea
cherne	**shern**'	stone bass
chocolate	shoh-koh-**laht**'	chocolate
chocos	**shoh**-koosh	cuttlefish
chouriço	shoh-**ree**-soo	red, spicy sausage
churrasco	shoo-**rash**-coo	on the spit
cogumelos	koo-goo-**meh**-loosh	mushrooms
cozido	koo-**zee**-doo	boiled
enguias	en-**gee**-ash	eels
fiambre	fee-**añbr**'	ham
fígado	**fee**-guh-doo	liver
frango	**frañ**-goo	chicken
frito	**free**-too	fried
fruta	**froo**-tuh	fruit
gambas	**gañ**-bash	prawns
gelado	je-**lah**-doo	ice cream
gelo	jeh-**loo**	ice
goraz	goo-**rash**	bream
grelhado	grel-**yah**-doo	grilled
iscas	**eesh**-kash	marinated liver
lagosta	luh-**gohsh**-tuh	lobster
laranja	luh-**rañ**-juh	orange
leite	**layt**'	milk
limão	lee-**mowñ**	lemon
limonada	lee-moo-**nah**-duh	lemonade
linguado	leeñ-**gwah**-doo	sole
lulas	**loo**-lash	squid
maçã	muh-**sañ**	apple
manteiga	mañ-**tay**-guh	butter
mariscos	muh-**reesh**-koosh	seafood
meia-de-leite	**may**-uh-d' **layt**'	white coffee
ostras	**osh**-trash	oysters
ovos	**oh**-voosh	eggs
pão	**powñ**	bread
pastel	pash-**tehl**'	cake
pato	**pah**-too	duck
peixe	**paysh**'	fish
peixe-espada	**paysh**'-**shpah**-duh	scabbard fish
pimenta	pee-**meñ**-tuh	pepper
polvo	**pohl**'-voo	octopus
porco	**por**-coo	pork
queijo	**kay**-joo	cheese
sal	**sahl**'	salt
salada	suh-**lah**-duh	salad
salsichas	sahl-**see**-shash	sausages
sandes	**sañ**-desh	sandwich
santola	sañ-**toh**-luh	large crab
sopa	**soh**-puh	soup
sumo	**soo**-moo	juice
tamboril	tañ-boo-**ril**'	monkfish
tarte	**tart**'	pie/cake
tomate	too-**maht**'	tomato
torrada	too-**rah**-duh	toast
tosta	**tohsh**-tuh	toasted sandwich
vinagre	vee-**nah**-gre	vinegar
vinho branco	**veeñ**-yoo **brañ**-koo	white wine
vinho tinto	**veeñ**-yoo **teeñ**-too	red wine
vitela	vee-**teh**-luh	veal

NUMBERS

0	**zero**	**zeh**-roo
1	**um**	**ooñ**
2	**dois**	**doysh**
3	**três**	**tresh**
4	**quatro**	**kwa**-troo
5	**cinco**	**seeñ**-koo
6	**seis**	**saysh**
7	**sete**	**set**'
8	**oito**	**oy**-too
9	**nove**	**nov**'
10	**dez**	**desh**
11	**onze**	**oñz**'
12	**doze**	**doz**'
13	**treze**	**trez**'
14	**catorze**	ka-**torz**'
15	**quinze**	**keeñz**'
16	**dezasseis**	de-zuh-**saysh**
17	**dezassete**	de-zuh-**set**'
18	**dezoito**	de-**zoy**-too
19	**dezanove**	de-zuh-**nov**'
20	**vinte**	**veent**'
21	**vinte e um**	**veen**-tee-ooñ
30	**trinta**	**treeñ**-tuh
40	**quarenta**	kwa-**reñ**-tuh
50	**cinquenta**	seen-**kweñ**-tuh
60	**sessenta**	se-**señ**-tuh
70	**setenta**	se-**teñ**-tuh
80	**oitenta**	oy-**teñ**-tuh
90	**noventa**	noo-**veñ**-tuh
100	**cem**	**sayñ**
101	**cento e um**	**señ**-too-ee-ooñ
102	**cento e dois**	**señ**-too ee **doysh**
200	**duzentos**	doo-**zeñ**-toosh
300	**trezentos**	tre-**zeñ**-toosh
400	**quatrocentos**	**kwa**-troo-**señ**-toosh
500	**quinhentos**	kee-**nyeñ**-toosh
700	**setecentos**	set'-**señ**-toosh
900	**novecentos**	nov'-**señ**-toosh
1,000	**mil**	**meel**'

TIME

one minute	**um minuto**	ooñ mee-**noo**-too
one hour	**uma hora**	oo-muh oh-ruh
half an hour	**meia-hora**	**may**-uh-**oh**-ruh
Monday	**segunda-feira**	se-**goon**-duh-**fay**-ruh
Tuesday	**terça-feira**	ter-sa-**fay**-ruh
Wednesday	**quarta-feira**	**kwar**-ta-fay-ruh
Thursday	**quinta-feira**	**keen**-ta-fay-ruh
Friday	**sexta-feira**	**say**-shta-**fay**-ruh
Saturday	**sábado**	**sah**-ba-doo
Sunday	**domingo**	doo-**meen**-goo